Governing Disasters

'The challenges posed by risky decisions are well documented. These decisions become even more daunting when they must be made in a midst of a crisis. Using the European volcanic risk crisis as the principal case study, Alberto Alemanno and the other contributors to this thought-provoking volume derive valuable lessons for how policy makers can cope with the attendant time pressures, uncertainties, coordination issues, and risk communication problems. Once the next emergency risk situation occurs, it may be too late to learn about how to respond. *Governing Disasters* should be required reading for all policy makers and risk analysts in advance of the next international risk crisis.'

– W. Kip Viscusi, Vanderbilt University, USA and Editor,
Journal of Risk and Uncertainty

'Catastrophes present us with a paradox. Many people don't think they will happen, so before a catastrophe, regulations are typically viewed as unnecessarily invasive. But in the aftermath of a disaster everybody suddenly blames the government for not having been strict enough. Overregulation often follows. In light of the unprecedented series of catastrophes in recent years, more than ever, top leaders in government and business must understand and overcome this regulatory challenge. Alberto Alemanno's innovative book tells you how.'

– Erwann Michel-Kerjan, The Wharton School's Center
for Risk Management, USA

Governing Disasters

The Challenges of Emergency Risk Regulation

Edited by

Alberto Alemanno

Jean Monnet Professor of EU Law & Risk Regulation, HEC Paris, France

Edward Elgar

Cheltenham, UK • Northampton, MA, USA

Published by
Edward Elgar Publishing Limited
The Lypiatts
15 Lansdown Road
Cheltenham
Glos GL50 2JA
UK

Edward Elgar Publishing, Inc.
William Pratt House
9 Dewey Court
Northampton
Massachusetts 01060
USA

A catalogue record for this book is available from the British Library

Library of Congress Control Number: 2011929466

ISBN 978 0 85793 572 4

Typeset by Columns Design XML Ltd, Reading, Berkshire
Printed and bound by MPG Books Group, UK

Contents

Figures and boxes

FIGURES

BOX

Tables

Contributors

Alberto Alemanno is Jean Monnet Professor of EU Law & Risk Regulation at Ecole des Hautes Etudes Commerciales (HEC) Paris, where he teaches EU law, international economic law, global antitrust and risk regulation. He has been a qualified attorney at law in New York since 2004 and Adjunct Professor at Georgetown Law School, St Gallen University and Fribourg Law School. Originally from Italy, Alemanno earned a Laurea in Giurisprudenza *cum laude* from the Università degli Studi di Torino, LLM degrees from Harvard Law School and the College of Europe (Bruges), and a PhD in International Law and Economics from Bocconi University. He is the Editor of the *European Journal of Risk Regulation*.

Nick Bernard graduated in law from the Université Paris-XI and the University of Kent at Canterbury. After his Masters in International Trade Law from Paris-I Panthéon-Sorbonne, he took up posts at the University of Essex and at Queen's University Belfast. He joined Queen Mary in 2003 as Senior Lecturer.

Vincent Brannigan holds his juris doctor degree from Georgetown University and is a member of the Maryland and DC Bars. He has been a full-time faculty member at the University of Maryland since 1977. Prior to joining the faculty, he worked at the Consumer Product Safety Commission, the National Fire Prevention and Control Administration and the Center for Fire Research at the National Bureau of Standards. He authored the legal materials for the Open Learning Fire Service Programme and has been an adjunct faculty member at the US Fire Academy since it was founded.

Chad Michael Briggs holds a PhD in political science from Carleton University in Canada and is principal of GlobalINT LLC and also Minerva Chair of Energy and Environmental Security for the Spaatz Center, Air University, United States Air Force. He is a former senior advisor to the US Department of Energy, and was team leader for the Abrupt Climate Change and Security project under GlobalEESE. He is based in Berlin, Germany, where he is a senior associate with Adelphi

Consult. He has also taught at universities in Ireland, Canada, and the UK, covering subjects from European history and sociology to environmental security and hydrogeology.

Morten Broberg, PhD in law and HD in international economics was associate professor in international development law before being appointed professor at the University of Copenhagen. He is also consulting senior researcher at the Danish Institute for International Studies and has been a visiting researcher at Oxford University, London School of Economics and Université Robert Schuman in Strasbourg, amongst others.

Adam Burgess is currently senior lecturer in sociology, having previously held lecturing posts at the universities of Reading, Bath and Brunel, and a research fellowship at the Centre for the Study of Democracy at Westminster University. In the department he is the director of studies and also currently coordinates the teaching of introductory sociology. He is on the editorial board of the principal journal in his field, *Health, Risk and Society* and an editor of the new online journal, *Sociology Compass.*

Giuliano G. Castellano is Research Fellow at Bocconi University (Department of Law) in Milan (Italy) and Research Associate at the Ecole Polytechnique of Paris (PREG/CRG). He graduated in law at Bocconi University (Milan) and he holds a PhD from the Collegio Carlo Alberto (University of Turin) in comparative analysis of law, economics and institutions and a PhD in economics and social sciences at the Ecole Polytechnique of Paris (PREG/CRG), with highest honors. He was 'Vinci Fellow' (Université Franco-Italienne) and he was awarded from the Ecole Polytechnique a post-doctoral fellowship to conduct his research on financial markets regulation at the Center for Socio-Legal Studies (University of Oxford). He has been teaching law and economics, comparative law, financial markets regulation, and financial instruments at Bocconi University and at the International University College of Turin. He collaborates with different international organizations and he publishes and researches in the fields of: comparative law, law and economics, law and finance, and risk regulation and governance. He practises law in Milan.

Sweta Chakraborty is originally from New York City and is currently a post-doctoral fellow at the Centre for Socio-Legal Studies at Oxford University where she is working on drug safety and pharmacovigilance issues. She recently submitted her PhD thesis in 'The Role of Trust in

Chronic Prescription Drug Taking' at the King's Centre for Risk Management, King's College London. She is correspondent in risk communication for the *European Journal of Risk Regulation*.

Alfredo Fioritto is Associate Professor at the University of Pisa where he teaches administrative law, administrative justice and planning law at the law faculty. Doctor of law, University of Rome, 1980, with thesis on administrative law, he was Visiting Scholar at the Faculty of Law of Paris, La Sorbonne, with a NATO-Advanced fellowship programme (1987–88) grant and a CNRS grant. During the years his research interests ranged over many themes of administrative law (policy implementation in agriculture, central–local governments relationship, trends in the administration by contracts in France and Italy, the negotiation in public contracts, simplification in administrative procedure and legal language, emergency administration).

Francesca Hansstein is a PhD candidate in agri-food economics and statistics at the University of Bologna. She holds a BSc in communication sciences from the University of Milan and an MSc in development studies from the University of Bologna. She has been at the New York University as a visiting student during the last year of her PhD. Her research interests focus on food policy, obesity and behavioural economics.

Lorenza Jachia is Head, Regulatory Cooperation Unit, and Secretary, Working Party on Regulatory Cooperation and Standardization Policies (WP6) United Nations Economic Commission for Europe, Switzerland. She holds a master's degree from the Graduate Institute for International Studies (Geneva) and a bachelor's degree from Bocconi University (Milan).

Alain Jeunemaitre, an economist by training, has attachments to the Ecole Polytechnique as Director of Research (Paris) and to the University of Oxford. From 1988 to 2003, he has held visiting positions at the London School of Economics, Hertford College, Nuffield College and the Maison Française d'Oxford. He has been attached to the CSL since 2004 with PhD visiting studentships at the Centre and lecturing to the BCL/MJur option on regulation.

Chris Johnson is Professor of Computing Science at the University of Glasgow. His research focuses on the analysis of failures involving complex socio-technical systems. He helped to author the guidelines on accident investigation across European Air Traffic Management and was a member of the Eurocontrol contingency planning team, helping to author European guidelines on the management of high-consequence, low-probability mishaps. He is co-chair of the SESAR Scientific Advisory Board for the European Commission. He is presently helping to author training guidelines for European railway accident investigators and is working with organizations including the US Air Force, NASA and the European Space Agency.

Christopher Lawless is currently a teaching fellow within the Institute for the Study of Science, Technology and Innovation (ISSTI) at the University of Edinburgh. His research field includes: use of evidence and probability theory in decision-making, the law–science relationship, risk and regulation issues associated with science and technology, commercialization of science.

Francisco B. López-Jurado is the Director of the Department of Administrative Law at the University of Navara's Law School. He holds a JD and PhD from the University of Granada Law School. His research fields cover administrative law and risk regulation.

Donald Macrae is a member of the UK's Risk and Regulation Advisory Council. Before going independent in 2007 as a consultant in regulation and policy, he was Director General for Law and Regulation in the UK's Department for Environment, Food and Rural Affairs. Amongst his recent consultancy work, he has for over a year been advising Brazil's technical standards regulator, Inmetro, on applying impact assessment to conformity assessment procedures, in conjunction with the University of Sao Paulo.

Mario Mazzocchi is an associate professor in applied economics and statistics at the Department of Statistics, University of Bologna. He is also Visiting Research Fellow at the University of Reading, where he has previously served as a lecturer in applied economics and consumer behaviour. He has been a consultant to the European Commission and FAO. His publication record includes two books with Oxford University Press (*Fat Economics*) and Sage Publications (*Statistics for Marketing and Consumer Research*) and about 30 articles in international refereed journals on a variety of applied economics topics, including policy evaluation, consumer demand, health economics, marketing research methods, time series econometrics.

Valentin Nikonov is the ad interim coordinator of the UNECE Group of Experts on Risk Management in Regulatory Systems. He works as a consultant in a UNECE project to identify regulatory barriers to trade. At the Growth Trajectory Consulting Company since 2003, he has completed several projects to help service companies raise business efficiency through the application of international standards. Valentin has a PhD in economics, is a certified ISO/IEC 9001:2008 auditor and certified project manager. He authored a book on risk management and numerous articles on risk, information security and project portfolio management.

Maddalena Ragona is a research fellow at the Department of Statistics of the University of Bologna. She is currently involved in the EC-funded MoniQA Network of Excellence (Monitoring and Quality Assurance in the Food Supply Chain), where her work focuses on methodologies for the impact assessment of food safety regulations. She holds a PhD in food and environmental economics (University of Naples, Parthenope, Italy), an MSc in agricultural development economics (University of Reading), and a 'Laurea' degree in tropical and sub-tropical agricultural sciences (University of Florence). Her research interests include, among others, economics of social regulation, economics of risk communication, policy evaluation methods, cost-benefit analysis and multi-criteria analysis.

Marta Simoncini is a PhD in public utilities and regulation (majoring administrative law) at the University of Pisa. She is interested in comparative and european administrative law and she focused her research on the administrative law approach to the protection of fundamental rights. In 2007 she was also a visiting scholar at King's College London, where she spent a research term working on UK regulation on terrorism. In 2006 she attended an internship at the Italian Data Protection Supervisor, where she practised her legal expertise in the protection of personal data and privacy. She has recently published part of her findings in many peer review journals of both national and international relevance (*Rivista trimestrale di diritto pubblico, German Law Journal, European Journal of Law Reform, Civitas Europa, Panóptica, European Journal of Risk Regulation* (forthcoming)) and she has just finished a monograph on the foundations of standard-based regulation of catastrophic risks in counter-terrorism issues and environmental matters.

A.M. Viens is a postgraduate research student at Queen Mary University London, where he is preparing a thesis on 'Morality in Times of Emergency'. Most of AM Viens' work focuses on philosophical ethics and the philosophy of law. His research focuses on metaethics (practical reason and the nature of ethics) and applied ethics (especially public health ethics, research ethics, health policy ethics, and the ethics of bioscience and biotechnology).

Acronyms

ANSP	Air Navigation Service Provider
ANT	Actor Network Theory
ATM	Air Traffic Management
AUC	Air Transport Users Council
BA	British Airways
BSE	Bovine Spongiform Encephalopathy
BRC	Better Regulation Commission
CAA	Civil Aviation Authority
CEA	California Earthquake Authority
CFMU	Central Flow Management Unit
CI	Critical Infrastructure
CJD	Creutzfeldt–Jakob disease
DOE	US Department of Energy
EASA	European Aviation Safety Agency
EC	European Commission
ECAC	European Civil Aviation Conference
EFA	European Food Agency
EFSA	European Food Safety Authority
EMEA	Europe, the Middle East and Africa
EQC	New Zealand Earthquake Commission
EU	European Union
EUROCONTROL	European Agency for the Saftey of Air Navigation
FAB	Functional Airspace Block
GMO	Genetically Modified Organism
HPA	Health Protection Agency
HRO	High Reliability Organization
IATA	International Air Transport Association
IAVW	International Airways Volcano Watch
ICAO	International Civil Aviation Organization

IFALPA	International Federation of Air Line Pilots' Associations
IPCC	Intergovernmental Panel on Climate Change
NAME	Numerical Atmospheric-dispersion Modelling Environment
NASA	National Air and Space Agency
NATO	North Atlantic Treaty Organization
NATS	National Air Traffic Services
NEB	National Enforcement Body
NFZ	No-fly Zone
OECD	Organization for Economic Cooperation and Development
OPEC	Organization of the Petroleum Exporting Countries
PSR	Patell Standardised Residuals
RIA	Regulation Impact Assessment
RRAC	Risk and Regulation Advisory Council
SARF	Social Amplification of Risk Framework
SARS	Severe acute respiratory syndrome
SES	Single European Sky
SESAR	Single European Sky ATM Research
SSK	Sociology of Scientific Knowledge
TBT	Technical Barriers to Trade
TFEU	Treaty on the Functioning of the European Union
UAV	Unmanned Aerial Vehicle
UCL	University College London
UK	United Kingdom
UNECE	United Nations Economic Commission for Europe
UPS	United Parcel Service
US	United States of America
USAF	United States Air Force
VAAC	Volcanic Ash Advisory Centre
WEF	World Economic Forum
WHO	World Health Organization

Preface

This edited volume finds its origin in the 1st HEC Paris Workshop on Regulation, 'Emergency Regulation under the Threat of a Catastrophe – A Hard Look at the Volcanic Ash Crisis', which took place, on 10–11 November 2010 at HEC Paris University main campus. This first international workshop devoted to regulatory studies was an unforgettable event characterized by lively discussions among an unusually interdisciplinary group of scholars coming from virtually all over the world. Bringing together such a strong team of contributors has been a unique experience, and the final product reflects the hard work and quality of all of those involved.

The publication of this volume would have not been possible without the support of my university and that of several people. I am very grateful to HEC Paris Foundation, for sponsoring the 1st HEC Paris Workshop on Regulation, and to HEC Paris for hosting us in the magnificent *Le Château*. The generous funding received combined with the substantive as well as moral support of HEC Dean Bernard Ramanantsoa, HEC Dean of Research, Marc Vanhuele, and of the coordinator of the Law Department, Nicole Stolowy, have rendered this publication possible. I also would like to thank Professor Vincent Brannigan for being a source of inspiration at the time of the launch of the workshop and for helping me animate the event. I am in debt to Cliff Wirajendi, whose research assistance, friendship and logistical help before, during and after the workshop have been invaluable. Finally, I would like to thank my wife Mariana for the usual weekends spent at home instead of in the forests during the preparation of this volume. This book is dedicated to her.

Alberto Alemanno
Luxembourg–Paris, March 2011

Introduction

Alberto Alemanno

The specific analytical focus of the volume is the notion of emergency risk regulation, i.e. regulatory action undertaken in the immediacy of a disaster in order to mitigate its impact. By retrospectively looking at what happened during the European volcanic ash crisis and other recent contingencies, contributors from a variety of disciplines – including sociology, economics, political science, moral philosophy, management, risk analysis and law – consider the regulatory dilemmas characterizing emergency risk situations. The objective of this edited volume is twofold: (1) understanding which are the main features and challenges of emergency risk regulation; (2) examining the use of scientific advice and evidence when authorities are put under great pressure to deal with atypical situations. Moreover, this volume also has a wider goal. By generalizing some of the most salient features of the volcanic ash crisis and other recent emergencies, this book proactively suggests how the lessons learned can affect other regulatory systems that might be faced with similar emergencies.

The recent European volcanic ash crisis epitomizes the general problem of emergency response in a world of uncertain manufactured and natural risks. A cloud of volcanic ash preventing travelling across an entire continent probably neither featured in the risk-management scenarios of many firms nor in the contingency plans of public authorities. Therefore, it is of no surprise that the immediate and drastic regulatory response that followed soon became an uneven political dispute between industry economic power and regulatory science, with consumers caught in the middle. Regulatory systems designed for careful deliberation and cooperative action had to respond almost instantly to a barrage of scientific data arguments and conflicting legal interpretations, with threats of litigation on one side and the risk of loss of human life on the other.

The ash crisis is not the first or the only such problem to have occurred. It is one of a series of recent real or potential catastrophes – natural disasters, terrorist attacks, and pandemics – that have taken by surprise globalized firms and regulators. As such it represents a rich case study in the problem of emergency risk regulation and the questions that it raises should concern a wide variety of scholars, regulators and industry analysts whose normal areas of concern are far removed from aviation and volcanoes. Any industry could face a problem that involves the same rapid, fragmented and multi-layered regulatory response. Some industries may even encounter problems or situations that are even more complex than the ash crisis. Indeed, potentially devastating crises loom on the horizon (Boin, 2010; Rosenthal et al., 2001). According to many, the volcanic eruption, as well as the recent 2011 Japanese tsunami, will serve as a wake-up call for both companies and regulators that need to modernize their understanding of the risk management approaches aimed at averting disasters or mitigating their full effects.

How to respond to such emergency problems is a major source of complexities in risk analysis, crisis management, regulatory decision-making and, more in general, in any legal system. Hence, a growing international community of scholars coming from different disciplines recognize this problem and is beginning to examine and discuss the interlocking structures of governance and regulation that pertain to disasters (Ansell et al., 2010; Farber and Fauré, 2009; Bostrom and Cirkovic, 2008). This emerging field of study encompasses diverse and interdisciplinary areas of research, ranging from central normative issues of disaster law to technical crisis management systems as well as issues of institutional design in disaster prevention (Disaster Law and the Legal Academia, 2007). It also includes empirical research areas of risk and decision-making.

Is rational decision-making possible in a situation of emergency? How to determine a proportionate response to risk events? Who is competent to conduct the assessment of the hazard? Who is competent to take risk-management decisions? What is the role of government in an emergency situation? Who has the final word on the quality of the safety analysis? Does industry ignore the problem until it finally occurs? How accurate are estimates of costs and benefits? Which risks are insurable? Do regulators tend to overact? What if they do? To what extent do they manage a politically perceived risk rather than the actual one? What are the implications of different schools of technical thought that must be resolved by the regulator? How and by whom should risks be communicated? Which are the consequences stemming from bad emergency regulations adopted in a high stress environment?

The chapters that follow address these questions. Their authors are intentionally drawn from different disciplines, such as sociology, economics, political science, moral philosophy, management, risk analysis and law, in order to provide an original perspective on emergency risk regulation. While literature in the business management field often amounts to 'rules for effective crisis management', most other disciplines, such as Disaster Law and Policy and Risk Regulation, are sceptical that generic rules can be applied to each and every extraordinary event.

Before leaving you to the individual chapters gathered in this book, I would like to offer the reader some background. To this purpose, the next sections discuss the 'what, when and how' of emergency risk regulation.

WHAT IS EMERGENCY RISK REGULATION

In choosing as the analytical focus of the book the notion of emergency risk regulation, it is first necessary to address the question of what do we mean for 'emergency risk regulation'. This rubric encompasses virtually all regulatory actions undertaken in the immediacy of a disaster in order to mitigate its impact. On this definition, an immensely diverse collection of regulatory interventions could constitute emergency risk regulations: potential candidates include anti-seismic regulations, radiation safety standards, pandemics response plans, and disaster management. If the concept of risk characterizes a 'peculiar, intermediate state between security and destruction' (Beck, 2000), in an 'emergency risk' the balance between these two clearly tilts for the latter. As for any risk situation, emergencies call for more public than private action.

Being triggered by a disaster, emergency risk regulation presupposes the existence, or a mere threat, of a disaster. A disaster is a natural or man-made hazard resulting in an event of substantial extent causing significant physical damage or destruction, loss of life, or drastic change to the natural environment. A disaster can be generally defined as any tragic event with great loss stemming from events such as earthquakes, floods, catastrophic accidents, fires, or explosions. Yet as exemplified by both the 2010 volcanic ash crisis and the 2011 Japanese tsunami the lines between manufactured and natural risks are increasingly blurred.

Typically, one speaks of crisis or disaster when a threat is perceived against the core values or life-sustaining functions of a social system, which calls for urgent remedial action under conditions of uncertainty (Rosenthal et al., 1989). Yet although the category of disaster at first may seem unproblematic it is an elastic concept centred on the following commonplace three-part characterization: sudden, significant and natural (Dauber, 1998; Caron 2001). Suddenness is the most relevant criterion to define a disaster for the purposes of emergency regulation. It emphasizes the emergency dimension triggered by the catastrophe in its destabilizing influence on the social, physical and institutional infrastructure of a given community. As for significance, the significant risk of harm associated with disasters is different from what we typically experience in times of normalcy. As a result, determination of an event as 'disaster' may produce significant impact on the regulatory context by justifying the partial or total suspension of the ordinary decision-making process (Gerrard, 2006). Such departures from the rule of law, or simply from established procedures, are generally perceived as necessary if the 'significance' threshold has been met by the relevant event. Moreover, the relative importance given to a disaster by policy-makers and the public at large may vary according to the social values. In particular, prejudicial attitudes, often based on a long-standing socio-economic or racial bias, may influence disaster response systems as well as timelines (Dauber, 1999).

As for naturalness, there is growing agreement – reinforced by the Japanese emergency situation triggered by an earthquake followed by a tsunami and a nuclear safety emergency – that even the damage caused by naturally-occurring events, such as a tsunami or a volcanic eruption, is inextricably bound with human agency, thus making it impossible to distinguish between a man-made and a natural disaster (Farber et al., 2010). As illustrated by the volcanic ash crisis as well by the recent Japanese tsunami, 'physical phenomena are a necessary component of risk, but they are only the starting point in addressing safety concerns' (Farber, 2006).

WHEN IS THE TIME FOR EMERGENCY RISK REGULATION

Emergency risk regulation finds its natural regulatory space within the first two stages of the disaster cycle: mitigation and emergency response. In principle, mitigation efforts attempt to reduce the potential impact of a disaster before it strikes, while disaster response tends to do so after the event. Yet, as exemplified by the volcanic ash crisis, the distinction between emergency mitigation and emergency response is not always so sharp. When called upon to act under the threat of a catastrophe, the authorities happen to both mitigate and respond to such a threat in a situation characterized by suddenness (emergency) and significance.

As a result, emergency risk regulation is not directly interested with the other phases of the cycle. In particular, it does not operate in the disaster prevention phase (often defined 'crisis management') nor in those final stages, collectively called post-disaster assistance, such as insurance/liability compensation, government assistance and rebuilding.

Although there is a tight linkage between the various risk management categories, emergency risk regulation is clearly called to operate in the initial phase of the disaster cycle, when the mere menace of a disaster overshadows the regulatory context by emergency. This is where media and public attention tend to focus. As a result, a vital part of emergency risk regulation is represented by risk communication along the disaster cycle. In particular, in an emergency, the need of communicating risk effectively to the public is crucial to prevent distrust and anxiety. To this purpose a recent report by the Science and Technology Committee of the UK House of Commons recommends public authorities, while communicating emergencies to the public, to rely on the concept of 'most probable scenarios' rather than on the actual government's policy of 'reasonable worst case scenarios' (House of Commons, Science and Technology Committee, 2011). In any event, there is a need to strike a balance between confidentiality and disclosure when preparing for, and responding to, emergencies.

FEATURES OF EMERGENCY RISK REGULATION

In the immediacy of any disaster, industry representatives, public authorities, decision-makers at every level of government must mitigate and respond to disasters through emergency risk regulation. As a result, emergency risk regulation, by taking place in the immediacy of a disaster, is characterized by the following features: (1) it is triggered by (the threat of) an unpredictable, sudden and significant event; (2) it occurs under time pressure and in a situation characterized by uncertainty; (3) it reflects, being shaped by prevalent interests and public attitudes, a prevalent narrative; (4) it is often characterized by transnational nature, as it addresses transboundary risks spreading across jurisdictional borders and policies boundaries; (5) it requires, and is conditioned by, emergency risk communication, as it multiplies the need for fast and effective information; (6) it questions the applicability of existing regulatory schemes, even those that expressly codify an emergency response to risk.

Unpredictable, Sudden and Significant Event

The event typically triggering emergency risk regulation is the threat of a disaster, i.e. a natural or man-made hazard resulting in an event of substantial extent causing significant physical damage or destruction, loss of life, or drastic change to the natural environment. As mentioned above, it is not only the significance of the risk that differentiates a disaster from a non-disaster event, but also its suddenness. As a result, public leaders, being caught by surprise by these events, typically qualify emergencies caused by a disaster as unthinkable and impossible to foresee. Due to its unpredictable character, the manifestation of a disaster, or the threat of its appearance, tends to be characterized by its abruptness. These features (unpredictability and abruptness), which have been defined as being of 'Hollywood quality', trick the imagination and contribute to make emergencies difficult to recognize in time (Boin, 2010).

Both the suddenness and abruptness surrounding any disaster scenario presents emergency risk regulation with the challenge of 'paralysis in decision-making'. This paralyzing situation can also be caused by the immediate and on-going search for better information typical of an emergency. In turn, this may give rise to a cascade of incoming data that are difficult to interpret. To avoid such a paralyzing effect of emergencies, Chad Briggs (Chapter 11) illustrates the potential use of scenario planning, a risk emergency tool aimed at creating systematic decision-making through decisions that can be made in advance concerning potential contingencies and disasters. Also, Lorenza Jachia and Valentin Nikonov (Chapter 10) illustrate that paralysis in decision-making due to emergency situations can be overcome by elaborating contingency plans. In particular, they identify issues that regulators should consider when designing, testing, implementing and maintaining crisis management plans and developing legislation that covers situations of emergency. They argue that actions taken by regulators in the immediacy of crisis will only be effective if the regulatory system embraces all functions of the risk-management process. Yet an abundant literature shows that plans, even disaster plans, work well for predictable and well-known events, not for those capable of generating emergencies situations. This is because the suddenness, abruptness and lack of information and coordination typical of emergencies make it impossible to control 'each and every move of first responders', especially in the initial phase of an emergency (Boin, 2010). Far from being useless, crisis planning may not only induce a false sense of security, but also – more critically – may reduce the imagination, creativity and flexibility that are badly needed during an emergency situation (Clarke, 1999). Along these lines, Giuliano Castellano (Chapter 16) attempts to identify the core policy issues to be addressed through a risk-based governance model that stimulates preventive strategies and minimizes losses. In particular, he illustrates how changing policy objectives might lead to establish a correct set of incentives that – with different insurance and reinsurance techniques – helps to reduce the impact of unexpected events ensuring a recovery of large-scale losses.

Time Pressure and Uncertainty

Another feature of emergency risk regulation is uncertainty and the lack of suitable scientific evidence. Typically, in times of emergency, uncertainty, interpreted as discordance between facts and beliefs, intensifies. This is because, in emergencies, hazards tend to be mutable, not static, and rumours and incorrect information make it difficult to understand the nature of the hazard. In those circumstances, any regulatory effort is hampered by the lack of knowledge as to the hazard at stake and, more critically, about the actual and potential consequences stemming from it.

As a result, risk managers typically find it hard to collect, share and interpret the right information (Boin, 2010). In particular, the scientific evidence underpinning regulatory action instead of stemming from 'normal science' tends to be derived from 'secret and often inadequately tested approaches that are routine in forensic science', i.e. any scientific enterprise whose primary market is the legal and regulatory system (Brannigan, Chapter 7). No surprise that the use and misuse of this science instead of 'normal science' may lead to suboptimal results. Moreover, the lack of adequate information makes it difficult to weigh the possible consequences of a 'false positive' (i.e. investing resources in a non-event) against those of a 'false negative (i.e. ignoring a crisis) (Boin, 2010). All of these aspects are compounded when there are few recognized trans-European frameworks for the exchange of credible scientific advice (Olson, 2009). Thus in the European volcanic ash crisis, individual member states relied on input from different scientific experts who provided inconsistent and partial advice. In consequence, as shown by Chris Johnson and Alain Jeunemaitre's chapter (Chapter 4), it took extraordinary intervention on behalf of the European Transport Council to cut through the *ad hoc* applications of the precautionary principle. A key finding from this work is that we need to prepare a framework for the involvement of leading scientific advice if we are to avoid any repetition in further contingencies. Yet – given the transboundary nature of most of those emergency risks – rapidly to share information and coordinate regulatory action under the threat of a catastrophe is a challenge in itself (Ansell et al., 2010).

If epistemic uncertainty (i.e. lack of understanding of basic rules of nature), aleatory uncertainty (i.e. lack of adequate data for use in analysis) and intentional (i.e. lack of knowledge of human intentions) uncertainties characterize risk regulation, it is normative uncertainty that causes more concern in emergency regulation. As illustrated by A.M. Viens in Chapter 9 drawing on moral philosophy, normative uncertainty (i.e. lack of consensus as to the truly desired social course of action) may 'prolong the intensity or duration of the emergency, since the diminished ability of the regulation to coordinate and regulate the behaviour of the 'regulatees' means that regulators will have less time and resources to devote to the source of the emergency itself'. In his view, since normative uncertainty exists to a much higher degree in times of emergency, the regulators should take into account its moral significance. Critically, normative uncertainty increases the possibility that conventional moral standards may or may not hold up in the same way. Likewise, because of uncertainty, any act of balancing between conflicting values, such as safety and economic reasons, may be exacerbated in an emergency situation. Indeed, one may doubt whether in emergency circumstances often characterized by the threat of a catastrophe an act of balancing between safety and economic reasons (i.e. continued operations) is likely to be biased in ways that ought to be recognized and account for. In particular, the pressures exercised on the decision-maker combined with certain unique features of crisis mind-set may result in systematic under-valuation of one interest and overvaluation of another so that the resultant balance would be tilted in favour of safety concerns at the expenses of economic or other concerns. This shows that when regulating under emergency risk situations there exist certain challenges to the rational actor model. Indeed, according to cognitive psychologists, indi-viduals are subjects to cognitive heuristics, i.e. shortcuts that people use when making decisions, as a means of countering the lack of sufficient time to properly assess the situation (Twersky and Kahneman 1974, 185). This typically occurs when individuals, and also decision-makers, make decisions under conditions of risk and uncertainty. Decision-making that takes place under conditions of uncertainty caused by emergency is particularly prone to suffer from distortions that result from the interplay of informational and reputational influence and cascades (Burgess, Chap-ter 5; Chakraborty, Chapter 6). Indeed these intuitive rules of thumb typically shape people's judgment under uncertainty, and often in ways that contravene the norms of the probability theory ('probability neglect') (Slovic, 2000; Sunstein and Zeckhauser, 2010). Hence, the concern, shared by a significant number of risk regulation authors that biased risk perceptions may be reproduced in public policy, law and regulation by governments responsive to the demand of its citizens (Sunstein, 2005; Eskridge, 2002). The question on how better to use the results of cognitive theory in regulating risk remains open, yet high, on the agenda of several countries today (Eskridge et al, 2002; Obama, Executive Order 13563, 2011).

Prevalent Interests and Public Attitude Shaping a Prevalent Narrative

Staged risk shapes its perception and inevitably its reaction (Beck, p. 137 ss). In particular, media set the stage on which the performance of risk managers is assessed in the aftermath of the emergency (Boin, 2010). Yet public leaders are not the only ones trying to frame an emergency situation. Their messages compete with those of other actors, who – as they typically hold diverging interests – depict the ongoing crisis differ-ently and support alternative courses of action (Sunstein, 2007). Both prevalent interests and public attitudes about risk might indeed influence the emergency risk regulation that will be enacted, given that political officials, in their pursuit for political security, seek to gratify the prefer-ences of their more vocal or powerful constituencies (Noll and Krier, 2000; Downs, 1957). This might give rise to the problem of the 'omitted voice', wherein the interests, values and preferences of stakeholders are disregarded from the decision-making process, often with the result that they will endure the damage, be it of economic or health nature, stemming from regulatory action or inaction (Graham and Wiener, 1996). In particular, in an emergency, well-connected parties may exploit epistemic and normative uncertainty to circumvent burdensome safety requirements and avoid transparent science in the regulatory process. As illustrated by Vincent Brannigan, they may do so by trying to reverse the burden of proof and make regulators prove the hazard rather than the industry prove safety (Brannigan, Chapter 7). In his view, this is what occurred in the volcanic ash crisis. Here the shift of burden of proof from the industry to the regulators and acceptance of 'substandard evidence' marked a 'paradigm shift' that redefined the regulatory environment. The concept of paradigm shift has been and remains a topic of major debate in the history and philosophy of science and seems particularly promising in the analysis of emergency risk regulation (Kuhn, 1962; Casti, 1990). In turn, not only prevalent interests but also media reporting shape public attitudes. In an emergency situation, the media are central to determining the outcome of government efforts as well as the crucial post-event perception of their adequacy (Rosenthal, Boin and Comfort, 2001). Although media coverage is often ill suited for 'sustaining high level coverage of long-term threats' (Kitzinger and Reilly, 1997), it plays an active role in framing risk controversies and can stigmatize technological risks (Flynn, Slovic, and Kunreuther, 2001). In particular, medias can generate an amplification of risk, perpetuating public distrust (Lofstedt and Horlick-Jones, 1999). In this type of environment where misperception is mounting, trust plays a considerable role in public perceptions of the severity of risk (Siegrist and Cvetkovich, 2000). Yet, as illustrated by Adam Burgess (Chapter 5) and Donald Macrae (Chapter 2), the demand for safety or feelings of distrust were not particularly acute in the volcanic ash crisis. The issue never became salient enough to trigger a phenomenon of 'social amplification of risk' (Sunstein, 2007). In particular, Burgess, by categorizing the stories generated by the ash cloud, illustrates how coverage of this emergency risk did not extend, despite the uncertainty inherent in the crisis, far beyond the immediate impact made by the cloud. In his view, this outcome confirms that the representation of hazards as significant risks remains contingent upon the nature of the hazard (an 'act of God' here) and its legacy as well as the context in which it becomes manifest (lack of major accidents). Although it would have been quite easy to spin the crisis and contribute to make it gain momentum thus generating unwarranted concerns, this did not occur. This would prove that there exist limits to the ability of the media, also in a situation of emergency regulation, to do so.

Transnational Character due to the Increasing Transboundary Nature of the Risks

As more and more citizens come to reap the benefits of open trade on a global scale, as well as extended lifespan and high quality of life, they also seem to expect public authorities to deliver more protection against threats to health, safety and the environment (Alemanno, 2011). Yet due to their inherent global dimension, risks today call for global and coordinated governance solutions. In particular, due to the increased world interconnectedness and rapid technological development, emergencies are increasingly becoming transboundary in nature. As such they affect multiple jurisdictions, they undermine the functioning of various policy sectors and evolve rapidly. Moreover, due to their nature, those risks tend to involve more participants who tend to be dispersed and struggle to share information and coordinate their actions. New forms of large-scale disasters, usually defined as emerging systemic (or catastrophic) risks, have gained more attention at international level, as the frequency of these occurrences increased and policy actions are required to prevent and minimize losses (OECD, 2003; Castellano, 2010).

It is against this backdrop that the very legitimacy, accountability and effectiveness of emergency regulatory action are increasingly measured today. Indeed, being modernity an enterprise for constructing order and control, transboundary risks call this very assertion of control by the nation-state into question today. Indeed the institutional and administrative structures for responding to emergency situations are not designed to deal with transboundary scenarios. In particular, their administrative toolbox for routine problems is of limited use in dealing with transboundary emergencies (Lagadec, 1990). Moreover, as illustrated by several social studies of scientific knowledge production, risks are culturally constructed, socially contested, and differently perceived not only across societies but also across time and space (Jasanoff, 1990; Wynne and Dressel, 2001). As a result, different countries have shown to possess significantly diverse cultures of scientifically informed regulation (Jasanoff, 1993). This poses governments the challenge to rationalize decision-making and urgently call them to coordinate their regulatory actions. Transboundary risks accentuate the challenges that public and private authorities confront in the face of urgent threats, and as such they represent a further experiment for emergency risk regulation (Ansell et al., 2010). An in-built tension in the EU relates to the division of responsibilities between the national and the EU-level. Being crisis management issues are regarded as the core responsibility of the nation-state by the citizens of the EU member states, European political leaders are in many instances unwilling to surrender policy-making autonomy in exchange for coordination at the EU-level (Olsson, 2009). Interestingly enough, the EU member states have included a 'Solidarity Clause' in the Treaty of Lisbon, thus introducing a legal basis for institutionalizing emergency risk regulation in the EU legal order. This provision (article 222) reads: 'The Union and its Member States shall act jointly in a spirit of solidarity if a Member State is the object of a terrorist attack or the victim of a natural or man-made disaster' (Consolidated Version of the Treaty on the Functioning of the European Union, 2009).

By drawing on the literature on organizational studies of risk and regulation, Christopher Lawless (Chapter 15) argues that a holistic, integrated and sociologically oriented approach is needed to understand risk regulation, especially in an increasingly global context. By taking as a point of departure in his analysis the volcanic ash crisis, he discusses how localized risks may become transformed into transboundary risks through organizational dynamics.

In turn, Francisco Lopez-Jurado (Chapter 12), by focusing on the European regulatory framework of network industries, discusses the systemic nature of transboundary risks. In his view, the concept of 'systemic risk' rapidly exceeded the boundaries of the financial sector, as a 'side-effect' of globalization, or as an intrinsic consequence of the multiplication of highly complex interconnected systems. He concludes that the balkanized structure of EU law concerning air transport and energy, in addition to the balance of power between EU institutions and the member states, should be re-examined in order to provide better responses to systemic risks affecting network industries.

Communicating with the Public

Risk communication, i.e. providing information on levels of health, safety and environmental risks, their significance and their management, is a critical component of effective emergency response, especially when dealing with a high perceived risk event. Indeed, the way an emergency is communicated to the public tends to influence the final emergency risk regulation. In general risk communication is concerned with the effectiveness with which messages are presented to the public: are they understandable? Do they under- or over-simplify?

Essentially, communicating risks may take many forms, such as written, verbal or pictorial. As such, it may include a wide range of different sources of information and may involve many different types of organizations (Covello et al., 1988). The *raison d'être* of risk communication within the broader framework of risk regulation lies in the assumption that scientific results as well as risk management options cannot always be easily converted into simple guidelines and advice that non-scientists, like the public or the media, can easily understand or follow. This seems especially true at a time in which we learn about crises via new media tools, such as Twitter, Facebook and YouTube. Moreover, public opinion having become more sceptical about the neutrality and effectiveness of science, there is a growing call for more transparency, especially in times of emergencies. Indeed, pre-existing distrust in government does not vanish in times of crisis. Moreover, in a typical emergency crisis, due to the significant number of actors involved, it is hard to produce one clear and univocal message capable of relieving collective stress. Against this backdrop, Sweta Chakraborty (Chapter 6), placing herself at the interface between risk communication and risk perception research, first highlights the main challenges existing in emergency risk communication. Second, she ventures to provide a plausible blueprint for the best risk communication strategy in emergency situations. In so doing, she illustrates how emergency communication approaches developed from previous similar borderless threats (i.e. pandemics and terrorist attacks) and how such lessons learned were not anticipated and adapted for the type of crisis presented in this book.

Even in the immediacy of disasters, it is evident that peoples' judgment and decision-making processes must be taken into account in order to produce effective risk communications. Today it seems undisputed that the current most widely accepted best practice approach towards risk communication in emergency situation is to first understand how lay publics cognitively perceive risks. Yet, notwithstanding the existence of this sophisticated body of knowledge, public leaders and risk managers often fail to recognize the importance of media in times of emergencies (Macrae, Chapter 2).

Challenge to Existing Regulatory Schemes

The institutional structures, legislative schemes and administrative processes for crisis and disaster management are periodically subject to 'stress tests' in each and every emergency situation. This is generally due to the fact that it is hard, from both an institutional design and normative point of view, to predict unforeseen and unimagined events. On the one hand, planning for each possible threat of hazard that may occur may lead not only to overspending but also to too detailed planning. On the other hand, adopting broader regulatory frameworks can lead to abstract schemes that may fail to provide guidance during an emergency. Yet an emergency requires some form of action, generally with great urgency and involving the possibility of unintended consequences. Moreover, as discussed in Christopher Lawless' chapter (Chapter 15), the transboundary nature of more and more emergencies renders even more difficult the task to design effectively a regulatory response to crises. In this context, Alfredo Fioritto and Marta Simoncini (Chapter 8) argue that given the difficulty in assessing the 'if and when' of catastrophes, due to a lack of scientific knowledge towards disasters, science-based risk regulation is not the optimal solution. They thus recommend the use of standard-based risk regulation that strikes a balance between the state's duty of protection from catastrophes, the exercise of fundamental rights and the costs of implementing the regulation. This 'Pareto optimum' – or acceptable level of protection – represents the point up to which a state is willing to or allowed to protect without constraining too much an individual's liberty.

The EU Air Passengers' Rights Regulation aimed at protecting passengers flying within Europe in case of boarding denial, delay and cancellation was unequivocally challenged by the volcanic ash crisis. When drafting this Regulation the EU legislator unambiguously anticipated having it covering both ordinary and extraordinary circumstances. However, the Icelandic ash cloud, as noted by Morten Broberg (Chapter 13), was not merely extraordinary; rather it brought about exceptional circumstances, or, to be more precise, it produced an emergency situation. In examining the application of the Air Passengers' Regulation in emergency situations like the one experienced during the ash cloud, Morten Broberg and Nick Bernard (Chapter 14) illustrate the limits to the legislator's ability to predict, respond and institutionally design effective protective emergency risk regulation coping with unusual, unforeseen and unimagined events. Both authors seem to agree that when it comes to emergency situations like the one experienced during the Icelandic ash cloud, the present Regulation provides an inadequate scheme for achieving its declared goal of consumer protection. At the time in which the EU legislator is laying down dedicated regulations aimed at recognizing passengers' rights also in the road and maritime transport sectors, they recommend a set of original and insightful suggestions for a possible reform of the Air Passengers' Rights Regulation. The Commission has recently unveiled its plans to draw the necessary lessons from the crisis and, after conducting an impact assessment evaluating further possible measures, is likely to revise the Regulation (Council of the European Union, 2011).

STRUCTURE OF THE BOOK

After this introductory chapter setting up the general framework of the volume, the first part aims at describing the volcanic ash crisis and to explain the lessons learned. The second describes the ideologies, narratives and communication challenges of emergency regulation. The third part goes beyond the ash crisis itself and addresses the many facets of emergency regulation. Whereas part four will be devoted to the organizational mechanisms of emergency regulation, some examples of codified

emergency regulation will be dealt with in part five. Finally, part six
suggests several new ideas for emergency risk regulation, and a closing
chapter critically concludes the volume with a modest set of recommendations on how to regulate risk in emergencies. Each of the chapters ends
with some references to the literature for those who wish to learn more in
that specific sub-field of risk research.

BIBLIOGRAPHY

Alemanno, A. (2012), 'Regulating the European Risk Society', in
    A. Alemanno, F. den Butter, A. Nijsen and J. Torriti, *Better Business Regulation
    in a Risk Society*, Springer, forthcoming (2012).
Alexander, D. (2002), *Principles of Emergency Planning and Management*, New
    York: Oxford University Press.
Ansell, C., A. Bojn and A. Keller (2010), 'Managing Transboundary Crises:
    Identifying the Building Blocks of an Effective Response System', *Journal of
    Contingencies and Crisis Management*, **18** (4), 195–207.
Beck, U. (1992), *Risk Society: Toward A New Modernity*, London: Sage Publica-
    tions.
Beck, U. (1999), *World Risk Society*, Cambridge: Polity Press.
Beck, U. (2000), 'Risk Society Revisited', in B. Adam, U. Beck and J. van Loon, *The
    Risk Society and Beyond: Critical Issues for Social Theory*, London: Sage,
    pp.211–29.
Boin, A. (2010), 'Preparing for Future Crises: Lessons from Research', in
    B. Hutter, *Anticipating Risks and Organising Risk Regulation*, Cambridge: Cam-
    bridge University Press, pp. 231–48.
Boin, A. and P. 't Hart, E. Stern and B. Sundelius (2005), *The Politics of Crisis
    Management: Public Leadership Under Pressure*, Cambridge: Cambridge Univer-
    sity Press.
Boin, A. and M. Rhinard (2008), 'Managing Transboundary Crises: What Role for
    the European Union', *International Studies Review*, **10**, 1–26.
Bostrom, N. and M.M. Cirkovic (2008), *Global Catastrophic Risks*, Oxford: Oxford
    University Press.
Brannigan, V. (2010), 'Alice's Adventures in Volcano Land: The Use and Abuse of
    Expert Knowledge in Safety Regulation', *European Journal of Risk Regulation*, **1**
    (2), 107–14.
Canton, L. (2007), *Emergency Management: Concepts and Strategies for Effective
    Programs*, New Jersey: Wiley.
Caron, D.D (2001), 'Addressing Catastrophes: Conflicting Images of Solidarity and
    Self Interest', in David D. Caron and Charles H. Leben (eds), *Les Aspects
    Internationaux des Catastrophes Naturelles et Industrielles/The International
    Aspects of Natural and Industrial Catastrophes*, The Hague Academy of Interna-
    tional Law.
Castellano, G. (2010), 'Governing Ignorance: Emerging Catastrophic Risks –
    Industry Responses and Policy Frictions', *The Geneva Papers*, **35**, 391–415.
Casti, J.L. (1990), *Paradigms Lost*, Harper perennial.

Clarke, L.B. (1999), *Mission Improbable: Using Fantasy Documents to Tame Disasters*, Chicago: University of Chicago Press.

Consolidated Version of the Treaty on the Functioning of the European Union (2009).

Council of the European Union (2011) 'EU Volcanic Ash Crisis: Follow-Up and the Wider Scope of Crisis Management', Information from the Commission, March 25, 2011.

Covello, von Winterfeldt, and Slovic (1986), cited in OECD, Risk Communication – Chemical Product Risks – An OECD Background Paper, Berlin, 2000.

Farber, D.A. and M. Fauré (2010), *Disaster Law*, Cheltenham, UK and Northampton, MA: Edward Elgar.

Farber, D.A, R.G. Bea, K. Roberts, E. Wenk and K. Inkabi (2006), 'Reinventing Flood Control', *Tulane Law Review*, **81** (1085).

Dauber, M.L. (1998), 'Let Me Be Next Time "Tried By Fire": Disaster Relief and the Origins of the American Welfare State', *Northwestern University Law Review*, **92**, 967–71.

Dauber, M.L. (1999), 'Fate, Responsibility and 'Natural' Disaster Relief: Narrating the American Welfare State', *Law &Society Review*, **33**, 257–61.

Disaster Law and the Legal Academia (2007), 'Curriculum, Research and Law Reform', Report on a Workshop held at UC Berkeley Law School, 25 June 2007.

Downs, A. (1957), *An Economic Theory of Democracy*, New York: Harper.

Drennan, L.T. and A. McConnell (2007), *Risk and Crisis Management in the Public Sector*, New York: Routledge.

Eskridge, W.N. Jr. and J. Ferejohn (2002), 'Structuring Lawmaking to Reduce Cognitive Bias: A Critical View', *Cornell Law Review*, **87**, 616.

Flynn, J., P. Slovic and H. Kunreuther (2001), *Risk, Media and Stigma; Understanding Public Challenges to Modern Science and Technology*, London, Sterling, VA: Earthscan.

Gerrard, M.B. (2006), 'Emergency Exemptions from Environmental Laws After Disasters', *Natural Resources & Environment*, **20** (10), 10–14.

Graham, J. and J. Wiener (1996), *Risk versus Risk: Tradeoffs in Protecting Health and the Environment*, Cambridge, MA: Harvard University Press.

Hood, C., H. Rothstein and R. Baldwin. (2001), *The Government of Risk: Understanding Risk Regulation Regimes*, Oxford: Oxford University Press.

Hutter, B.M. (2010), *Anticipating Risks and Organising Risk Regulation*, Cambridge: Cambridge University Press.

Hutter, B.M. and M. Power (2005), 'Organizational Encounters with Risk: An Introduction', in B.M. Hutter and M. Power (eds), *Organizational Encounters with Risk*, Oxford: Oxford University Press, 1–32.

House of Commons, Science and Technology Committee, Scientific advice and Evidence in Emergencies, Third Report of Session 2010–11, February 2011.

Jasanoff, S. (1990), *The Fifth Branch: Science Advisers as Policy Makers*, Cambridge, MA: Harvard University Press.

Jasanoff, S. (1993), 'Bridging the Two Cultures of Risk Analysis', *Risk Analysis*, **13** (2), 123–9.

Kitzinger, J. and J. Reilly (1997), 'The Rise and Fall of Risk Reporting', *European Journal of Communication*, **12**(3), 319–50.

Kuhn T.S. (1962), *The Structure of Scientific Revolutions*, Chicago: Univ. of Chicago Press.

Lagadec, P. (1990), *States of Emergency: Technological Failures and Social Destabilization*, London: Butterworth-Heinemann.

Löfstedt, R.E. and T. Horlick-Jones (1999), 'Environmental Regulation in the UK: Politics, Institutional Change and Public Trust', in G. Cvetkovich and R.E. Löfstedt (eds), *Social Trust and the Management of Risk*, London: Earthscan, 73–88.

Majone, G. (1984), 'Science and Transcience in Standard Setting', *Science, Technology and Human Values*, 9 (1), 15–22

Noll, R.G. and J. E. Trier (2000), 'Some Implications of Cognitive Psychology for Risk Regulation', in C.R. Sunstein, *Behavioral Law & Economics*, Cambridge: Cambridge University Press.

Obama, B. (2011) Executive Order 13563 of January 18, 2011, Improving Regulation and Regulatory Review.

OECD (2003), *Emerging Systemic Risks in the 21st Century: An Agenda for Action*, Paris: OECD.

Olson, S. (2009), *Crisis Management in the European Union – Cooperation in the Face of Emergencies*, Berlin-Heidelberg: Springer.

Posner, R.A. (2004), *Catastrophe: Risk and Response*, New York: Oxford University Press.

Rosenthal, U., R.A. Boin and L.K. Comfort (eds) (2001), *Managing Crises: Threats, Dilemmas, Opportunities*, Springfield: Charles C. Thomas.

Siegrist, M. and G. Cvetkovich (2000), 'Perception of Hazards: the Role of Social Trust and Knowledge', *Risk Analysis*, **20**, 713–9.

Slovic, P. (2000), *The Perception of Risk*. London: Earthscan Publications.

Smith, D. and D. Elliot (2006), *Key Readings in Crisis Management: Systems and Structures for Prevention and Recovery*, New York: Routledge.

Sunstein, C.R. (2000), *Behavioral Law & Economics*, Cambridge: Cambridge University Press.

Sunstein, C.R. (2005), *Laws of Fear: Beyond the Precautionary Principle*, Cambridge: Cambridge University Press.

Sunstein, C.R. (2007), *Worst-Case Scenarios*, Cambridge, MA: Harvard University Press.

Sunstein, C.R. and R. Zeckhauser (2010), 'Dreadful Possibilities, Neglected Probabilities', in E. Michel-Kerjan and P. Slovic (eds), *The Irrational Economist*, New York: Public Affairs Press.

Twersky, A. and D. Kahneman (1974), 'Judgement under Uncertainty: Heuristics and Biases', *Science*, **185** (4157), 1124–31.

Weinberg, A.M. (1985), 'Science and its Limits: The Regulator's Dilemma', *Issues in Science and Technology*, **2** (1), 59–72.

Wynne, B. and K. Dressel (2001), 'Cultures of Uncertainty – Transboundary Risks and BSE in Europe', in J. Linnerooth-Bayer, R. Lofstedt and G. Sjostedt (eds), *Transboundary Risk Management*, London: Earthscan, 121–54.

PART 1

The volcanic ash crisis: what happened and lessons learned

1. What happened and lessons learned: a European and international perspective

Alberto Alemanno

More than 20 years after the EU eliminated its internal land borders, the Union still lacks an integrated airspace. This seems to the most immediate regulatory lesson learnt from the recent volcanic ash crisis. In this introductory chapter, I provide a first-hand analysis of the regulatory answer developed across Europe in the aftermath of the eruption of the Icelandic volcano Eyjafjallajökull and qualify it as a case in point for an analysis of the concept of 'emergency risk regulation'. While reconstructing the unfolding of the events and the procedures followed by the regulators, I will attempt to address some of the following questions: What did the assessment of the danger of volcanic ash mean for airplanes? Who was competent to take risk-management decisions, such as the controversial flight bans? Is it true that the safe level of volcanic ash was zero? How to explain the shift to a new safety threshold (of 2,000 mg/m^3) only five days after the event? Did regulators overact? To what extent did they manage the perceived risk rather than the actual one?

1.1 THE EMERGENCY REGULATORY RESPONSE

Following the eruption of Icelandic volcano Eyjafjallajökull on 14 April 2010, a cloud of ash quickly spread across Europe, helped by favourable winds. As a result, most European civil aviation authorities closed their respective airspaces.[1] The flying bans came amid fears that the volcanic ash – a mixture of glass, sand and rock particles – could seriously damage aircraft engines. The national measures were based on the scientific advice provided by the Volcanic Ash Advisory Centre, London (VAAC)[2] and were implemented by the European Organisation for the Safety of Air Navigation (Eurocontrol).[3] From an average of 28,000 flights a day in Europe, by

17 April, when less than half of European's airspace was in use, there were only 5,335 actual flights. Yet, even before the bans were lifted, recriminations began. The national authorities came under pressure from European airlines, several of whom had conducted allegedly successful test flights in the supposed danger zone. After three days of flying bans, all major airlines vocally claimed that authorities had been overly cautious by overestimating, in the name of the controversial precautionary principle, the extent of the ash cloud and the hazard it represented for jet engines. In particular, critics have disputed the model used by the VAAC London, which was originally developed to track radioactive fallout from the Chernobyl nuclear disaster in 1986,[4] and dismissed it as 'theoretical'.[5] National authorities defended their 'zero-risk' regulatory response by claiming that their position was consistent with the guidelines developed by the International Civil Aviation Organisation (ICAO).[6] In turn, scientists have strenuously defended the predictions made by the NAME atmospheric dispersion model underpinning the ICAO guidelines (ICAO, 2007, section 3.4).

Meanwhile, the cloud was not moving. As Europe was facing another week of disruption, the European Commission took the initiative over the weekend of 17–18 April, with the Spanish Presidency and Eurocontrol, to propose a coordinated European approach. As the situation evolved, the model and the national risk-management procedures were tested. It became clear to the EU member states, national air safety authorities, national air traffic controllers and Eurocontrol that a more differentiated assessment of risk from the ash cloud was needed. But, under a 'prisoner's dilemma'-like scenario, no member state could act independently by departing from the ICAO guidelines and taking the first step to introduce change. These guidelines are crystal clear: 'The recommended procedure in the case of volcanic ash is exactly same as with low-level wind shear, regardless of ash concentration – AVOID AVOID AVOID' (ICAO, 2007, point 3.4.8). Five days after the enforcement of the national flying bans, European member states unanimously agreed, following an extraordinary meeting co-chaired by Eurocontrol and the European Commission on 19 April, to move to 'a co-ordinated European approach in response to the crisis' (EU Commission, 2010 b).

As a result, new procedures were defined that led to a partial reopening of European air space and hence reduced the human and economic impact on passengers, airlines and cargo.[7] The new measures came into force at 08.00 hours CET on 20 April and established three types of zones, depending on the degree of contamination. The first zone was located in the central nucleus of the emissions, where a full restriction of operations was maintained; the second consisted of an intermediary zone where member states could allow flights 'in a coordinated manner [with other members]' but with additional restrictions and safety controls; and the third zone, not affected by the ash, had no restrictions. These procedures based on a more differentiated risk assessment and paving the way for more coordinated decisions across the states allowed for 'a progressive and coordinated opening of European Air Space' (EU Council, 2010). By 22 April, eight days after the eruption began, flights were back to normal, with 27,284 flights compared to 28,578 expected on the same day two weeks earlier.[8] Interestingly enough, transport ministers agreed to ask the Commission, 'as long as the air traffic in Europe is not totally open', to contribute to 'a smooth coordination that allows the mobility of European citizens through other modes of transport' (EU Council, 2010).

The calm after the storm – one might have thought. Yet, the situation created by the protracted closure of the European airspace has been so extraordinary that the regulatory action responsible for the disruption remained at the centre of a growing controversy. Beyond the personal dramatic situation for millions of passengers who were stranded, and the difficult implementation of the passenger's rights regulation,[9] the air industry has incurred significant costs and suffered reduced revenues.[10] Also, airports, as well as ground handling services and tour operators, had been severely hit.[11]

1.2 THE SCIENCE BEHIND REGULATIONS FOR VOLCANIC ASH

It seems undisputed that volcanic ash can cause jet engines to fail in flight.[12] An engine's heat melts the finely-ground rock, which in turn proceeds to encrust the cooler parts of the mechanism, stopping it from working. This phenomenon is called sand-blasting and it came to wide public attention in 1982 when two jumbo passenger jets lost engine power due to the planes flying through clouds of ash from the eruptions of the Galunggun volcano in Indonesia (Casadevall, 1991, pp. iii–iv). Since then, volcanic ash has been internationally recognized as a source of potential hazard for aviation and triggered a wide range of initiatives by ICAO aimed at mitigating that hazard.

These incidents undoubtedly served to increase interest in the aviation community in volcanic hazard. Yet, although they revealed that mitigation of the hazard posed by volcanic ash to aviation safety would require the cooperation and efforts of volcanologists, meteorologists, air traffic managers, engine manufacturers and pilots, they were not enough to capture the interest of the airline industry. It seems that the same airline companies that today blame the authorities and the scientists for being overly cautious have always been rather reluctant to commission studies on the impact of ash on their aircraft. As a result, given the lack of technological tools capable of detecting volcanic ash, the only strategy left that guarantees flight safety seems to be the complete avoidance of these ash clouds. As mentioned above, this is the risk-management strategy enshrined in the ICAO's Manual, which explains why national authorities have consistently held that the presence of virtually any volcanic ash was a threat to aviation.

The major obstacle to resuming flights has been understanding aircraft tolerance levels to ash. It seems that manufacturers have agreed on increased tolerance levels in low ash density areas, but have refused to disclose their data. It remains therefore to be seen how exactly authorities moved from the ICAO's recommended zero safety level to a 2,000 micrograms of ash per cubic metre within the space of five days.

By implicitly acknowledging the inherent limits of the predominant risk analysis model, the EU Commission has decided to take two initiatives addressing the wider international dimension:

- the creation of a working group of experts, encompassing representatives from Eurocontrol, the European Air Safety Agency, member states, ICAO and the air industry. The idea is to entrust this group with the task of establishing an inventory of the relevant technological and methodological tools at European level and in the member states, and a research roadmap to make the most up-to-date and validated tools available to facilitate making appropriate decisions;
- the elaboration of a new methodology and coherent approach to safety risk assessment and risk management in relation to the closure of airspace to be proposed to ICAO.

The results of both initiatives were, as originally planned (EU Commission, 2010 a), submitted by the EU to the ICAO general assembly in September 2010. After that, the ICAO International Volcanic Ash Task Force (IVATF) elaborated a new international standard within ICAO for flying in volcanic ashes.[13] This is a globally applicable process to facilitate the management of flight operations into, or near, areas of known or forecast volcanic cloud through the provision of appropriate information to assist in minimizing safety risk in such operations. The emerging new standard, developed by the IVATF, represents, first, a shift from a zero-risk policy to a threshold level, which has been rendered possible by the data obtained by engine manufacturers in the aftermath of the crisis. Second, it signals a change in the responsibility for the decision to fly in those circumstances by shifting it from the public authorities to the airline operators. Indeed, under the ICAO Draft December 2010 Guidance:

For States whose airspace is potentially contaminated by volcanic ash, it is intended that the control measures specified in this document should be sufficient to satisfy their need to be confident in the ability of operators from other States to undertake operations safely into airspace that is known or forecast to be contaminated by volcanic ash; no further action on the part of States whose airspace is potentially contaminated by volcanic ash is intended. (ICAO, 2010)

In essence, the approach is based on formalizing a risk-assessment process for use by an operator wishing to conduct such an operation and an evaluation process for use by that operator's state in assessing whether or not the risk of that operation is minimized to an acceptable level by that operator's use of this process. It is intended that the state of the operator or state of registry, as appropriate, would make this determination on behalf of all other provider states through whose airspace the resultant flight operations are planned to be conducted.

1.3 THE NOT-YET EUROPEAN SKY

As is well known by now, EU integration does not yet extend to air traffic management.[14] Only member states can decide whether or not to close their airspace. As a result, the EU boasts 27 different air traffic zones, each able to impose a flying ban. Fragmentation in the European Union is the result of a history where air traffic control has been (and still is) closely associated with sovereignty, and hence confined within national borders. Indeed, air traffic control is still perceived as governed by both national defence and sovereign interests. This also reflects one of the tenets of the Chicago Convention according to which each state is responsible for safety oversight in civil aviation within its jurisdiction.[15]

Yet, it would be a mistake to think that efforts have not been made towards integration of EU airspace.[16] Following the adoption of the Single Europe Sky (SES I) legislation in 2004, air traffic management was brought under the EU common transport policy.[17] The idea was to redesign the European sky according to traffic flows rather than national borders. Yet, as unambiguously exemplified by the patchwork regulatory response to the current crisis, a truly 'single' sky has not been achieved.

To remedy this situation, another reform, the 'Single Sky Package' (SES II) was adopted by the European Parliament and the Council in November 2009.[18] To accelerate the full implementation of the SES, the Commission has been leveraging the volcanic ash crisis to create political momentum. In the aftermath of the crisis, it came out with a set of encouraging proposals. Most of them have been implemented by now.[19]

First, the creation of a crisis coordination cell, gathering together Euro-control, EASA,[20] member states and air transport stakeholders. This is exactly what the EU did not have available during the crisis. This cell institutionalizes some of the *ad hoc* mechanisms born during the crisis and would be empowered with the possibility of launching unmanned aircraft vehicles (UAV) to collect data.

Second, nomination of the Functional Airspace Blocks (FAB) coordina-tors to facilitate their quick creation. FABs are airspace blocks, nine in number, based on operational requirements. They have been established regardless of state boundaries, where the provision of air navigation services and related ancillary functions are optimized and/or integrated. They were foreseen in SES II and their implementation was adopted on 3 December 2010, which together with the nomination of the FAB Coordi-nator will provide support in facilitating the respect of the FAB implemen-tation deadline of 4 December 2012.[21]

Third, appointment of the central European Network Management. It could reasonably be argued that if the network management function had been designated prior to the crisis, the EU would have benefited from a more harmonized and coordinated approach to the risk and flow/capacity assessment; this would have given it the ability to formulate proposals for solutions quickly to be tabled in the context of SES governance structures, taking also into account the need for coordination with other neighbouring countries and regions. The Implementing Rule for Network Functions was adopted by the Single Sky Committee, along with the decision on the designation of the Network Manager, on 15 February 2011.

Fourth, acceleration of the implementation of EASA's competences in Air Traffic Management (ATM) safety. Following the opinions issued by EASA on 28 Mary 2010, the agency will be assuming these new compe-tences before 2012 to ensure the safety of the European network, thus ensuring a 'full system, gate-to-gate' approach to safety.

1.3.1 Lessons Learned and Open Questions

The protracted closure of the European airspace following the volcanic eruption in Iceland, together with the initially fragmented regulatory answer, has shown that while precautionary measures may be life-saving, they may also be not only logistically disrupting but also economically very costly. Whether and how these costs should be taken into account at the risk-management stage represents one of the most difficult questions surrounding the principle. According to many, this is also one of its greatest weaknesses.[22] Should the expected value of the precautions have been compared against their expected costs?[23] The EU version of the principle, reflecting the Judaeo-Christian belief that life is without price, does not seem to admit any room for this kind of regulatory exercise. However, a comparative analysis of expected costs and expected benefits of precautionary measures could serve as a useful check against overreaction to recent incidents.

This seems especially true if one considers the incentives that regulators have in the aftermath of a crisis to pay undue attention to the worst-case scenarios. Moreover, it is often argued that the inclusion of precautionary costs could also induce regulators, when examining risk vs risk tradeoffs, to spot 'substitute risks', i.e. hazards that materialize or are increased by risk-regulation policies (Graham et al., 1995). Thus, for instance, after the attacks of '9/11', many Americans switched from flying to driving and because driving is more dangerous than flying, thousands of people have died as a result of the switch. It is probably too early to detect the impact that flying bans have had on other public transport accidents but it might be interesting to look at these data.

On the other hand, one may wonder how costs can be realistically computed in a situation in which, by definition, it is not possible to assign probabilities to the various scenarios because of the alleged level of uncertainty involved. But is it true that authorities did not know how much ash a jet could safely tolerate? Or perhaps they knew this but had no means of measuring the average density of ash in the atmosphere. Should it emerge that authorities at the time of the eruption did not know either of the two, their regulatory response would seem to be justified and could escape criticism. On the other hand, if they did know, or could have known, this information with some more diligence and/or cooperation with airline industries and engine manufacturers, then some claims of precautionary abuse might be justified. A question worth asking is whether in these circumstances some forms of regulators' liability should emerge. However, if it is true that airlines and engine manufacturers have been reluctant to commission studies on the impact of ash on their aircraft, the claim of overreaction would lose some of its evocative power.

For the time being, the European Commission seems more prone to look into the future than into the past. At the time this book went to press, the EU legislator adopted a wide range of measures designed at better integration of the EU airspace through the Single European Sky (SES).[24]

By leveraging the disruption caused by the volcanic ash crisis, the Commission successfully accelerated the implementation of SES II, thus institutionalizing some of the *ad hoc* mechanisms and procedures developed during the outbreak. Undoubtedly, this crisis has added new impetus to the long-running struggle to unite Europe's airspace. The costs of a non-European sky have turned out to be higher than expected. As if any proof were needed, it is time for the EU to conquer its own sky.

NOTES

1.   At its height on 17–18 April 2010, 17 EU member states had a full airspace closure and two were partially closed. At the same time, six non-EU states were fully closed.
2.   Nine Volcanic Ash Advisory Centres around the world are responsible for advising international aviation of the location and movement of clouds of volcanic ash. They are part of an international system set up by the International Civil Aviation Organization (ICAO) called the International Airways Volcano Watch (IAVW). In particular, the London VAAC is responsible for monitoring and forecasting the movement of volcanic ash over the UK, Iceland and the north-eastern part of the North Atlantic Ocean.
3.   Contrary to what was reported by most media, Eurocontrol is an international, not an EU, organization. It was established in 1960 by Germany, Belgium, France, UK and Northern Ireland, Luxembourg and the Netherlands through the Eurocontrol International Convention relating to Co-operation for the Safety of Air Navigation signed in Brussels with the main purpose 'to strengthen their cooperation in matters of air navigation and in particular to provide for the common organisation of the air traffic services in the upper air space.' This convention entered into force in 1963 and has 38 member countries, including the European Union.
4.   The Numerical Atmospheric-dispersion Modelling Environment (NAME) has evolved into an all-purpose dispersion model capable of predicting the transport, transformation and deposition of a wide class of airborne materials, e.g. nuclear material, volcanic emissions, biomass smoke, chemical spills, foot-and-mouth disease. See ICAO's *Manual on Volcanic Ash*, Radioactive Material and Toxic Chemical Clouds – Doc 9691.
5.   Statement by Giovanni Bisignani, Director General and Chief Executive of the International Air Transport Association (IATA), on 19 April 2010, available at http://www.iata.org/pressroom/pr/Pages/2010-04-19-01.aspx (accessed 8 April 2011).
6.   ICAO was created in 1944 by the Convention on International Civil Aviation and is headquartered in Montreal, Canada. The guidelines are contained in the *Manual on Volcanic Ash*, Radioactive Material and Toxic Chemical Clouds – Doc 9691.
7.   These procedures were presented by EU Commission Vice-President Kallas to an extraordinary meeting of Transport Ministers, chaired by Spanish minister José Blanco, and finally endorsed at the same meeting.
8.   See Eurocontrol Volcanic Ash Could Timeline, available at http://www.eurocontrol.int/category/keywords/ volcanic-ash-cloud-timeline (accessed 1 April 2011).
9.   Despite the exceptional circumstances, the EU Commission considers that the Regulation on Air Passengers Rights (EC Regulation 261/2004) remains fully applicable. Yet, it admits that, in the ongoing review of the regulation, it will 'take into account the experience of the volcano ash crisis to decide whether improvements are necessary'. See EU Commission (2010 a), at para. 26.
10.   Although at the end of April it was too early to measure the impact, since some traffic that did not occur during the closure of the airspace might have taken place later on, the first figures provided by the sector calculate losses of several hundred million euros.
11.   Under EU law, tour operators are required to provide repatriation of stranded passengers and to refund or offer alternative arrangements to customers who have not started their journey as a result of the European airspace's closure.
12.   To know more on volcanic ash and its effects on aviation, see V.M. Branningan (2010). On volcanism and its consequences, see M.R. Rampino (2008).

13. International Civil Aviation Organization International Volcanic Ash Task Force Guidance Material Management Of Flight Operations With Known Or Forecast Volcanic Cloud Contamination Preliminary Issue – Draft Version 3.1 – 19 December 2010.

14. Air Traffic Management (ATM) encompasses the functions required to ensure safe and efficient movement of aircraft during all phases of operations (Air Traffic Services (ATS)), airspace management (ASM) and air traffic flow management (ATFM).

15. Convention on International Civil Aviation, signed in Chicago in 1944.

16. Efforts to shape an EU airspace date back 1996 when the European Commission published a White Paper on Air Traffic Management ('Freeing Europe's Airspace') and were followed by the 1997 initiative of Eurocontrol members to open up Eurocontrol membership to the European Community.

17. The SES I consists of a Framework Regulation plus three technical regulations on the provision of air navigation services, organisation and use of the airspace and the interoperability of the European air traffic management network. See EC Regulation 549/2004 of the European Parliament and of the Council of 10 March 2004 laying down the framework for the creation of the Single European Sky.

18. EC Regulation 1070/2009.

19. Council of the European Union (2011) EU Volcanic Ash Crisis: Follow-Up and the Wider Scope of Crisis Management, Information from the Commission, 25 March 2011.

20. The European Air Safety Agency is based in Cologne and employs some 500 professionals from across Europe. It provides expert advice to the EU for drafting new legislation and is in charge of the implementation and monitoring safety rules, including inspections in member states as well as of the approval of organizations involved in the design, manufacture and maintenance of aeronautical products.

21. In accordance with article 8 of the Framework Regulation, the European Commission has issued a mandate to the Eurocontrol Agency for support in the establishment of Functional Airspace Blocks (FABs).

22. See for example C. Sunstein (2007).

23. Even in the US, where value has been conceived for long time solely in monetary terms, there is an emerging consensus that both expected value and expected costs should be measured in terms of well-being. Yet, to say the least, people disagree on how to define well-being (or welfare). See, e.g., R. Revesz et al. (2008) and M. Adler et al. (2006).

24. EU Commission Regulation 1191/2010 of 16 December 2010 amending EC Regulation 1794/2006 laying down a common charging scheme for air navigation services ; EU Commission Regulation No 691/2010 of 29 July 2010 laying down a performance scheme for air navigation services and network functions and amending EC Regulation 2096/2005 laying down common requirements for the provision of air navigation services. See Note d'information de M. Kallas 'Conséquences du nuages de cendres générée par l'éruption volcanique survenue en Islande sur le trafic aérien', SEC(2010) 533.

BIBLIOGRAPHY

Adler, M. and E. Posner (2006), *New Foundations of Cost-Benefit Analysis*, Cambridge, MA: Harvard University Press.

Brannigan, V. (2010), 'Alice's Adventures in Volcano Land: The Use and Abuse of Expert Knowledge in Safety Regulation', *European Journal of Risk Regulation*, **1** (2), 107–14.

Casadevall, T. (ed.) (1991), *Volcanic Ash and Aviation Safety: Proceedings of the First International Symposium on Volcanic Ash and Aviation Safety*, US Geological Survey Bulletin 2047.

EU Commission (2010 a), Note d'information de M. Kallas 'Conséquences du nuage de cendres généré par l'éruption volcanique survenue en Islande et sur le trafic aérien – Etat de la situation, available at http://ec.europa.eu/commission_2010–2014/kallas/headlines/news/2010/04/doc/information_note_volcano_crisis.pdf (accessed 1 April 2011).

EU Commission (2010 b), Volcanic Ash Crisis: Frequently Asked Questions, MEMO/10/143, available at http://europa.eu/rapid/pressReleasesAction.do?reference=MEMO/10/143 (accessed 1 April 2011).

EU Council (2010), Extraordinary Meeting of Minister Of Transport, available at http://www.consilium.europa.eu/uedocs/cms_data/docs/pressdata/en/trans/1138 99.pdf (accessed 1 April 2011).

Graham, J.D. and J.B. Wiener (1995), *Risk vs. Risk: Tradeoffs in Protecting Health and the Environment*, Cambridge, MA: Harvard University Press.

IATA (2010), Re-Think Volcano Measures – Governments Must Base Decisions on Fact Not Theory (Press release), available at http://www.iata.org/pressroom/pr/Pages/2010-04-19-01.aspx (accessed 1 April 2011).

ICAO (2007), 'Manual on Volcanic Ash, Radioactive Material and Toxic Chemical Clouds', available at http://www.paris.icao.int/news/pdf/9691.pdf (accessed 27 February 2011).

ICAO (2010), 'Management Of Flight Operations With Known Or Forecast Volcanic Cloud Contamination – Preliminary Issue – Draft Version 3.1', available at http://www.paris.icao.int/Met/Volc_Ash/docs/IVATF-AIR04-Draft%20Version%203.pdf (accessed 27 February 2011).

Rampino, R. (2008), 'Super-Volcanism and Other Geophysical Processes of Catastrophic Import', in N. Bostrom and M.M. Cirkovic (eds), *Global Catastrophic Risks*, Oxford: Oxford University Press, 205–21.

Revesz, R. and M. Livermore (2008), *Retaking Rationality,* Oxford: Oxford University Press.

Sunstein, C. (2007), *Worst-Case Scenarios*, Cambridge, MA: Harvard University Press.

2. Which risk and who decides when there are so many players?

Donald Macrae

2.1 INTRODUCTION

There was a time that a voyage across the North Atlantic involved praying to Thor and Odin for calm seas and favourable winds but these old practices have fallen into disuse. For a few months in 2010, prayers may have become appropriate again, for favourable winds to blow away the cloud of volcanic ash that could prevent a flight to North America from many places in Europe. Whether modern risk-management systems are more effective than praying to the Norse gods is beyond the scope of this chapter but we certainly saw a time when many of the advances of modern life disappeared and Fate seemed to reassert itself in all its pre-Cartesian power.

To have been a catastrophe, people would have had to have died and it is a feature of this incident that nobody is know to have died as a direct result of volcanic ash in jet engines. But the image of catastrophic engine failure that captured imaginations in the first two days soon faded as millions of lesser disasters and inconveniences surfaced across the globe. It was a remarkable instance of the possibility of a severe loss being set against the certainty of multiple lesser losses, a risk equation that is always difficult to manage.

It all seemed a bit of a mess as well. Could it have been handled better? This chapter tries to analyze the situation using the methodology developed by the UK's Risk and Regulation Advisory Council to manage 'public risk' incidents. It will show that what appeared at one level to be a binary fly/no fly issue for government to decide was only one part of a complex adaptive system of many risk actors, each with their own incentives. It will also speculate on how the system might have adapted had different decision-making taken place.

2.2　MANAGING PUBLIC RISK

The Risk and Regulation Advisory Council (RRAC)[1] was a temporary successor body to the Better Regulation Commission (BRC), established when Gordon Brown became Prime Minister in 2008. The BRC had achieved some fame with its report 'Risk, Responsibility and Regulation: Whose Risk is it Anyway?', known more simply as The Risk Report, which listed many instances of regrettable regulation that derived from incidents of high public anxiety and led the government of the day to conclude that 'something must be done'. The Risk Report was stimulating in its many examples of bad regulation but still left a 'so what?' question in terms of what could be done about this unfortunate regulatory phenomenon. It was essentially the task of the RRAC, in 18 months, to tease out what could be done to manage better these instances of public risk.[2]

2.2.1　The Concept of Public Risk

'Public risk' was defined by them as 'those risks that may affect any part of society and to which government is expected to respond'. It was defined in terms of its characteristics, rather than of its subject-matter, the chief characteristic being that the public perceived it to be a risk that government ought to manage on its behalf. This made the content unpredictable. There could be cases of risks that were not serious but gave rise to anxiety but equally there could be risks that were profound yet somehow just did not excite attention (such as climate change).

Following the BRC's thinking in The Risk Report, the RRAC started out by wanting the management of risks to be devolved to those best placed to manage them, rather than government assuming it was automatically better at managing them. There was a broad view that it would generally be preferable for the government to leave people and organizations free to manage their risks themselves, rather than stepping in with regulatory solutions. However, that view soon changed when analyzing instances of 'public risk' as a social phenomenon. It was realized that it was not a simple alternative of government regulation or individual freedom. Government was not the only player in managing these risks. The RRAC started to identify many 'risk actors' who each contributed to a complex adaptive system, which was described as 'the risk landscape'. In that complex system ministers and officials were only two risk actors – and not always the most influential. It was a key message of the RRAC that the actual government regulation was only one part of the regulatory reality and more needed to be understood.

2.2.2 The Business of Risk Management

There are many people and many occupations that have an interest in managing other people's risks. Insurers and lawyers probably spring to mind. These are perfectly legitimate businesses in risk management services but they add cumulatively to the risk landscape (and were integral to the ash cloud incident, as we shall see). They can deal directly with individual clients but contact may be through intermediaries, such as insurance brokers or citizens' advice bureaux. Again, these are legitimate and respectable services but the web of actors is already extending. Businesses often feel the need to hire consultants to navigate through some of the varied risks they face and they too will add to the complexity. Each layer can add value or can add confusion: there is nothing inherently wrong with it. But those whose business is managing risks can have an interest in escalating risk perception of their clients, even if only to then save them from a worse fate than just paying their fees. Consultants on occupational safety are often blamed for the more extreme urban myths about what safety regulations require but there must be more profit in advising on corrective measures than in simply telling a business that what it is doing is perfectly fine. These urban myths are spread by the media who also are key risk actors and perhaps have a more blatant interest in escalating risk perceptions. So the business of risk management has, at the very least, the seeds of aggravating rather than smoothing the citizen's management of his own risks.

The next stage is the internalizing of the cumulative perceptions, in a reverse 'wisdom of crowds',[3] by a fear of the myths that itself becomes a new myth, such as the 'compensation culture'. People and organizations fear the threat of litigation itself, quite apart from any actual consequences of litigation, and may act to avoid even that threat. Lawyers and the judiciary are certainly RRAC risk actors but that is not always because of actual decisions or behaviours but because of the cultural assumptions about them made by others. Standard setters are then brought into the web even though their standards may have no express legal effect in themselves but many people or businesses will be reticent to fail to follow a standard in case of subsequent litigation if something goes wrong.

2.2.3 Internalizing the Myths

All this can be illustrated in the case of the 'Killer Trees' that the RRAC helped stir debate around. The British Standards Institute was approached in 2007 by the arboriculturalist industry for a standard on tree safety management, which it duly devised and published for public consultation.

It proposed measures that could have led to significant costs if tree owners followed it faithfully for all relevant trees.[4] The chances of death resulting from an interaction of a person with a tree (with one either falling on or from the other) is apparently around 1:10,000,000 so this was not a pressing social issue.[5] But the subsequent media derision (Timmins, 2008; The Economist, 2008; Bennett, 2008) of the BSI was based on assumptions about how tree owners would react to there being such a standard, namely that many would prefer to fell their trees than pay for the inspections or take the risk of litigation. So this proposal for an industry standard became a scare story about massive tree-felling across the country, all based on the internalization of the assumptions about risk-management behaviours. Nothing more has been heard of that standard.

It is against this background that government has to make decisions about risks to the public. Quite apart from any questions about how 'rational' the public are, they operate in this complex web of interests, advice, myths and assumptions and government can no longer assume that its message is the one that gets across when there is so much noise from other actors. Even where the government acts, its actions (including regulations) will be subject to interpretation and advice, which may lead to unintended consequences and perverse results.

2.3 THE ASH CLOUD AS A PUBLIC RISK INCIDENT

The ash cloud incident was certainly a case of 'public risk'. There was a very real threat to the public and a possible role for government in managing that risk. Passenger aircraft falling out of the sky is clearly of public concern. However, the public reaction that the government had to deal with was not one that demanded more safety but one that pressed for more liberty. The high public anxiety was not so much about dying in an air crash but in a million and one other ways that the incident affected individuals personally.

At first, the position for each government to take seemed straightforward enough. It was accepted in the aviation world that aircraft should avoid volcanic ash because of a very real threat of total engine failure. Any government would want to step in and ground all flights until the threat passed or could be managed. However, even at this stage there was no necessity for government to become involved. The danger was well enough known in the aviation industry that all flights would have paused anyway. For the first 24 hours or so, there was a pretty clear consensus that no flights should go through the cloud and that meant closing the three big European hubs, Heathrow, Schiphol and Charles de Gaulle. It was an easy message for ministers to give – safety is paramount.

The public was prepared to tolerate a delay in resuming normal daily life, as with occasional snowstorms, industrial action or other interruptions. There were hints that the danger of Icelandic volcanoes would be with us forever and that modern life would change in that part of the globe but these did not gain much prominence (despite the media's interest in escalating threats) (Burgess, Chapter 5). It was probably too awful to contemplate. But the public could contemplate it continuing for a few more days and that was beginning to be bad enough. Commercial interests were also recalculating their positions and beginning to see losses mount.

It became much more difficult for government because the consensus was evaporating. Saying that safety was the overriding concern was no longer carrying the same weight or political assurance. Safety is a relative term, not an absolute, and the phrase loved by politicians that safety will never be compromised is, in practice, a nonsense. It was an extreme example of the *possibility* of a serious danger balanced against the *certainty* of lesser dangers, as the implications for a remarkably huge number of people began to be realized. Tens of thousands of people were in the wrong place. They were perhaps safe but that was not enough. They wanted to be safe somewhere else. From those people and things that were in the wrong place, there were consequences for people who were not travelling or even for people in another part of the globe. There were reports of schools in Surrey that were closed because the teachers were in Florida. Flights from China to Africa were disrupted, even though nowhere near the North Atlantic, simply because so much of the world's airline fleet was grounded in Europe.

The consensus broke first from the airlines, who were at the sharp end of the crisis. Some sent up aircraft to test the cloud, which was enough for the public to start challenging the international standard of zero tolerance of volcanic ash. There was then speculation about the possibility of gradations of ash and attendant dangers or challenges to the meteorology of the cloud's whereabouts. The relativity of safety asserted itself quickly and the simplistic ministerial reliance on safety being paramount sounded out of touch. But it was not clear at all to ministers what their new message should be.

Then, as cheap fiction used to say, 'in a bound, our hero was free'. It was announced that, within a few hours, flights would recommence. This was not met with howls of public anxiety about safety but relief that life was getting back to normal and, for many, a chance to repair their personal losses. The crisis was passing, with no deaths or injury directly from ash-induced disaster.

2.4 THE RISK LANDSCAPE OF THE ASH CLOUD

2.4.1 The Risk actors

In terms of the RRAC analysis, there were the following risk actors:

- government, or actually governments in the plural. No one government could have resolved this crisis. Each controlled its own airspace but few flights would have remained within one national airspace;
- airspace regulators – International Civil Aviation Authority (ICAO), Eurocontrol and national bodies like the UK's NATS and Civil Aviation Authority;
- supra-national governance through the EU Council, with Commission support;
- airlines;
- trades unions, especially for pilots (International Federation of Airline Pilots' Associations (IFALPA)) and air crew;
- engine manufacturers;
- insurers to the engine manufacturers and to the airlines;
- lawyers, advising all parties on powers and potential liabilities;
- scientists (meteorologists, volcanologists, engineers);
- the media;
- passengers.

But these players each have their own interests, and few of them have an interest in taking a risk. Plotting them against axes of their influence in decision-making against their incentive to take a risk might look like Figure 2.1.

The most striking aspect of Figure 2.1 is how few actors had a strong incentive to take a risk on flying. Most of the key players had no pressing interest in giving any assurance about safety. If ever there was a case of 'not betting the company on a single throw', this was it. Getting this one wrong would be disastrous, both for the company and for the unfortunate people who would tragically prove the point.

The parties with the biggest influence were the engine manufacturers. But they had no incentive to underwrite the risks of flying through ash. It was the airlines who had the greatest incentive to take a risk but they were not the decision-makers and their influence over the politicians carried negative political value. And if some airlines were to start taking risks and, in so doing, damage their engines, the manufacturers would happily sell them more engines.

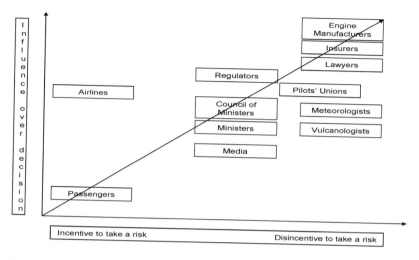

Figure 2.1. Influence and incentive

When then plotting formal decision-making capability against the level of knowledge with which to make that decision, something like Figure 2.2 may have been the case. Once again, it was the engine manufacturers who held the key.

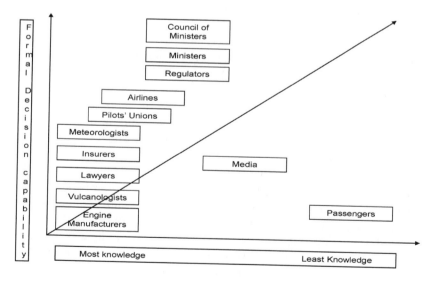

Figure 2.2. Decision-making and knowledge

2.4.2 Options for Ministers

In some ways, Figure 2.2 is an inversion of Figure 2.1 because, in this crisis, knowledge was the key. The system was locked into safety and ministers were powerless just to 'deem' something to be safe. There had to be some evidence. The power that the minister had was a negative one of closure of airspace. Even if they had a legal power to open their airspace again, flying within the airspace still depended on safety assessments. Operators had to lodge safety risk assessments with the airspace regulators who had to approve them, therefore the regulators still required to be satisfied regarding safety, even if the airspace was not closed or was reopened. So perhaps the system might still have operated without any ministerial intervention at all?

2.4.3 Options for the Airlines

But even if there had been no closure of airspace, the airline companies were not free to make their own risk assessment. They were constrained first by their own concern for safety. It would be very unfair to present them as straining at the leash to fly again regardless of the consequences. They recognized that the first carrier to send up an airliner that then crashed would sooner or later go the way of Pan Am after the Lockerbie bombing. The market would kill the company as passengers shifted to the 'safer' airlines. It was in nobody's interests to have a crash. But the airlines did have huge commercial pressure to resume flying. It was not just losing throughput but also stacking up additional liabilities to the booked passengers, plus the logistical challenge of getting back to normal. The commercial pressures were acute on both sides of the equation, if a fatal flight were to be the cost of flying again. And, of course, the problem with the fatal flight was not just the reputational damage but that the incident would have locked down the safety precautions even tighter. It would be much longer before anyone flew.

Even then, the board decision for the airlines would have to have taken account of legal advice and insurance cover. It would probably not have been enough simply to make a 'test' flight and then claim that the commercial balance was in favour of resuming. Both the lawyers and the insurers would be looking to the engineers and scientists. For as long as the engine manufacturers said that there was no safe level of ash tolerance and for as long as the meteorologists said that the cloud was in their flight path, the insurers would walk away and the lawyers would list the inevitable liabilities.

Even if the airlines decided to resume, that would then pass the decision on any particular flight to the 'pilot in command'. It is a trite example of assurance that in a crash the pilot is first to die therefore he / she can be trusted to keep safety in proportion. However, pilots face strong pressures to do what they are paid for, to fly. The position of the pilots' representative body, IFALPA, would also have been influential in being, as their strapline has it, 'The Global Voice of Pilots'.[6] There would have been no strong incentive for IFALPA to stretch the safety limits.

2.4.4 The Scientists

For the scientists, they would not see it as a matter of risk but a matter of knowledge: they would just give their best understanding of the facts that they were asked to provide and it was not for them to assess these facts in terms of outcomes. However, they would have been naïve to believe that others would not try to place the assessment on them and push them towards predicting an outcome, one way or another. The volcanologists could give their best view of the nature of the ash and the meteorologists their forecast of dispersal. Sooner or later, there would have been pressure on the grey area of the boundary of the cloud. Even if there were truly no safe level of ash, there had to be a boundary somewhere between clear skies and cloud. That would be the wedge to be driven into the scientific assessment. As it turned out, this graduated approach was indeed adopted.

2.4.5 The Media

The media could have it both ways, as is often the case in an acute crisis. They could focus on the horrors of crashes or on the misery of stranded passengers, or the reputed instances of life-saving surgery being denied people unable to travel. They may have acted as some sort of conscience if the mood were to get too gung-ho about the risks but they also built the pressure from the frustrated passengers. There was no shortage of stories to report on that side of the equation (Burgess, Chapter 5). They are the one actor whose position does not change from Figure 2.1 to Figure 2.2. They were in no position to force a decision because they were not a source of the evidence needed to unblock the situation.

The crisis did not last long enough for the media to develop its own narrative, as noted by Adam Burgess in his chapter. Coverage was fragmented, with whatever stories made good copy at the time, and did not coalesce into a particular angle, or even into competing angles. Where the media can have influence tends to be where there is a clear, simplistic issue and the tension between the high drama of airline disasters and the mundane reality of airport-bound refugees stopped the media settling into a particular line.

2.4.6 Passengers

Passengers might arguably not have been risk actors but rather the passive beneficiaries of all the other actors' stated motivations. It was the safety of passengers rather than of physical or corporate assets that all this was ostensibly being done for. But passengers became active players by the increasing demand for flights to be resumed. The passengers had no formal lever to pull in making the decision. But the passengers are also the market.

In terms of the BRC's pleas to devolve risk management to the lowest level at which it can be properly managed, it is doubtful that this was a risk that could have been devolved to the travelling public. Although much information was readily available on the internet, it would have been difficult for an ordinary passenger to make a proper risk assessment. What would have overridden recourse to scientific evidence would have been the simple fact that the airlines were flying again. If the planes were going up, that would be good enough for most people. We are back to trusting the pilot not to have a death wish.

But perhaps there is more to it than that. For the politicians to devolve the decision down to the appropriate level, it was not just the level of the airlines deciding to fly. The flying public also had to decide to fly. They could have chosen to stay away.

This was another risk in this crisis that, perhaps surprisingly, did not materialize. Even if the airlines had worked their way through all the obstacles to resuming flying, they still remained vulnerable to passengers deciding to stop flying. The air disasters of 9/11 led to a significant reduction in air passenger traffic yet it is worth noting that this did not happen after the ash cloud (Alemanno, Chapter 1). As it was, there was a kind of captive market anyway in the first few weeks just repatriating the displaced, most of whom would have found an alternative by then if one had been available. But the cloud had none of the deterrence of Al Qaeda. Perhaps it was because there was no crash, no graphic pictures, no gruesome iconography. Or perhaps the public is more rational than normally presented and recognizes that ash-related issues are far more predictable and manageable than terrorist attack.

2.4.7 The Law

It is worth reflecting that none of this was strictly speaking controlled by law or by regulation. All the factors that determined actions and decisions were extra-legal. A different regulatory system would not necessarily have led to a different result. The real 'regulatory' system was effectively the risk landscape of incentives, interests and decisions, not the framework of rules.

2.5 COULD IT HAVE BEEN DONE BETTER?

It could certainly have been done worse but it could also have been done better.

2.5.1 The Solution was Known

What resolved it was that one of the engine manufacturers actually had done the research some time before and had the data. Perhaps they all had but only one took the risk of coming forward with it. Contrary to speculation that safety simply gave way to public pressure, the graduated zones for flying were based on much earlier studies of engines in these different levels of ash concentration and type. They did know the answer.

Had they not had that data, the crisis would have forced the research to be done but that would have taken time. What would have happened if it had taken longer? The cloud remained in the area for a few weeks after the graduated zones had been established and flying resumed so Nature would not have stepped in and blown it all away. What is most likely is that the research would have been rushed, with more and more aircraft being sent up to see what happened. The problem with these test flights, however, was that they only provided evidence in relation to where they had been and would not necessarily have led to the same criteria for developing graduated zones.

2.5.2 The Problem was Easily Predictable

But it is a crisis that should never have happened. For ministers and the airlines, the pressure was relentless, with a staggering burn rate of costs for every minute that so much of the world's fleet remained grounded. Yet the crisis had been totally predictable, the dangers had been well known for many years and the engine impact data was already researched. Iceland's capacity to produce volcanoes is well documented and understood. Wind patterns that could coincide with one of the relatively frequent eruptions would easily take the plume over the northern European airport hubs. Exactly what happened was very easily predictable.

2.5.3 So Why Did it Happen?

One of the most amazing aspects of this crisis was that there was a crisis at all.

It is amazing partly because of the amount of regulation already in place and the emphasis on safety throughout the aviation industry. In regulatory terms, this was a type I error.[7] Type II is where regulation is too heavy and is either counter-productive or produces unnecessary costs, and is the sort most commonly criticized. Type I is where lack of regulation allows a predictable damage to occur that could have been prevented by regulation. In one sense, this was both types in that the international standard for the product safety of jet engines in volcanic ash was too heavy – zero tolerance. At the same time, it was both too heavy and led to massive costs but it was also an almost meaningless standard.

2.5.4 International Standards

Amongst the risk actors identified by the RRAC were the standards setters. The example referred to earlier of the proposed standard for safety management of trees was about the impact of standards.

The world of commerce, trade and industry operates on vast web of standards and regulation. The British Standards Institute of the UK lists 27,000 standards[8] and the International Standards Organisation (ISO) list 18,000 at international level.[9] Standards for products are necessary for safety but also for trade, in order that tariffs are not circumvented on spurious grounds and this vast web of product standards is overseen by the WTO's Technical Barriers to Trade (TBT) Committee. Standards themselves are voluntary but can become mandatory if adopted in Technical Regulation by national or supra-national legislatures. As such, they can be subject to the normal regulatory controls of impact assessment and accountability of the executive to the legislature. But there are few controls on the production of standards or political accountability of standard-setting bodies.

But a key message of the RRAC is that the world of regulation does not operate exclusively at the legislative level. The mandatory rules are only part of the picture and their interpretation (or misinterpretation), enforcement and adaptation by a range of interested players can change the outcome significantly. This chapter's analysis of the ash cloud crisis argues that a different regulatory structure would not have made any difference because all the drivers were extra-legal. What would have made a difference, however, and wholly avoided the crisis would have been international standards of the sort that emerged from the crisis for the tolerance of jet engines to types and concentration of volcanic ash. This need not be mandatory regulation but only a recognized standard.

The international regulatory community has institutional measures to counter type II errors, through the TBT Committee and the *corpus* of technical regulation.[10] What was missing here was any way to counter type I errors. But these are always more difficult to counter, with some of the futility of trying to prove a negative. It is easier to assess what is there than to assess the infinite possibilities of what is not there. Yet that is not an answer here. The problem was not only well known but there were advocates of change (Brannigan 2010, pp. 107–14). They lacked an institutional remedy.

The TBT is there when things go wrong with international standards but what is needed is a more proactive solution to prevent things going wrong in the first place. One new possibility may come from an initiative of the UN's Economic Commission for Europe and its Working Party 6 for Regulatory Cooperation and Standardisation Policies.[11] Although it has Europe in its title, its membership is global and it can provide a forum for exploring issues in this field of regulation. On 1 November 2010, it decided to establish a new Group of Experts on Risk Management in Regulatory Systems.[12] It is over-ambitious to expect that group to prevent an incident of the ash cloud simply through monitoring the application of risk to this area of regulation but it may have been a forum to which the advocates of better standards of volcanic ash might have appealed. Lorenza Jachia and Valentin Nikonov's chapter (Chapter 10) takes up that theme in looking at generic approaches to risk management in regulatory systems where the system as a whole and the context in which it operates both need to be seen together. As the RRAC stressed, the framework of rules is not the chief determinant of outcomes but rather the way in which many players act out their interests within that framework. The framework still matters, especially in trying to find ways of tackling type I errors. There was no institutional remedy for those campaigners, long before the crisis occurred, who saw it coming. To end as this chapter begun, with characters from mythology, the patron of type I errors was Cassandra.

NOTES

1. http://webarchive.nationalarchives.gov.uk/ (accessed 20 February 2011) and http://www.bis.gov.uk/policies/better-regulation/reviewing-regulation/better-regulation-commission/risk-regulatory-advisory-council (accessed 20 February 2011).
2. For a summary of their findings, see Risk and Regulation Advisory Council publication *Response with Responsibility: Policy Making for Public Risk in the 21st Century.*
3. For the proper version of this concept, see Surowiecki (2004, p. xiii, Introduction, section II).
4. The draft standard is still available from the BSI shop: http://shop.bsigroup.com/en/ProductDetail/?pid=000000000030174363 (accessed 20 February 2011).
5. See the Health and Safety Executive report on tree safety, *Management of the Risk from Falling Trees* (2007).
6. http://www.ifalpa.org/ (accessed 20 February 2011).

7. For one exposition of this typology, see Bounds (2010, p.18).
8. Available at http://www.bsigroup.com/# (accessed 20 February 2011).
9. Available at http://www.iso.org/iso/store.htm (accessed 20 February 2011).
10. Marceau et al. (2002).
11. http://www.unece.org/trade/wp6/AboutUs.htm (accessed 20 February 2011).
12. See   http://www.unece.org/trade/wp6/AreasOfWork/RiskManagement/RiskManage
    ment.html (accessed 20 February 2010). For an account of its approach to developing a
    reference model of risk management in this area, see ECE/TRADE/C/WP.6/2010/3.

BIBLIOGRAPHY

Bennett, R. (2008), 'Plans to Check Safety of All Garden Trees will Cost Home-
    owners Dear', *The Times*, available at http://property.timesonline.co.uk/tol/life_
    and_style/property/article4176060.ece (accessed 20 February 2011).
Bounds, G. (2010), 'Challenges to Designing Regulatory Policy Frameworks to
    Manage Risks', in *OECD Reviews of Regulatory Reform: Risk and Regulatory
    Policy – Improving the Governance of Risk*, 15–41.
Brannigan, V. (2010), 'Alice's Adventures in Volcano Land: The Use and Abuse of
    Expert Knowledge in Safety Regulation', *European Journal of Risk Regulation*,
    1 (2), 107–14.
Health and Safety Executive (2007), *Management of the Risk from Falling Trees*,
    available at http://www.hse.gov.uk/foi/internalops/sectors/ag_food/1_07_05.pdf
    (accessed 20 February 2011).
Marceau, G. and J. Trachtman (2002), 'The Technical Barriers to Trade Agreement,
    the Sanitary and Phytosanitary Measures Agreement, and the General Agree-
    ment on Tariff and Trade: A Map of the World Trade Organization Law of
    Domestic Regulation of Goods', *Journal of World Trade*, 5, 811–81.
'Red Tape: The Wood for the Trees' (2008), *The Economist,* available at http://
    www.economist.com/node/11591407 (accessed 20 February 2011).
Risk and Regulation Advisory Council (2009), *Response with Responsibility –
    Policy-Making for Public Risk in the 21st Century*, available at http://www.
    berr.gov.uk/files/file51459.pdf (accessed 20 February 2011).
Surowiecki, J. (2004), *The Wisdom Of Crowds*, New York: Doubleday.
Timmins, N. (2008), 'Stricter Rules on Tree Safety "Not Necessary"', *The Financial
    Times*, available at http://www.ft.com/cms/s/0/093992d6–3e37–11dd-b16d-0000
    779fd2ac.html#axzz1ERrxBEeg (accessed 20 February 2011).

3. The financial impact of the volcanic ash crisis on the European airline industry[1]

Maddalena Ragona, Francesca Hansstein and Mario Mazzocchi

3.1 INTRODUCTION

In April 2010, the European air traffic was heavily disrupted by the volcanic ash cloud originated by the eruption of the Icelandic volcano Eyjafjalla-jökull. Even if the explosion was of low intensity, it produced an enormous cloud of ash moving through the European sky. The fact that the ash was much finer than usual, moving quickly and possibly affecting aircraft engines, led aviation authorities of concerned countries to declare most of European skies no-fly zones (NFZs). On the basis of the information immediately available, there were claims of huge economic impact on the air travel industry, even bigger than the impact engendered by the US air traffic halt following the terrorist attacks on 11 September 2001 (European Commission, 2010).

It is obviously difficult to obtain accurate estimates of the overall economic impact that can be ascribed to a natural disaster like this. Besides the unpredictable behaviour of nature (in this case not only the eruption but also weather conditions), one should consider the adaptive behaviour of people, whose complexity increases with the number of actors involved, each with different interests and motivations in managing the emergency situation (Macrae, Chapter 2). For example, after five days of air disruptions the relevant authorities raised the safety threshold at which flying was admitted, a decision that is likely to have softened the potential impact (Alemanno, 2010). Restriction measures that led to the closure of large sections of European skies, as part of the emergency regulatory process that was developed in response to the volcanic ash, had been established on the basis of two previous accidents in the 1980s, where aircraft engines were compromised without any reported air crash (Brannigan, 2010). The mass

27

media interest raised by this type of event, together with the higher risk perception that is inevitably generated in travellers, may also alter economic behaviours (Burgess, Chapter 5; Chakraborty, Chapter 6). Thus, although flight operations may rapidly go back to normality, many potential air passengers (for example holiday-makers) are likely to cancel their trip or alter their plan (e.g. change mode of transport or destination country). When psychology comes into play, an accurate estimate of economic outcomes is even harder (Burns et al., 1993; Slovic et al., 1980). Travelling with the worry that your flight could be disrupted or, even worse, that your aircraft engines might be suffering could by itself generate a welfare loss, even if the travel and aircraft are not affected. On the other hand, avoiding a risk may imply facing another, possibly higher, 'countervailing' risk (Graham and Wiener, 1995). Switching from flying to driving could result in an increase in the number of people who might die in car accidents, as driving is more dangerous than flying (Alemanno, 2010). The literature on response to risk information (see e.g. Becker and Rubenstein, 2004) also shows that economic agents invest their money to take countermeasures, hence generating profits for other economic agents. For example, disrupted air passengers may have opted to take a train, rent a car or stay in a hotel, with different costs and economic outcomes, including (possibly) additional income for railway, car rental, and accommodation industries.

A further reason that makes it difficult to estimate the overall economic impact is the number of offsetting factors that need to be considered. Accountability is quite complex for airplane and airport industries, due to the weight of counterbalanced effects as, for example, the tonnes of fuel saved or car-parking filled in. The International Air Transport Association (IATA) estimates that the airline industry uses around 4.3 million barrels of fuel per day. At the peak of the airline space closure, the demand for fuel was estimated to have fallen by 1.2 million kerosene barrels per day (about US$110 million saved) (IATA, 2010).

There are a few industries that could have benefited from the volcano's eruption, at least in the short term, especially those linked to alternative modes of transport, like car rentals and railways. Eurostar reported an increase of 50,000 passenger on 15 April 2010, and 33 per cent extra passengers on 17 April 2010. P&O Ferries of France declared their services between Spain, France, the Netherlands, and the UK were fully booked and drafted extra personnel to face the huge volume of phone calls to their info centres.[2] Besides this, industries other than airlines have been negatively hit by the disruption, for example courier services, air cargos and those industries that rely on air transport to trade perishable commodities. The European Commission pointed out that air cargo traffic faced a fall between the scheduled flights the week before and the 'ash days' of

61 per cent within the EU-27 (compared to a decrease of 64 per cent in passenger traffic) (EC, 2010).

A (partial) solution to the impossible task of estimating and aggregating all those impacts lies in the exploration of financial markets. Assuming that investors make the best use of available information and choose their purchasing or selling behaviour on the basis of their rational economic assessment and expectations (which rules out speculative behaviours), returns on equities may be seen as the 'thermometer' of the current and predicted performance of a certain industry. In this respect, one might be able to account for both the losses suffered by the air industry and potential gains by other stakeholders (i.e. alternative transport companies). A strong assumption of this evaluation route is that the behaviour of listed securities is also representative for industries not listed in stock exchanges, for example small and medium enterprises.

The welfare loss of disrupted travellers or the productivity losses for all firms indirectly affected by the ash crisis cannot be evaluated. However, the analysis of stock returns seems an easy, fast, and reasonable way to explore the magnitude of such a complex event.

In this chapter, we provide a first basic estimation of some of the economic effects of the Eyjafjallajökull volcano's eruption, focusing on the airline industry and with some evaluations on potential gainers, namely alternative transport industries. To this purpose an event study analysis is employed in order to provide some estimates of financial losses that may be ascribed to the volcanic ash cloud.

Firstly, an overview of the earliest estimates of the economic consequences for the airline industry made by different organizations is given. Then, we briefly summarize the procedure for conducting an event study, before exploring the related literature that covers the financial impacts of various events on the airline industry. In the final sections, the key results are discussed and some conclusions are drawn.

3.2 FIRST ESTIMATIONS OF THE ECONOMIC IMPACT ON THE AIRLINE INDUSTRY

As usually happens with crises of this scale, a number of attempts at quick – albeit rough – quantification of the magnitude of the economic impact have been produced. Straight after the eruption, most estimates were provided by the main airline association, like the International Air Transport Association (IATA), and by the European Commission, DG Mobility and Transport. Table 3.1 reports some of these quantifications, all produced in the week following the first closure of airspace.

Governing disasters

In terms of operations, on 17–18 April 2010, 17 EU member states had full airspace closure, two member states had partial closure, and six non-EU states also decided for full closure. On 22 April, airspace was fully operational with the exception of partial closure in southern Finland (EC, 2010). In terms of passenger flows, the UK, French, and German domestic markets were the most affected by the closure, while the largest blow to airline revenues derived from the cancellation of US–UK flights.

In terms of economic impact, the revenue loss for airlines from scheduled services was estimated at US$1.7 billion (this figure is considered 'conservative') during the period 15–21 April. The revenue loss per day varies according to the daily airspace closure, and reaches US$400 per day on the peak period (17–19 April). During the five days disruption, British Airways, as well as Air-France KLM, reported a loss of £20 million per day.[3]

Table 3.1. Estimated effects of the volcanic ash cloud on the airline industry (15–23 April)

Source	Outcome	
ACI Europe	313 airports	European airports totally disabled (75% of the European Airport Network)
IATA	100,000 flights	Flights cancelled within the EU, to/from the EU and overflying the EU
	19,000 flights	Peak of flights cancelled on 18 and 19 April
EUROCONTROL	10 million passengers	Estimated passengers unable to travel
	1.2 million passengers	Average of scheduled passengers affected each day
	–24% (–9% worldwide) passengers flow reduction	Reduction of the within-Europe and Europe-rest of the world passenger flows
Source	Economic Impact	
IATA	US$1.7 billion	Revenue loss for airlines during the period 15–21 April
IATA	US$400 million	Per day revenue lost for airlines over the peak period (17–19 April)

Source	Outcome	
AEA	€850 million	Loss for airlines including profitability, assistance to passengers, costs for stranded crew, parking and positioning of aircraft and other cost issues (for the period 15–23 April)
ERAA	€110 million	Estimated loss for members of ERAA
ELFAA	€202 million	Estimated loss for members of ELFAA
IACA	€310 million	Estimated loss for members of IACA
ACI Europe	€250 million	Overall European airports losses
IAHA	€200 million	Direct financial loss for independent handlers pertaining to the IAHA
ANSPs	€25 million	Loss per day for Air Traffic Management (ATM)
EC–DG Mobility and Transport	61%	Fall in air traffic cargo between the scheduled flight per week in the EU-27

Notes:
ACI: Airport Council International
IATA: International Air Transport Association
AEA: Association of European Airlines
EUROCONTROL: European Organisation for the Safety of Air Navigation
ERA: European Regions Airline Association
ELFAA: European Low-Fare Airlines Association
IACA: International Air Carrier Association
IAHA: International Aviation Handlers Association
ANSPs: Air Navigation Server Providers

Source: Mazzocchi et al. (2010).

3.3 THE STANDARD EVENT STUDY METHODOLOGY AND ITS APPLICATIONS TO THE AIRLINE INDUSTRY

A rapid assessment of the financial impact of the volcanic ash cloud can be pursued through an event study analysis (MacKinlay, 1997). In this section we briefly explain the underlying logic of this methodology, while the technical details for this specific application are provided in the original article by Mazzocchi et al. (2010).

The event study methodology is a widely used and consolidated econometric method that was designed for financial markets. It consists of 'an empirical investigation of the relationship between security prices and economic events' (Strong, 1992, p. 533).

Events that could affect security prices are, for example, regulatory changes, release of financial news, or other external shocks relevant to the market. The ash cloud crisis of April/May 2010, as well as all 'contingency events' (as defined in Johnson and Jeunemaitre, Chapter 4), can be considered as an external shock.

An event is considered to have a statistically significant (positive or negative) impact on the price of a security when it generates an abnormal return on the security. A return is regarded as abnormal when it is significantly different from the return that would be expected in the absence of that event.

In an ordinary situation, returns to an individual security listed on a stock exchange follow the trend of the average market return, which is generally identified as the stock index (e.g. the FTSE index of the London Stock Exchange). Ordinary deviations ('excess residuals') of the returns to an individual security from the market index should be random. Non-random deviations suggest that some event may have caused such 'abnormality'. The event study methodology is used by economists to detect 'abnormal' behaviours of excess residuals. Large and prolonged excess residuals that are inconsistent with the randomness assumption lead to the conclusion that the price of the selected security/ies has been significantly affected by the event. The procedure to be followed in an event study analysis can be summarized in the following five key steps:

- identify the date when the event has occurred (or an 'event window' around the event date);
- estimate, in accordance with a certain benchmark model, the 'ordinary' behaviour of the returns of the selected securities on the basis of the behaviour registered prior to (or excluding) the event period;
- predict the expected returns over the event period using the benchmark model;
- compute the difference between actual and expected returns during the event window (such difference is the excess return or excess residual);
- test for the significance of the excess returns. Excess returns that are significantly different from zero are abnormal returns.

In order to estimate the expected returns had the event not occurred, i.e. the (unobserved) ordinary behaviour of security prices over the event window, it is necessary to adopt an economic model. On the basis of the actual returns observed over a given 'estimation period' (prior to the event window), such model is used to 'predict' the 'ordinary' returns that were to be expected over the event window (Figure 3.1).

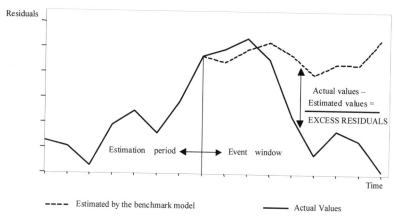

Figure 3.1. Illustrative representation of the event study method

In principle, the estimation period should not be affected by other major security-specific events, or it should be long enough to absorb previous shocks.

Several economic models may be used to estimate the expected returns. In this analysis, we adopt the market model, which assumes a linear relationship between the return of any individual security and the average market return.[4]

The ordinary behaviour is projected through the 'event window' and significant departures from the ordinary behaviour are detected through statistical tests, as those described in Patell (1976), hence the name of Patell Standardised Residuals (PSR).

It is theoretically possible to test for abnormal returns on a single security and on a single day (event date). However, the event study statistical procedure is not very powerful unless events are really conspicuous. Thus, it is possible to aggregate excess residuals over time or across securities. Aggregation over time is achieved by defining an event window, which contains several observations after the first occurrence of the event. Aggregation through securities, besides increasing the detection power, is also useful to estimate aggregated effect, at different aggregation levels. For example, it may be the case that some securities gain and others lose as a consequence of an event and aggregated excess returns help determining the overall effect or compare the positive and negative effects. In this analysis, various event windows are considered (plus a large event window that includes all the smaller event windows), and securities are aggregated in order to identify a loser industry (airlines) and a group of potential gainers (alternative transport companies).

Several studies have employed the event study approach, or other similar econometric methods, to analyze the impact of various events on the airline industry.

Zhang and Aldridge (1992) estimated the impact of news regarding the merger/foreign alliance possibilities on the Canadian airline industry for the 1992–93 period. Through a standard event study methodology, Gong (2007) estimated the stock price reaction of US airlines seeking bankruptcy protection, as well as that of their domestic rivals, at the time of the filing and during up to three years following the filing. He found considerable improvement in the financial conditions of airlines entering bankruptcy protection, and, interestingly, a positive stock market performance also for their rivals.

Binder (1985) used a multivariate regression model to solve some problems in the standard event study methodology, in order to measure abnormal stock returns caused by the Airline Deregulation Act of 1978 on the US airline industry. The same Act was also taken into account by Whinston and Collins (1992), who investigated, through an event study approach, the stock reactions following announcements of entry of a US airline company (People Express) into airport-pair markets. The authors provided interesting insights on the competitive interaction between airline companies in deregulated markets, among others a dramatic decrease in fares in the entered airport-pair.

Davidson et al. (1987) determined the impact of 57 crashes on the stock returns of 22 airline companies. Whilst in some cases the losses were statistically significant in the day of the crash, the authors did not find significant abnormal returns in the longer term. Bosh et al. (1998) intended to clarify the possible reasons for the loss of market value incurred by airline firms involved in serious air crashes: expectations of adverse consumer reaction, increased regulatory surveillance, and/or higher insurance premiums. They explored the stock price reaction of both 'crash' airlines and a sample of airlines not involved in crashes, and found a switching effect to 'non-crash' airlines by consumers, together with a little negative spillover effect, i.e. consumers also reacted by flying less.

A few studies estimated the impact of the terrorist attacks of 11 September 2001. Gillen and Lall (2003) employed a standard event study analysis to investigate the impact of the 9/11 attacks on more than 50 US and non-US airline companies. They found that US companies were the most negatively affected and their market value continued to decrease even eight weeks after the event, while Asian airlines were the least hit. Low-cost carriers like Ryanair were not affected as much and recovered within the first four weeks. Furthermore, other econometric models were used to show the role of the alliance effect (airlines that belong to an affected alliance), the wake-up call effect (by which a country-specific shock can be transmitted to companies in other countries) and the trade effect (how closely firms are linked to the affected country, the US in this case) as transmission mechanisms of shocks (e.g. 9/11) at the international level.

Carter and Simkins (2004) employed a multivariate regression model methodology instead of the standard event study approach to investigate the rationality of market's reaction to the terrorist attacks on 11 September 2001. They found that investors believed that airline firms would have been differently affected by the impact of the attacks, based on the level of their cash reserves. In addition, they examined the period when the Air Transportation Safety and System Stabilization Act passed into law (18–24 September 2001) and found that investors believed only the major airlines would have benefited; however, airlines with revenue coming mainly from international operations would have been penalized. Overall, their results supported the rational behaviour within the US financial markets, despite the strong emotional impact of such a tremendous event, designed to spread fear and irrationality.

Drakos (2004) preferred various econometric models to the event study approach, in order to explore not only short-term abnormalities, but also the possibility of structural shifts in the risk profile of companies affected by the 9/11 terrorist attacks. The author found that the risk of stocks had significantly increased in the period following the attacks, revealing enhanced uncertainty surrounding the airline industry.

To our knowledge, other studies estimating the economic and financial impact of the air traffic disruption caused by the eruption of the Icelandic volcano are not yet available, except for the work by Nippani and Washer (forthcoming). This study looks at the daily returns of eight airlines (Aeroflot-Russian Airlines, Air France-KLM, British Airways, Lufthansa, Easyjet, Iberia, Ryanair, Turk Hava Yollari) for the Bloomberg EMEA (European, Middle Eastern and African) Airlines Index, throughout the event window from 15 to 22 April 2010. The results from their econometric analysis revealed a significant underperformance of the index, and a quite slow response of investors, as the largest declines occurred on 16 and 17 April. They also calculated a cumulative loss of €2.3 billion in market capitalization.

3.4 APPLICATION AND RESULTS

For this event study, we make use of Datastream daily data on share prices for selected securities in the London, Frankfurt, Paris, and Stockholm stock exchanges. The estimation window is chosen to be relatively short (100 observations, from 24 December 2009 to 14 April 2010) in order to minimize the risks of major structural changes associated with the economic crisis and emphasize short-run dynamics.[5] Nine airlines (seven flag carriers and two low-cost companies) were included, considering their listing in the most relevant stock exchange. We also selected six potential gainers, five car rental companies and Eurotunnel, the company that runs Eurostar trains and the Eurotunnel channel. Our assumption, partially confirmed by the results, is that these companies may have benefited from a decrease in airplane transport, through an increase in car rental and train services demand. The selected companies and the reference stock exchange are listed in Table 3.2.

Table 3.2. Selected securities and reference market returns

Security	Reference market return (Stock Exchange)
Airlines	
Aerlingus	FTSE-All (London Stock Exchange)
Air France – KLM	CAC (Paris Stock Exchange)
British Airways	FTSE-All (London Stock Exchange)
Easyjet	FTSE-All (London Stock Exchange)
Finnair	DAX (Frankfurt Stock Exchange)
Iberia	DAX (Frankfurt Stock Exchange)
Lufthansa	DAX (Frankfurt Stock Exchange)
Ryanair	FTSE-All (London Stock Exchange)
SAS	OMX (Stockholm Stock Exchange)
Potential gainers	
Avis Europe	DAX (Frankfurt Stock Exchange)
Avis Budget Group	DAX (Frankfurt Stock Exchange)
Eurazeo	CAC (Paris Stock Exchange)
Eurotunnel	CAC (Paris Stock Exchange)
Hertz	DAX (Frankfurt Stock Exchange)
Sixt	DAX (Frankfurt Stock Exchange)

Source: Mazzocchi et al. (2010).

The period affected by the ash cloud goes from 15 April to 20 May 2010 (the day when European skies were declared 'ash-free') and a detailed timeline of events and effect on air operations is provided in Table 3.3.

Table 3.3. Timeline of events associated with the ash cloud and effects on flights

Date	Actual Flights	Estimated flights in a normal day	EUROCONTROL's expectations declared each day (summary)
Wed 14 April	28,087	28,000	None
Thu 15 April	20,842	28,000	None
Fri 16 April	11,659	28,000	Airspace is not available for operation of civilian aircraft in the following countries/ areas: Ireland, the UK, Belgium, the Netherlands, Denmark, Sweden, Norway, Finland, Estonia, the north of France, parts of Germany, parts of Poland. Forecasts suggest that the cloud of volcanic ash is continuing to move east and south-east and that the impact will continue for at least the next 24 hours.
Sat 17 April	5,335	22,000	No landings and take offs are possible for civilian aircraft across most of northern and central Europe: Austria, Belgium, Croatia, the Czech Republic, Denmark, Estonia, Finland, Northern France, most of Germany, Hungary, Ireland, northern Italy, the Netherlands, southern Norway, Poland, Romania, Slovakia, Slovenia, Sweden, Switzerland and the UK. Forecasts suggest that the cloud of volcanic ash will persist and that the impact will continue for at least the next 24 hours.

Date	Actual Flights	Estimated flights in a normal day	EUROCONTROL's expectations declared each day (summary)
Sun 18 April	5,204	24,000	Air traffic control services are not being provided to civil aircraft in the major part of European airspace: Austria, Belgium, Croatia, the Czech Republic, Denmark, Estonia, Finland, most of France, most of Germany, Hungary, Ireland, northern Italy, the Netherlands, Norway, Poland, Romania, Serbia, Slovenia, Slovakia, north Spain, Sweden, Switzerland, Ukraine and the UK.
Mon 19 April	9,330	28,000	Air traffic control services are not being provided to civil aircraft in the major part of European airspace: Belgium, the Czech Republic, Denmark, Estonia, Finland, parts of France, Germany, Hungary, Ireland, the Netherlands, northern Italy, Poland, Romania, Slovenia, Switzerland, parts of Ukraine and the UK.
Tue 20 April	13,101	28,000	The new procedures agreed yesterday have been in place since 06.00 UTC. Air traffic control services are not being provided to civil aircraft, or are being provided with significant restrictions, in the lower airspace in north-western Europe: Denmark, Estonia, Finland, north France, north Italy, Latvia, Slovenia, Slovakia and UK. In the upper airspace above 20,000 feet, all European airspace is available. In the evening almost 75% of the total continent area is free of any restrictions.
Wed 21 April	21,916	28,000	All European airspace is available above 20,000 feet. Below 20,000 feet, restrictions are still in force in a few areas (southern Sweden, part of Finland, parts of Scotland). It is anticipated that these restrictions will gradually be lifted throughout the day. It is anticipated that almost 100% of the air traffic will take place in Europe tomorrow.

Date	Actual Flights	Estimated flights in a normal day	EUROCONTROL's expectations declared each day (summary)
Thu 22 April	27,284	28–29,000	A small number of cancellations can be expected due to some limited restrictions and the logistical problems of airlines. Almost all European airspace is available, with a few exceptions in parts of Southern Finland, southern Norway, northern Scotland, and western Sweden.
Fri 23 April		29,000	Almost all European airspace is available, with the exception of part of Northern Scotland.
Wed 28 April	Normal	Normal	The Ash Concentration Charts produced by VAAC London show that there has been no area of high potential volcanic ash coverage within the CFMU area for several days now.
Tue 4 May		28,000	Airspace in Ireland, northern Ireland and small parts of western Scotland was closed between 08.00 and 14.00 CET (cancellation of some 150 flights). The latest Ash Concentration Charts show that the area where ash concentrations could exceed engine manufacturer tolerance levels has shrunk and is no longer affecting any substantial part of European airspace. This situation is expected to remain stable for the coming hours.
Wed 5 May	27,904	29,000	Several Ireland airports will be closed for limited hours. Edinburgh is currently operating at reduced capacity and the western part of Scottish airspace is closed. The situation is not expected to improve in this area during the day. The whole of Ireland, west Scotland and north-west England could be affected. Greek airspace is also closed for all traffic as a result of industrial action.
Thu 6 May	30,202	28,500	No closures of airspace or airports within the European area. The predicted area where ash concentration areas could exceed engine manufacturer tolerance levels lies to the west/north-west of Ireland. In the night of 5–6 May, renewed and more intensive ash eruptions took place.

Date	Actual Flights	Estimated flights in a normal day	EUROCONTROL's expectations declared each day (summary)
Fri 7 May	30,342	28–29,000	Some airports were closed in the west of Ireland overnight. The main predicted area where ash concentration could exceed engine manufacturer tolerance levels lies to the west of north-west Europe. Renewed and more intensive ash eruptions took place overnight, and the area of potential higher ash contamination is forecast to extend from Iceland as far south as the western edge of the Iberian peninsula during the day. Transatlantic flights are being rerouted south of the affected area which could cause delays to these flights.
Sat 8 May	22,424	22,600	Ash eruptions are ongoing. Airports are closed or expected to close in northern Portugal, the north of Spain and parts of southern France. Transatlantic flights are being rerouted around the affected area which is causing substantial delays to these flights.
Sun 9 May	23,491	25,000	Ash eruptions are still substantially affecting European airspace. Airports in northern and central Portugal, north-western Spain, northern and central Italy are unavailable, and are expected to open later. Transatlantic flights continue to be affected by the ash cloud (reroutings, delays).
Mon 10 May	29,155	29,000	Areas of high ash concentration have dispersed overnight over continental Europe. There is an area of ash cloud in the middle of the North Atlantic which is impacting transatlantic flights (reroutings, delays). No airports are closed in Europe. During the afternoon, areas of higher ash concentration could move in a north-easterly direction from the Atlantic into the Iberian Peninsula.

Date	Actual Flights	Estimated flights in a normal day	EUROCONTROL's expectations declared each day (summary)
Tue 11 May	27,807	29,000	Airports on the Canary Islands, some in south-west Spain and some in Morocco are closed. At the same time, ongoing work by the UK Met Office and the UK CAA has confirmed the effectiveness of the model used to determine the areas where ash concentration could be above engine tolerance levels.
Wed 12 May	29,935		Areas of high ash concentration at lower altitudes, which are still causing some difficulties for trans-Atlantic flights, are currently found in the Mediterranean between the Spanish mainland and the Balearic Islands, and are moving north east. All airports are available, however with the Balearic Islands airports operating at reduced capacity. The areas of higher ash concentration are expected to dissipate further during the day.
Thu 13 May	26,852		The areas of high ash concentration at high altitude have now dispersed. The areas of higher ash concentration are not expected to cause any disruption to air traffic during the next 24 hours.
Fri 14 May	Normal	Normal	The areas of ash concentration are mainly at low levels in the vicinity of Iceland, and are not expected to cause any disruption to air traffic during the next 24 hours.
Sun 16 May	25,088	25,000	None.
Mon 17 May		29,000	The areas of ash concentration are mainly at low levels. During the course of the day, the current cloud is expected to disperse somewhat. The cloud is expected to mainly affect Northern Ireland, parts of Scotland and parts of south-west UK. On Sunday 16 May, the disruptions in Ireland and north-west UK resulted in a reduction in expected number of flights by about 400.

Note: Blanks in the actual flight number indicate that EUROCONTROL did not provide official information, which happened in days when air traffic was normal.

Source: Mazzocchi et al. (2010) based on EUROCONTROL' Updates on European air trafficsituation (http://www.eurocontrol.int).

Based on the events listed in Table 3.3, several event windows were explored, as summarized in Table 3.4.

Table 3.4. Event windows

	Event window	Flights affected
EW1	15–19 April	Peak negative effect on most EU flights.
EW2	15–23 April	All period until return to normal flights operation (April).
EW3	3–7 May	Negative effects on UK, Ireland, and southern European flights.
EW4	17–19 May	Some disruption in flights to/from UK and northern Europe.
EWTOT	15 April–20 May	All period until return to normal flight operations (May).

Despite the fact that the event study approach was employed in its simplest and basic form, results were econometrically robust to choices on the size of estimation and event windows. Figure 3.2 shows the day-by-day excess residuals aggregated over the two groups of firms through the overall event window going from 15 April to 20 May 2010. Significant abnormal returns

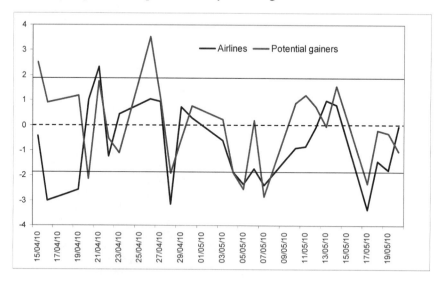

Figure 3.2. Excess residuals by group of firms

at the 95 per cent confidence level are those below or above the two horizontal lines. The aggregate airlines value (darker line) is below the zero line over most of the considered period, although it is only significant during the first peak period (17–19 April), on 28 April, over the second 'wave' of ash (5–7 May) and with the last occurrence of the ash cloud (around 17 May). On 21 April there is a positive significant return, a 'rebound' after the negative peaks of previous days. Instead, on aggregate, evidence on positive returns for potential gainers is quite weak, with positive values on the first few days (only significant on 15 April).

As already explained in the previous section, more powerful tests can be obtained by aggregating over time, as well as over securities. We consider the various event windows described in Table 3.5.

Table 3.5. Aggregate financial impact over various event windows (excess residuals)

	EW1	EW2	EW3	EW4	EWTOT
	15–19 April	**15–23 April**	**3–7 May**	**17–19 May**	**15 April–20 May**
Airlines	**–3,48**	**–1,29**	**–4,04**	**–3,80**	**–3,79**
Potential gainers	**2,66**	0,98	**–3,13**	–1,65	–0,18

Note: Values in bold indicate significant abnormal returns at the 95% confidence level.

Source: Mazzocchi et al. (2010).

Table 3.5 clearly shows that a persistent negative impact on the selection of listed airlines has been observed through all event windows, with the exception of the second event window ending on 23 April. This might be explained by the rebound observed on 21 April and presumably with the positive expectations driven by the return to normality and the debate about rising ash concentration thresholds to allow for air traffic, which happened towards the end of the event window. The recurrence of the ash cloud in May resulted in new major negative effects, probably worsened by the expectation that the issue could be long lasting. The overall effect over the longest event window is strongly negative, despite the fact that increasing the length of event windows usually reduces the power of tests because of forecast errors. Again, the evidence on potential gainers is mixed and confined to the short term in the first occurrence of the crisis, while on the longest event window there is no detectable effect.

Finally, in Table 3.6, we provide an estimate of the overall effect of the crisis (longest event window) on individual companies, based on the individual excess residuals. The residuals were negative for all airlines, but only Easyjet and Lufthansa registered significant abnormal returns. We also give a rough estimate of the associated financial loss, based on the excess residuals on single days and the market value of firms. As a reference company market value we use Datastream estimates for May 2010. Of course these figures only refer to a small selection of companies and stock exchanges, but they may help to give an idea of the magnitude of the effect. Considering the period between 15 April and 20 May 2010, the nine airlines considered for this study have experienced a loss of about €3.3 billion in terms of market value.

Table 3.6. Impact by individual security (Patell Standardized Residuals and impact on firm market values)

	PSR	Firm value impact (millions of €)
Airlines		
Aerlingus	−0.12	−7
Air France – KLM	−1.34	−368
British Airways	−1.43	−365
Easyjet	**−2.20**	−338
Finnair	−1.91	−83
Iberia	−1.52	−525
Lufthansa	**−2.20**	−670
Ryanair	−1.58	−791
SAS	−1.25	−229
Potential gainers		
Avis	1.10	123
Budget	−1.14	−225
Eurazeo	0.56	110
Eurotunnel	−1.02	−201
Hertz	−0.46	−306
Sixt	−0.56	−76
Aggregate results		
Airlines	**−3.79**	−3374
Potential gainers	−0.18	−575

Note: Values in bold indicate significant abnormal returns at the 95% confidence level.

Source: Mazzocchi et al. (2010).

3.5 FINAL CONSIDERATIONS

This study provides an exploration of the impact of the volcanic ash cloud, using financial data and a traditional event study approach that allows for a timely assessment. The volcanic ash cloud and its effect on air traffic represent a major example of the complexities that economists face to produce a rapid estimate of the magnitude of the monetary impacts of a natural disaster. Albeit the event study approach is a relatively basic and traditional method in financial econometrics, this simple procedure is still a fast and efficient instrument to monitor the patterns of these complex effects.

With respect to the ash cloud application, a few key results can be summarized. First, as experienced with other risk-related events, the initial occurrence of the crisis generated major negative impacts on airlines, then return to normal financial operations was quite rapid and one week after the first closure of European airports and airspace there was no major sign of significant losses. However, as the ash cloud returned to affect flight operations in May, despite the relatively low impact in terms of disrupted flights and grounded passengers, the financial reaction was quite strong. Recurring events raise the risk level for affected companies and may engender a structural impact on the economic performance of firms, at least in the short/medium term. Albeit our limited sample of securities does not allow for general conclusions, potential gains for economic agents that can benefit from the disruption of air travel seem to be short-lived, consistently with the adaptive behaviour of agents and the time needed for structural adjustments (e.g. increasing capacity for car rentals). Our overall estimate for nine selected European flag carriers is a financial loss of about €3.3 billion over one month, a figure that is well above the overall economic impact estimated by various air traffic organizations in the aftermath of the event for all European airlines.

NOTES

[1.] This chapter is an extended version of the article M. Mazzocchi, F. Hansstein and M. Ragona (2010), 'The 2010 volcanic ash cloud and its financial impact on the European airline industry', *CESifo Forum*, **11** (2), 92–100.
[2.] From BBC News, www.bbc.co.uk.
[3.] From the Economist, www.economist.com.
[4.] In a linear relationship, any given change in the independent variable (the average market return) produces a corresponding (proportional) change in the dependent variable (the return of an individual security).
[5.] However, estimation windows with 200, 300 and 400 observations produced similar results.

BIBLIOGRAPHY

Alemanno, A. (2010), 'The European Regulatory Response to the Volcanic Ash Crisis: Between Fragmentation and Integration', *European Journal of Risk Regulation*, **1** (2), 101–6.

Becker, G.S. and Y. Rubinstein (2004), 'Fear and the Response to Terrorism: An Economic Analysis', *University of Chicago mimeo*, revised version (February 2010) available at http://www.econ.brown.edu/fac/yona_rubinstein/Research/Working%20Papers/BR_FEB2010.pdf (accessed 20 February 2011).

Binder, J.J. (1985), 'Measuring the Effects of Regulation with Stock Price Data', *The RAND Journal of Economics*, **16** (2), 167–83.

Bosch, J.-C., E.W. Eckard and V. Singal (1998), 'The Competitive Impact of Air Crashes: Stock Market Evidence', *Journal of Law and Economics*, **41** (2), 503–19.

Brannigan, V. (2010), 'Alice's Adventures in Volcano Land: The Use and Abuse of Expert Knowledge in Safety Regulation', *European Journal of Risk Regulation*, **1** (2), 107–14.

Burns, W.J., P. Slovic, R.E. Kasperson, J.X. Kasperson, O. Renn and S. Emani (1993), 'Incorporating Structural Models into Research on the Social Amplification of Risk: Implications for Theory Construction and Decision Making', *Risk Analysis*, **13** (6), 611–23.

Carter, D.A. and B.J. Simkins (2004), 'The Market's Reaction to Unexpected, Catastrophic Events: The Case of Airline Stock Returns and the September 11th Attacks', *The Quarterly Review of Economics and Finance*, **44**, 539–58.

Davidson, W.N., III, P.R. Chandy and M. Cross (1987), 'Large Losses, Risk Management, and Stock Returns in the Airline Industry', *Journal of Risk and Insurance*, **54** (1), 162–72.

Drakos, K. (2004), 'Terrorism-Induced Structural Shifts in Financial Risk: Airline Stocks in the Aftermath of September 11th Terror Attacks', *European Journal of Political Economy*, **20** (2), 435–46.

Gong, S.X.H. (2007), 'Bankruptcy Protection and Stock Market Behavior in the US Airline Industry', *Journal of Air Transport Management*, **13** (4), 213–20.

European Commission (2010), 'The Impact of the Volcanic Ash Cloud Crisis on the Air Transport Industry', SEC(2010) 533, 27 April 2010.

Gillen, D. and A. Lall (2003), 'International Transmission of Shocks in the Airline Industry', *Journal of Air Transport Management*, **9** (1), 37–49.

Graham, J.D. and J.B. Wiener (1995), *Risks vs. Risks: Tradeoffs in Protecting Health and the Environment*, Cambridge, MA: Harvard University Press.

International Air Transport Association (2010), 'IATA Economics Briefing: the impact of Eyjafjallajokull's volcanic ash plume', available at http://www.iata.org/whatwedo/Documents/economics/Volcanic-Ash-Plume-May2010.pdf (accessed 15 May 2010).

MacKinlay, A.C. (1997), 'Event Studies in Economics and Finance', *Journal of Economic Literature*, **35** (1), 13–39.

Mazzocchi, M., F. Hansstein and M. Ragona (2010), 'The 2010 Volcanic Ash Cloud and its Financial Impact on the European Airline Industry', *CESifo Forum*, **11** (2), 92–100.

Nippani, S. and K. Washer (2011), 'A Note on the Immediate Impact of the Eyjafjallajökull Volcanic Eruption on Airline Stocks', forthcoming on *International Review of Applied Financial Issues and Economics*, available at http://www.

southwesternfinance.org/conf-2011/swfa2011_submission_20.pdf (accessed 4 February 2011).

Patell, J.M. (1976), 'Corporate Forecasts of Earning per Share and Stock Price Behavior: Empirical Tests', *Journal of Accounting Research*, **14**, 246–76.

Slovic, P., B. Fischhoff, and S. Lichtenstein (1980), 'Facts and Fears: Understanding Perceived Risk', in R.C. Schwing and W.A. Albers, Jr. (eds), *Societal Risk Assessment: Safe is Safe Enough?*, New York: Plenum Press, 81–216.

Strong, N. (1992), 'Modelling Abnormal Returns: a Review Article', *Journal of Business Finance & Accounting*, **19** (4), 533–53.

Whinston, M.D. and S.C. Collins (1992), 'Entry and Competitive Structure in Deregulated Airline Markets: An Event Study Analysis of People Express', *The RAND Journal of Economics*, **23** (4), 445–62.

Zhang, A. and D. Aldridge (1997), 'Effects of Merger and Foreign Alliance: An Event Study of the Canadian Airline Industry', *Transportation Research Part E: Logistics and Transportation Review*, 33 (1), 29–42.

PART 2

Revisiting the volcanic ash crisis: ideologies, narratives and communication of emergency risk regulation

4. Risk and the role of scientific input for contingency planning: a response to the April 2010 Eyjafjallajökull volcano eruption

Chris Johnson and Alain Jeunemaitre

4.1 INTRODUCTION

This chapter focuses on the insights that the Eyjafjallajökull eruption in April 2010 provided for the coordination of scientific input to decision-making across the European aviation industries. Volcanic eruptions are part of a wider class of natural risks, including earthquakes, pandemics, and regional fires etc., that have to be managed collectively. These, in turn, form a sub-set of adverse events that also include man-made catastrophes, such as terrorist attacks, pollution etc. Natural and man-made risks are collectively known as contingency events. They are characterized by relatively low expected probabilities but extremely high potential consequences. The public increasingly expect commercial and regulatory agencies to adopt a precautionary approach to such events. These expectations extend not just from the time before any incident occurs but also under the stress and time pressure of decision-making during a contingency. If we are to meet these expectations, it is important that operational decision-making is informed by accurate scientific information on a wide range of issues. It should not be shaped by *ad hoc* political pressures, although these will inevitably play a role.

The assessment and management of risk depends upon a clear scientific understanding of the contingency under consideration. Without significant prior consultation, Air Navigation Service Providers (ANSPs), regulators and government agencies are forced to gather what scientific advice they can find in response to an adverse event as it develops. This undermines decision-making processes because prior scientific information is seldom available in an appropriate form. It may be based on limited laboratory studies or environmental observations.

There is a need to scrutinize the chain of decisions from before an incident to the aftermath if we are to identify opportunities for improvement. This creates further problems because it can be difficult to avoid hindsight bias when considering these rare events. It is easy to identify 'optimal' responses after a crisis has passed. Finally, remedies to improve the management of future events have to be considered. Previous research in decision theory has identified ways of looking beyond hindsight bias and regret. These techniques offer some hope of identifying appropriate structures for regulatory intervention in contingency planning.

4.2 THE ROLE OF SCIENTIFIC INPUT TO RISK AND UNCERTAINTY IN AIR TRAFFIC MANAGEMENT CONTINGENCIES

A number of general concepts support a scientific analysis of contingency planning. Such concepts support a general mode of reasoning that might be applied to a number of different natural and man-made hazards characterized by low probabilities and extremely high potential consequences. One component of such a framework can be built upon risk in everyday decision-making. Risks involve *ex ante* assessments of gains and losses from particular actions and their alternatives. For instance, we make informal risk assessments every time we select an airline schedule. We assess the probability of failing to make a tight connection and missing our plane. In such circumstances, we can make contingency plans by booking an alternate flight or using a carrier that supports alternate transfers.

From this it follows that we can introduce a distinction between situations where individuals assess possible outcomes according to 'more or less' accurate distributions of event probabilities and situations where the occurrence of outcomes cannot be objectively evaluated. By analogy, we can assess the risks associated with airline connections because we have experienced previous delays on a particular route. However, it can be very difficult to assess the likelihood of very rare outcomes for which there may have not been any previous direct experience within our lifetime. For instance, it is very difficult to make accurate assessments of the potential impact of pandemic flu when making our travel plans.

For some contingency events, whose outcomes are reversible or whose consequences can be mitigated by different forms of insurance, we can take measures to reduce the impact on various stakeholders. In such situations, we may be less concerned by the risks because prior investments soften the impact of even relatively rare risks. Many ECAC states have adopted this approach, following the requirements in EC Commission Regulation 2096/2005 of 20 December 2005. Some have built fall-back systems that provide support in the event of earthquakes or terrorist attacks. At least one has bought insurance that will help them meet the costs incurred if they cannot provide ATM services during a contingency. However, the events of April 2010 illustrate the limitations of these piecemeal strategies across European ATM; they also illustrate the need to recruit more direct scientific advice to inform policy and planning in this area.

Previous research has identified a number of decision-making strategies and these are illustrated by ANSP responses to the EC Common Requirements, cited above. Some individuals may rationally choose to reject the mitigation strategies mentioned above. These 'risky' positions can be justified by arguments such as 'it is impossible adequately to inform investments when we cannot be sure of the contingency events that we will face' or 'even if we can identify potential hazards, it is impossible to ensure that any investments will be useful in the aftermath of an earthquake, pandemic, volcanic ash cloud etc.' Problems arise because these 'risky' individual behaviours will have a collective impact on any other states that rely upon those service providers to support their traffic. From this it follows that we must understand the aggregate impact of European contingency plans. Such collective actions can help to improve disaster and emergency planning in a number of ways. For instance, Eurocontrol has developed simulations of what might happen following the closure of air space across a number of ECAC states. These were still being refined at the time of the Eyjafjallajökull eruption. However, they provided important indications of the disruption that was in fact experienced.[1]

From a collective perspective, objectively assessed and predictable outcomes assume preventive actions. In other words, if we can be certain about the outcome of a potential contingency then we should be able to identify actions that would help to mitigate any potential future adverse event. In contrast, uncertain outcomes, typically, force decision-makers to act with precaution *before* adverse events occur. We must take steps to reduce the likelihood of failure because we cannot predict or control the likely consequences. Unfortunately, this classical approach to decision-making is complicated within contingency planning because it is extremely hard to influence the probability of volcanic eruptions or terrorist attacks.

Crises may take place in 'stabilized' or ideal conditions when ANSPs have all the necessary decision-making processes, financial resources and technical infrastructures. In such situations, it can be relatively easy to coordinate and recruit scientific expertise needed to resolve any ambiguity in assessing the risks posed by a contingency event to the continued provision of air traffic services. However, adverse events also occur in less optimal conditions, for example during economic downturns when financial resources are scarce or during major changes in higher levels of management. Decision-making processes operate in a confused environment where industry bodies must recruit scientific advice at a time when the media, public and politicians are also trying to influence operational decisions. At such times, a lack of clear responsibilities both at a national and a European level can interfere with the management of any crisis. Under such interference, social and political controversies overwhelm technical considerations. Decisions are unlikely to be based on a clear scientific rationale. Diverse representations of the risk and possible outcomes compete, which may lead to an ill-considered application of the precautionary principle minimizing risks towards zero with enormous social, political and economic costs.

The more sudden the crisis, the more urgent is the need for scientific input to inform decision-making. However, few operational organizations know where to begin an informed dialogue with external scientific experts. If these links do not exist before a crisis then delays will occur. If ambiguity exists over the available expertise, contradictory advice can be offered with little relevance to the contingency at hand. Following any contingency, it is equally important to reinforce links between service providers and the scientific community in order to identify appropriate lessons for future intervention.

4.3 THE STATE OF SCIENTIFIC RESEARCH INTO THE IMPACT OF VOLCANIC ERUPTIONS ON AIR TRAFFIC MANAGEMENT

A number of scientific studies have been conducted into volcanic eruptions and their potential impact on air transport. Much of this work was motivated by concerns over the loss of power during flights into ash clouds by British Airways in 1982 and KLM in 1989.[2] A series of symposiums, workshops and seminars have been held in many different areas of the world during 1987, 1991, 2004, 2007. These were sponsored by agencies including the International Civil Aviation Organization (ICAO), the International Airways Volcano Watch (IAVW) and Volcanic Ash Advisory Centres (VAAC). These topics have received increased attention since the disruption of April 2010 with meetings hosted by university and research organizations, sponsored by Eurocontol, NASA, ICAO and the World Meteorological Organization etc. A number of common concerns can be identified across the previous scientific work in this area. For instance, there remain inherent difficulties in distinguishing hazardous volcanic clouds from more mundane meteorological clouds. Further concerns can be summarized as follows:

- What is the concentration of ash required to damage different types of aircraft?
- How can we detect or predict those eruptions that are likely to create significant ash clouds?
- What observational techniques provide the most accurate/cost-effective estimates of ash dispersion?
- What meteorological conditions (wind, precipitation, pressure) must we consider in modelling and predicting future dispersions?

These issues are intertwined. They are influenced by the scale of the eruption; by the quantities of volcanic ash projected into the atmosphere at different altitudes, by the specific gravities of different particles and by the range of volcanic gases that travel at different speed, height and directions according to different meteorological conditions etc. Each of these factors increases the difficulty in predicting the consequent impact of volcanic eruptions and the associated ash clouds on aviation operations. However, a range of observational techniques, simulation tools and pattern analysis algorithms have been developed to address these concerns. Ground-based, airborne[3] and satellite-sensing technologies as well as 'reverse absorption' models handle residual data. However, none of these technologies provides perfect predictions.

Scientific input cannot simply focus on the dispersion of volcanic products. It must also be informed by the risk-based perspective adopted within decision theory. No human casualties have yet been caused by volcanic ash. However, traffic growth over areas of volcanic activity in the Pacific and North Atlantic will exacerbate potential hazards. These additional risk factors must be offset by the increasing sophistication of engine management systems and fabrication techniques. Risk assessments must also consider a host of lesser consequences. An aircraft crossing ash clouds will suffer some reduction in the expected life of its engines and consequent maintenance costs. The scientific analysis of operational decisions during volcanic activity must offset each of these factors against the obvious costs of disruption from a precautionary approach that would leave many flights and passengers on the ground.

Academic research papers are, typically, not an appropriate means of informing strategic management decisions. For instance, the findings from these studies need to be assessed against multiple channels of information providing real-time data about rapidly changing situations. These observations illustrate the relevance of other branches of research. Computational research offers techniques for identifying and resolving the contradictions and omissions in scientific and operational data. Risk management also depends on knowledge management. Without risk management there is little benefit to be gained from the collection and integration of diverse information sources. These two technologies together provide means of integrating scientific and operational knowledge in a manner that enables network optimizations during contingency events.

4.4 REVIEW OF THE CRISIS

A number of reports have been issued into the events that took place from 14 to 22 April 2010. Many of these accounts disagree about the meetings and decisions that helped to shape the response across ECAC states. Estimates also vary over the total costs of the disruption; from €1 billion to €3 billion, and beyond.

Most accounts recognize the lack of coordination across Europe. This undermined network optimization as airspace was closed at relatively short notice. Further concerns focus on the need to tailor scheduling information to the broader needs of the aviation industry, especially for airports and airlines. Reports also agree on the domino effect that propagated the cancellations, diversions and airport closures beyond national airspace. They also agree that it was difficult, if not impossible, for ANSPs to use existing risk-assessment tools to determine whether or not it was safe to fly at various thresholds for the concentration of ash. Existing regulatory guidance provided a framework for considering likelihood and consequence but not how to resolve inconsistent and competing scientific advice. Previous reports have also argued that members of the public were poorly informed about the impact of the eruption. In consequence, they could not reschedule flights even where these were available. Uncertainty created bottlenecks as travellers tried to book alternate modes of transportation. ANSPs were, typically, viewed as responsible for the inconvenience caused to members of the public.

Many of these problems had been anticipated by Eurocontrol's Contingency Task Force. Unfortunately, few ANSPs had sufficient time after the publication of their guidance to implement the recommendations from this group. Further problems arose because the Eurocontrol contingency guidelines were focused on ANSPs. They were not intended to help airline or airport operations respond to the eruption. They also failed to anticipate the speed with which the ash cloud spread through the airspace of northern

Europe. The rapid propagation of cloud imposed unexpected demands on the chain of decision-making that extended both within and between ECAC states. The UK Meteorological Office's London Volcanic Ash Advisory Centre issued an initial warning following advisories from the Icelandic Met Office. The VAAC alert triggered a swift reaction from Eurocontrol; the Central Flow Management Unit (CFMU) sent warnings to individual ANSPs around Europe. They also prepared for worst-case scenarios with zero-rate regulation, assuming there was a possibility of prolonged closures to national airspace. This decision was taken after an emergency video conference with UK NATS.

The second day saw the consequences of the precautionary approach, as many areas of airspace around Europe were closed. CFMU acted as an information exchange passing data and information between ANSPs, coordinating with the European Commission and national meteorological services. However, the crisis imposed considerable stress upon key members of staff. The challenges of keeping these communications channels updated over time left little opportunity to identify the underlying scientific research that might have helped to inform or direct subsequent risk-based decision-making.

The work of CFMU was complicated by the need to respond to decisions made in each member state. Sectors were often open or closed with relatively little warning in the early stages of the contingency. This undermined attempts to optimize the revised traffic flows. The lack of agreed tools for risk assessment also prevented the coordinating bodies from anticipating the impact of changing meteorological conditions. In consequence, there was a 25% reduction in air traffic across ECAC states on the first day of closures.

Over the next three days, the ash cloud expanded south. This triggered additional airspace closures. However, there was still little consistency in the decision-making processes that were advocated and followed by individual NSAs. For example, Ireland initially opened her southern sectors to transatlantic flights. This decision was later reversed. Across Europe, airport operators were often left to decide whether or not to remain open while airspace closures were in place. This led to further confusion as members of the public did not know whether they should try and check-in for their flights. Similarly, airlines used different algorithms to determine which flights would be cancelled and which would be scheduled.

Airlines and airports initially struggled to cope with the impact of the closures. Over time, more and more questions were raised about the evidence for the 'risk-averse' approach of ANSPs. Partly in consequence, member states authorized more than 30 test flights into the ash cloud over different areas of Europe during 18 April. The results took time to analyze.

It was also difficult to explain to the public that a small number of successful flights did not provide a sufficient sample to reopen European air space.

By 19 April, direct ground observations indicated that the eruption was beginning to diminish. There were signs that the emission of ash was declining. However, operational decision-making continued to be complicated by a lack of consensus amongst the scientists making different predictions about the extent of the ash cloud. Traffic disruption created political pressure from the media who raised concerns about the fate of thousands of stranded passengers. These concerns were mirrored by mounting financial pressures as the airlines struggled to meet legal obligations to support their customers. It is against this background that the EU Transport Council held an extraordinary videoconference meeting. It was decided to allow governments to reopen airspace on a limited basis. In order to do this, the meeting introduced a three-tier categorization: fully restricted; at the discretion of national authorities and unrestricted. ANSPs gradually began to open sectors at reduced capacity. The next 24 hours saw an 80 per cent increase in traffic volumes, up to almost 30 per cent of normal capacity.

From 19 April, airlines were allowed to operate in airspace that would previously have been closed under the precautionary approach previously adopted by ANSPs. Special operating procedures and permits enabled flights under visual rather than instrument flight rule restrictions. These measures created considerable confusion for many members of the public who legitimately asked whether or not it was now safer to fly than it had been over the previous 48 hours. Between 19 and 22 April, many sectors reopened but others closed with shifting patterns in the ash cloud and changes in the local risk assessments across ECAC states.

The previous paragraphs have identified a number of issues that are relevant for the integration of scientific advice in anticipation of future contingencies:

- *Need for scientific input into 'real-time' risk assessment and decision-making.* In the early stages of the eruption, many ANSPs implemented a precautionary approach. By closing air space to reduce the safety risks, they increased business risks to passengers and airlines. There was also a significant loss of support from politicians and the public, with a growing perception that *ad hoc* decisions were being made without any proper scientific justification. While the precautionary principle was applicable in the hours following the eruption; subsequent events showed the need for closer cooperation between scientific agencies and service providers.

- *Need for exchange of scientific expertise in contingency planning around the globe.* There was some complacency in the European aviation industry. Ash clouds were not considered to be a significant threat by many ECAC states. This created vulnerabilities when operators struggled to find coherent information about the nature of the threats that they faced. This attitude is understandable given the relative frequency of ash clouds. From October 2008 to March 2010, the London Volcanic Ash Advisory Centre (VAAC) did not report any volcanic activity in its area of responsibility. In a comparable period, the Buenos Aires VAAC issued just under 500 ash advisories associated with four different volcanoes. The Wellington VAAC issued 76 warnings for ash clouds emanating from Tonga and Vanuatu while the Tokyo VAAC gave out 76 warnings for a single Russian volcano.

- *Need for integration of scientific input into proportionate responses.* Research results are seldom published in a form that can easily inform operational decision-making. Unless appropriate communications channels are created before an emergency then there is little chance that external scientific input will reduce the uncertainty and confusion that can undermine any response. Closer cooperation between scientific bodies and service providers can deliver mechanisms for ensuring a proportionate response based on scientific evidence where uncertainty persists. Decisions can then be grounded in evidence and revised as more data becomes available. For example, flight tests could have been coordinated in conjunction with the use of satellite visualization, ground volcano observations and simulation algorithms. In contrast, many activities were rapidly scheduled by different agencies around Europe with little coordination. It is equally important for the public and for politicians to be informed. During the Eyjafjallajökull eruption, most European citizens were completely unaware of the scientific appraisal of the situation that their taxes supported.

- *Need for scientific input into European crisis management.* It was clear at many stages of the contingency that scientific input was needed to support a host of operational decisions. Each NSA and ANSP looked to different national and international agencies. In consequence, confusion, inconsistency and rumour led many states to adopt a precautionary approach. There were few clear mechanisms for translating VAAC warnings into policy decisions. The interactions between the warning centres, CFMU and individual member states provided a clear starting point for a more coordinated response.

However, the airports, airlines and travelling public often felt isolated from the decision-making processes.

- *Need for scientific input to inform media and political influence.* Many ANSPs found it hard to justify to the travelling public and to politicians the closure of their airspace. These difficulties were exacerbated when neighbouring states kept sectors open. The intervention of the European Extraordinary Transport Council provided some resolution to a growing conflict in which service providers were seen to oppose public and political consensus. However, the need for such an 'extraordinary' intervention illustrates the need to reform the European response to crises. At present, responsibility is distributed between a host of intersecting European and national agencies including but not limited to ANSPs, NSAs, airlines, airports, government ministries of transport and the economy, Eurocontrol/CFMU, EASA, ICAO etc.

4.5   REGULATION AND GOVERNANCE

Many aspects of the Eyjafjallajökull response raise wider questions about the resilience of European governance in the face of international contingencies. Similar questions have been posed by previous adverse events in many different industries, ranging from recent problems across the financial services industries through to the blackouts in electricity distribution across France, Italy and Germany. The experience from these rare, high consequence failures creates a requirement for supranational regulatory coordination in drawing scientific and operational lessons from previous contingencies. They also suggest a framework to coordinate the future European response to potential adverse events, which could be based on structures that are already in place as part of the SESAR programme mapping out the future of European air traffic management.

4.5.1   Coordinating the European Response to Contingency Events

A number of different approaches have been taken to structuring the European response to contingency events in different industries. Each technique has strengths and weaknesses; a complete analysis is omitted for the sake of brevity.[4] However, the different approaches can be summarized as follows:

- *a network of national entities* that coordinate through interaction. This can be seen in the direct operational coordination that, for instance, characterizes adjacent states within the European energy distribution market. Each neighbour establishes common letters of agreement and may act collectively to develop regional plans for emergency response. This local focus creates problems for establishing European consistency at a higher level. Additional complexity arises when one member state dominates regional policy or where there are political tensions between neighbouring states;

• *a European meta-organization* that coordinates semi-binding guidance. Eurocontrol and EASA have achieved their greatest results in areas where it is too costly or difficult to ensure consistency through a series of bilateral and multi-lateral regional agreements. However, their work is often complicated when different member states progress at very different speeds towards the implementation of common guidance. The more that views diverge, the less confidence can be placed upon the effectiveness of any future response to major contingencies. This caveat is particularly important when the decisions made by European meta-organizations are seen to be detrimental to the independence and interests of national entities.[5]

Many of the problems that complicated the response to the Eyjafjallajökull eruption were created because the governance and regulation of European air traffic management was based on elements of both approaches at the time of the contingency. The Common Requirements devolved many aspects of policy and decision-making to NSAs in conjunction with their ANSPs. There were also fledging attempts to establish regional groupings around Contingency Planning Teams within Functional Airspace Blocks (FABs).

4.5.2 Governance and Organization Structures

Governance is multifaceted. The term encapsulates decision-making, the acceptance and assignment of responsibility, the supervision and implementation of procedures and of enforcement actions. It is impossible to provide an exhaustive analysis of each aspect of the response to the Eyjafjallajökull eruption across each European state. Instead, we focus on the constitution of decision-making bodies and the interfaces between those bodies between different nations. In most cases, ANSPs and NSAs formed *ad hoc* committees that prepared tactical and operational responses to the changing threat posed by the ash cloud. These groupings often lacked scientific representation. In some cases, they did not regularly interact with members of the travelling public or even with other stakeholders, including the airlines and airports. In consequence, these stakeholders did not talk directly to ANSPs. Instead, they turned to the media, who sought the opinions of other scientific agencies. This led to conflict.

A number of alternatives can be identified. Many ANSPs have in-house research and development organizations. Financial considerations have curtailed their work in recent years. In consequence, some ECAC states have external scientific advisory boards to identify new areas of research that might guide the strategic direction for their organization, such as the development of small composite aircraft or on UAV operations. The work of these scientific groups is seldom visible to the public or other ANSPs. However, they provide a template for the integration of leading researchers to support decision making during contingency events. It is clear from these existing contacts that such relationships cannot be built up during the time pressures and political or economic tension that characterizes an on-going contingency.

4.6 SCIENTIFIC INPUT IN POST-CRISIS THINKING

There is a danger that the inconsistency and incoherence that characterized scientific input during the eruption will extend into the longer-term response. Reviews have been commissioned in many different regions of Europe and by parliamentary committees, regulatory agencies, industry bodies etc. Many of the conferences and workshops have been the result of local initiatives rather than a coordinated action plan. This proliferation of research interest is positive; it encourages further reflection on the technical problems that led to uncertainty during the initial response. However, the multiplicity of distributed events creates further challenges for ANSPs and other industry organizations. They must synthesize key lessons from all of these various meetings that are often not documented in a format that can easily inform operational decisions.

Many of the submissions to these meetings are based on a partial understanding of the events as they unfolded across Europe. They, typically, focus on the problems faced by an individual nation or by a particular region. They lack the European perspective that can only be provided by an authoritative analysis of the distributed response across ECAC states. For example, the problems and information needs for NATS were radically different from those facing individuals in NAV Portugal during different phases of the eruption. The need for an authoritative account of the handling of the ash cloud during April 2010 extends to the role that scientific bodies played in decision making across member states. As we have seen, there were significant differences in the degree of engagement both at a European level and within individual ANSPs. The future analysis of the Eyjafjallajökull response must analyze these differences in the hope that we can identify lessons for information-sharing across Europe.

4.7 CONCLUSIONS

This chapter has argued that scientific uncertainty, opaque decision-making processes and poor communication mechanisms impaired a coordinated response to the Eyjafjallajökull eruption in April 2010. These factors combined over time to undermine public and political confidence in the decision to close many European airspace. Many stakeholders felt excluded from the subsequent decision-making processes, leading to the intervention of the European Extraordinary Transport Council. Further action is now needed to ensure that lessons are learned for any similar contingency.

We are fortunate because many of the key elements are available to develop a coordinated response. CFMU, EASA are already set up. Eurocontrol has significant experience in promoting contingency planning in air traffic management. SESAR provides useful scientific and technical structures that can support contingency planning. However, we need to identify the detailed scientific decision-making structures that can help to implement a more consistent approach to the hazards that we face in an uncertain future.

NSAs and ANSPs were faced with exceptional circumstances. This justified the precautionary approach, which guided their decision-making processes after the initial eruption. However, a lack of coordinated scientific input into decision-making processes at a European level arguably led to inconsistency, confusion and lack of communication with the public and with politicians after the first closures. We have, therefore, argued that the Commission should form and maintain the core scientific knowledge needed to support European crisis management during future contingencies.

NOTES

1. For more information about the work of the Eurocontrol Contingency Task Force see http://www.eurocontrol.int/ses/public/standard_page/sk_sesis_guidelines.html (accessed 24 March 2011)
2. For summary accounts see witness statements included in the transcript of US Senate Committee on Commerce, Science and Transportation, Volcanic Hazards – Impacts On Aviation, US Senate Commerce Committee hearing in 2006, available at http://www.cusvo.org/docs/volcanichazards031606.pdf (accessed 24 March 2011).

3.   Examples include the well-publicized AVOID infra-red technologies being trialled by
     Easyjet and the Norwegian Institute for Air Research (Brannigan, Chapter 7).
4.   Johnson et al. (2008).
5.   Johnson et al. (2009).

BIBLIOGRAPHY

Johnson, C.W., G. Amar, T. Licu and R. Lawrence (2008), 'High-Level Architec-
   tures for Contingency Planning in Air Traffic Management', in R.J. Simmons,
   D.J. Mohan and M. Mullane (eds), *Proceedings of the 26th International Conference on Systems Safety, Vancouver, Canada 2008*, Unionville, VA: International
   Systems Safety Society.
Johnson, C.W., B. Kirwan, T. Licu and P. Statsny (2009), 'Recognition Primed
   Decision Making and the Organisational Response to Accidents: Ueberlingen
   and the Challenges of Safety Improvement in European Air Traffic Manage-
   ment', *Safety Science*, (47) 853–72.

5. Representing emergency risks: media, risk and 'acts of God' in the volcanic ash cloud

Adam Burgess

5.1 CRISIS MANAGEMENT, MEDIA AND RISK AMPLIFICATION

To an extent, at least, we live in a precautionary era whose imagination is exercised by the possibility of remote threats. As the example of international air travel security indicates, we are even prepared to reorganize aspects of everyday life around them and suffer routine inconvenience without question. Such responses often originate in demands following dramatic incidents, intensified by revelations and accusations articulated through the media. 'Something must be done!' is the common cry, with the underlying message that public health and safety must be paramount, and not compromised by politics or profiteering. This chapter is a preliminary consideration of media coverage around the volcanic ash cloud in the context of the distinctive late modern discourse of risk that has been influential in framing unforeseen events in the UK, the country, alongside Ireland, most affected by the unprecedented 'cloud of unknowing' in April 2010 (Marley, 2010). Here was a new and unpredictable threat – apparently able to bring down airliners, according to the implication of the flight ban put in place following the appearance of the cloud. Might the ash cloud also evoke the kind of media 'amplification of risk' (Pidgeon, Kasperson and Slovic, 2003) and political over-reaction seen in the UK around issues from genetically modified organisms (GMOs) to train crashes and child murders (BRC, 2006; RRAC, 2009)?

The potential to do so, and concern that it might, was indicated by the populist newspaper, the *Daily Star* and its headline: 'Terror as plane hits ash cloud' (21 April 2010), and the response that followed. The story concerned an incident back in 1982 – rather than now, as the story implied – when a Boeing 747's engines were knocked out by an ash cloud. The newspaper's picture was taken from television documentary on the incident by National Geographic. The documentary, luridly entitled *Volcanic Ash: Flight of Terror*, was then shown the same night by Channel 5, who managed to boost their normal viewing ratings by 77 per cent (Deans, 2010). The newspaper was removed from UK airport newsagent shelves over fears it could cause panic (Plunkett, 2010). At the same time, it should be remembered that responses to risk from the media and other actors remain selective and inconsistent, a process that follows patterns determined by culture and many other factors. As an 'act of God' without clear human actors, it lacks a focus for the blame, responsibility and accusation seen to be at the heart of how and why risk is constructed in human societies (Douglas and Wildavsky, 1982).

Waugh (2000, p. 6), in his drawing together of the field, notes that: 'whilst there is a tendency to view emergency management primarily as disaster planning and response, it involves much more …'. It is, 'intensely political'. This intensity stems from the often contested nature of how events should be understood and responded to. Emergency management and governing after crisis concerns blame and responsibility, often centred upon the (in) adequacy of official responses (Boin, McConnell and 't Hart, 2008). In a crisis situation, the media are central to determining the outcome of government efforts and the crucial post-event perception of their adequacy (Rosenthal, Boin and Comfort, 2001). The New Orleans floods following Hurricane Katrina is a clear example, and one where the government response was perceived as so inadequate that it even suggested a deliberate, perhaps racially tinged conspiracy (Spence, 2006; Preston, 2008; Putra, 2009). There, 'the media "framed" this event as a fiasco more completely than any kind of "spin" or speech could later undo' (Preston, 2008, p. 34).

Contesting the nature of crisis response is fought through the media, and those challenging the official government, state or corporate reaction have often more effectively engaged public imagination through better media management. Following the Madrid bombings of 11 March 2004, the opposition party won the election as their framing of events was more effectively communicated than the government's (Olmeda, 2008).

In the UK the classic example was the disposal of the Brent Spar oil storage buoy in 1995. Greenpeace's media campaign forced the oil corporation Shell to abandon its plans despite the later acknowledgement that dumping the facility in deep Atlantic waters was the safest and most environmentally sound solution (Ahmed 2006).

Media influence can be over-simplified, and the media 'are ill suited for sustaining high level coverage of long-term threats' (Kitzinger and Reilly, 1997, p. 320). News media lack a framework for discussing uncertainty, the essence of a typical story being, instead, a polarized discourse that implies irresponsibility and blame. Yet they can play an active role in framing risk controversies (Hansen, 2000) and stigmatize technological risks (Flynn, Slovic, and Kunreuther, 2001). The UK has a distinctively focused and single-minded media, particularly their newspapers, some of which, like the *Times* and the *Daily Mail*, are historic and powerful institutions. It is routine for the media to demand that future risk be eliminated even following incidents such as train crashes involving few or no casualties, insisting there be an official inquiry or new regulatory measures to prevent recurrence (Burgess, 2010b). One of those involved in communications management of the ash cloud in the UK told the author that in discussions with international colleagues it was only the British media who were asking: 'why the skies were shut?' Journalists in other countries were, by contrast, naturally inclined to ask instead: 'is it safe to open them?' Further, there was an expectation in the UK that the media would rally against *whichever* approach government and regulators adopted, as too risk averse or as indicating a cavalier approach to public safety.

A further and relatively unique phenomenon in the UK is the development of an explicitly campaigning stance among media outlets around the raising of risks (Burgess, 2010a). Newspapers in particular have adopted certain risks as a focus for sustained coverage without claiming they are simply reporting news. A wide range of hazards in the domains of technological innovation and child protection, in particular, have been adopted by media outlets since the 1990s. GMOs, for example, were dubbed 'Frankenfoods' by British newspapers and, alongside other actors, this was crucial to the successful stigmatization of the technology (Frewer et al., 2002). The predominant form of campaigning is to allege that a particular risk is not being taken sufficiently seriously and that authorities are compromised by their association with relevant commercial actors. This campaigning has frequently influenced the terms and speed of official response, such as leading the government to hold a public inquiry into possible health effects from mobile phones (Burgess, 2004). Media risk campaigning has been encouraged by such defensive government accommodation. By no means every publicly prominent hazard has become a focus for aggressive media attention, but there is clearly at least the potential for the ash cloud to have become the latest example.

There has been an enormous amount of research into risks, hazards and media, reflecting the central role they are perceived to have often played in the construction of risk in society (Kitzinger and Reilly, 1997). The predominant framework used in these studies is the *social amplification of risk*, reflecting the media's identification with heightening rather than attenuating risk perception (Pidgeon, Kasperson and Slovic, 2003). The main thesis is that events pertaining to hazards interact with psychological, social, institutional, and cultural processes in ways that can heighten or attenuate public perceptions of risk and shape risk behaviour. This is developed into a framework on the basis of a 'signal/receiver' metaphor, with social amplification conceived of as primarily a communication phenomenon.

Critics, adopting a more cultural approach, point out that SARF assumes that there is a 'correct' level of risk reaction from which amplification presumably deviates (Tansey and Rayner, 2008). In the case of ash cloud coverage we are confronted with the question of the level of media coverage against which we might judge whether there has been a process of amplification or attenuation. Realistically, it is only in a comparative sense that we might draw some conclusions, provided we can either compare reactions in different countries that faced a similar level of threat, or we can compare how reactions have changed over time when the same society was confronted with similar hazards in different eras, as was done in the case of mobile phones for example (Burgess, 2004).

But the potential to consider risk comparatively is more limited in the ash cloud case, where the hazard was unprecedented (previous ash clouds could always be circumnavigated) and very disproportionately affected two countries, the UK and Ireland. Whilst we can make some useful comparisons with other events occurring at the same time and the extent of their coverage, there are clear limitations to a quantitative focus on amplification. We need to also consider the qualitative character of discussion – its themes, targets and consistency. We will consider whether the ash cloud – like so many other hazards in the UK over recent years – has been configured as a late modern risk, at once both uncertain yet represented as a pervasive threat beyond control. This is by no means simply a question of the actual harm caused by a hazard, or even its potential to do so. Whilst 'Frankenfoods', for example, caused no known human harm they were successfully cast as being likely to do so, and we will here consider whether the ash cloud might also be framed in threatening terms beyond its immediate and visible impact.

5.2 FACTORS INFLUENCING AMPLIFICATION

It is useful to consider the themes of media coverage in the context of the distinctive characteristics of risk highlighted by Beck (1992), as has been done in the case of the BSE crisis, for example (Cottle, 1998; Washer, 2006). A first characteristic of contemporary risk is that it concerns 'the distribution of bads, not the distribution of goods' (Mythen, 2005). In risk framing the economic aspect is, at least, secondary, and often the antithesis of concerns that suspect economic interests are likely to compromise health and safety. Secondly, and proceeding from this 'postmaterialist' context, the highlighting of even speculative hazards such as a health threat from mobile phone radiation or GMOs becomes routinized. 'Unnatural' new technologies are particularly subject to suspicion, particularly those identified with corporate interests. A third characteristic of issues in the 'risk society' is the tendency towards absolute intolerance of risk as opposed to mitigation and balancing against costs and benefits. It was demanded that all products declare themselves 'GM Free', for example, and it will be similarly useful to examine evidence of such a 'zero-risk' approach in the ash cloud case. The acceptance of the accidental associated with classical modernity tends to be similarly rejected (Green, 1997). Instead, single negative incidents and experiences are regarded as necessarily symptomatic of a wider problem, rather than as technical matters susceptible to direct solution (Burgess, 2010b). A final characteristic of contemporary risk is its generalization. In the 'risk society' hazards are not so clearly confined and restricted by probability and exposure, but perceived as likely to make a more indiscriminate impact. Beck (1992) identifies radiation fall-out from the Chernobyl nuclear accident to illustrate this 'democratization' of risk. The extension of assumed negative impacts can be relatively immune to scientific evidence as negative impacts are projected into the future on the basis of worst-case assumption.

Some studies reveal a dramatically different character to risk perception even within advanced industrial nations, reflecting the extent to which countries have made the transition to a 'risk society'. A comparative study of risk perceptions in the US and Hungary in the early 1980s found that Americans' perception accorded with the distinctive character indicated by Beck, with fears reflecting uncertainty about the future and invisible threats such as radiation (Englander et al., 1986). Hungarians' risk perceptions, by contrast, were much more mundane in character, focusing on 'real' and immediate problems of workplace safety, for example, and still dominated by economic concerns. Such a contrast has been identified around particular crises, as reflected in differing media responses. For example, Höijer, Lidskog and Thornberg (2006) compare international reactions to the farmed salmon health scare in 2004 and found that the issue tended to be subject to extended problematization in the UK in the wake of a history of fiercely contested food scares. In countries like Norway, by contrast, the issue was presented in more straightforward economic terms as a threat to a national industry.

The widespread 'risk treatment' of a range of issues and concerns is understood by Beck to be the product of profound shifts within society and our impact on the environment. More socially it is the result of changing assumptions and relations between the individual and society, and social groups and elites. Despite being driven by such forces, this is not to say that every issue is subject to comparable treatment. Every crisis has its unique characteristics, both because of the nature of the hazard itself and the context in which it presents itself. The characteristics of the hazard itself have long been the subject of study in the perception of risk (Zinn, 2006). Whether particular hazards have the capacity to inspire dread, are visible, and appear subject to control and consent have long been understood as central to the perception of risk, and these factors constrain the capacity of 'risk amplifiers'. Hazards have been mapped according to the extent to which they are perceived as controllable and observable (Morgan et al., 2001). A particularly relevant factor to examining the ash cloud is the extent to which hazards can be regarded as 'acts of God' or, instead, can be identified with human error or man's general negative impact upon the environment. As Frumkin (2010, p. 1104) argues: 'risks generated by human action, failure or incompetence ... are judged to be greater than risks believed to be caused by nature or 'Acts of God' (for example, risks from earthquakes or cosmic rays).

Contextual factors are also vital to determining whether particular hazards become elevated into significant risks to society by the media, such as the impact of the legacy of associated risks (Flynn, Slovic and Kunreuther, 2001). Thus the weak non-ionizing 'radiation' associated with mobile phones suffers because it, nonetheless, shares the same basic name with the dangerous, 'ionizing' form, associated with nuclear accidents. Duration can also be an important factor in determining the impact made by particular hazards and the capacity of the media to influence this – particularly emergencies that appear unexpectedly and are not prolonged in their impact. This is important because it means media and the claimsmakers who might advance particular risks do not have a prolonged period to develop an effective language and terms through which risks might be seen as problematic. We can suggest that a key reason for the success of media campaigning against GMOs was the extended period over which it was in the public arena, allowing an alliance of actors to coalesce and a clear framework of understanding and language to evolve (Frewer, 2002). By contrast, the disease SARS never really developed into the international threat that some expected despite its coincidence with the start of the war in Iraq and 'bioterrorism' panic in America (Washer, 2004; Alcabes, 2009). Instead, 'surprisingly, militaristic language was largely absent, as was the judgemental discourse of plague' (Wallis and Nerlich, 2004). The disease was effectively isolated and eliminated through successful international scientific collaboration, before it could form part of any wider discourse of 'bioterrorism' and new disease threats. These are all factors that need to be considered when reviewing the coverage of the ash cloud and determining whether it was amplified and represented as an uncertain yet threatening risk.

5.3 COMPARING AND BREAKING DOWN THE ASH CLOUD COVERAGE

Google trends searches confirm that internet news activity around the cloud was overwhelmingly concentrated in the UK and Ireland. Other European and North American countries were a long way behind in their amounts of coverage, and scarcely distinguishable in quantity from one another. Similar trends are evident in print news media from the Lexis Nexis international database of media coverage. This is scarcely surprising, reflecting the disproportionate impact of the cloud on the British Isles. We can also identify the expected peaks of activity around the flight ban and a subsequent disappearance of the issue. Although this may also seem unsurprising, it is more significant in the context of considering whether the ash cloud was discussed and understood in similar terms to other high profile hazards of recent years such as BSE, GMOs and mobile phone radiation. In the latter cases the quantity of media discussion has not necessarily reflected peaks of direct impact from these hazards. Coverage of BSE and its human form, Creutzfeldt–Jakob disease (CJD), did not reflect the number of deaths, either of cows or people but was shaped by a range of other factors (Dawson and Lyons, 2003). Negative impacts from GMOs and mobile phone radiation remain, at most, uncertain and media discussion followed its own campaigning dynamics (Frewer, 2002; Burgess, 2004). A search on the Lexis Nexis database reveals the maximum 'over 3,000 hits' for all three issues compared to only around 397 for the ash cloud. This relatively limited media coverage suggests that the ash cloud did not become framed as a pervasive problem in the manner of GMOs, BSE and mobile phones. Instead it appears to have remained relatively confined to the precise periods during which flights were affected.

Some comparisons with other significant issues around the same time period are useful. There were 219 stories in national UK newspapers on the British Airways cabin crew dispute, for example, an issue that also concerned air travel disruption. This is around half the comparable figure for the ash cloud. Such figures stand in contrast to two other issues in the same month that made a much larger impact. The Deepwater Horizon crisis bears some comparison to the ash cloud as an emergency crisis involving major corporate players and national regulators. It generated more hits (664) than the ash cloud in UK newspapers, despite the fact that it took place in the US. Of course, it involved a major British company and this would be expected to increase British media interest. Beginning with a major and dramatic incident that involved casualties, many actors were drawn into both a technical search for solutions and a process of recrimination. A high stakes 'blame game' ensued as Obama deflected criticism onto BP, and BP onto others involved in the drilling. As well as targets for blame there were clearer victims. Coverage centred on the economic impact on the affected area, but also raised wider environmental concerns and discussion about the viability of fossil fuel sources that are increasingly difficult to access. In short, Deepwater Horizon involved and engaged with key themes of the 'risk society'.

April 2010 also saw the swine flu outbreak in Mexico and this generated more than 3,000 hits (1,100 linked with Mexico) indicating it was regarded as an issue altogether more serious than either the ash cloud or Deepwater Horizon. There was widespread alarm despite its relatively modest impact in Mexico, based on the widespread expectation that sooner or later there will be a flu outbreak approximating the 'Spanish flu' of 1918. Events in Mexico reignited and affirmed the powerful discourse of 'dread' around potentially devastating disease impacts (Alcabes, 2009). Flu is determinedly promoted by public health authorities in the UK as an inevitable occurrence that may have a devastating impact that cannot be easily contained, and it is in this context that the volume and dramatic tenor of coverage should be understood. The ash cloud does not readily fit into an existing paradigm of threat, but is rather shrouded in uncertainty.

Turning to the coverage of the ash cloud itself, in more detail, there were 397 articles where it was a 'major mention' (once repeat mentions were excluded) up until 25 October 2010. Breaking these down into general categories that were the focus of the articles we find:

- secondary reference (such as 'the ash cloud is another issue that …'): 71
- assorted stories (from 'ash is good for garden' to 'navy pick up stranded'): 7
- reporting of cloud, restrictions and prospects (such as 'cloud returned'): 85
- celebrity/traveller/human interest story (such as 'football game under threat'): 65
- travel displaced to other modes and places (such as 'Britons shun foreign holidays'): 13
- economic impact (such as 'air fares will rise'): 110
- insurance and claiming: (such as 'claiming unclear'): 14
- blame and (ir)responsibility: 29, made up of these stories:

-     –   1 'airlines avoid payouts'
-     –   1 'airlines look for blame'
-     –   1 'Met office's plane wasn't ready for week'
-     –   1 'airline shuns sick'
-     –   1 'fury against airline'
-     –   4 'airlines demand help/who pays?'
-     –   1 'Met office got it wrong'
-     –   1 'rescue thwarted by French'
-     –   1 'government under pressure to reopen'
-     –   1 'parties attacked for campaigning whilst millions stranded'
-     –   1 'anger that navy not picking up travellers'
-     –   4 'restrictions unnecessary'
-     –   3 'Salmond [Scottish politician] furious'
-     –   3 'Met office's satellite photos didn't exist'
-     –   1 'airline fury'
-     –   1 'pandemic of panic'
-     –   1 'was necessary'
-     –   1 'our reaction a shambles'
-     –   1 'Met office used probability not fact'
- other associated risk: 4 ('air conditioning health fear'; 'health risks low'; 'people with respiratory conditions advised to stay indoors'; 'water's safe').

The incident over the *Daily Star* headline proved to be an isolated one. There was no media frenzy around the ash cloud. There was no 'risk campaign' mounted by a newspaper, or anything approximating this – unlike in cases such as GMOs, mobile phones and BSE. The *Daily Mail* (26 April) gave space to a comment piece attacking the reaction as unnecessarily risk averse. It also highlighted the subsequent claim that the CAA's reaction was unnecessary, based on the examination of satellite imagery (following the story's printing in the London *Standard* title, a sister paper of the *Mail*). This was also covered by its sister paper, the *Mail on Sunday*, and by the *Mirror*. Yet no other media outlets appear to have followed the story. In its own terms this might be considered curious as, whatever the contested truth of the matter, this was an intrinsically interesting revelation in a country where the appropriate level of public risk aversion is much debated. It is also interesting that the airlines' attack on the slowness of response from European regulators ('can't they even organise a conference call on a weekend?!') did not become a focus of more sustained media attention.

Coverage did not extend far beyond the immediate impact made by the cloud. In so far as it did, stories are disparate. Risk was not projected forward into an uncertain future, despite the uncertainty inherent in the crisis. The furthest we appear to go is the straightforward: 'chaos may go on all summer' (*Daily Mail*, 6 May). There were few demands that 'something be done' or even the converse that 'too much' (risk aversion) had been done. The ash cloud was only the subject of one clear comment piece, where it was located in the context of a wider 'pandemic of panic'. More generally, there is little speculation about the significance or implications of the cloud, instead remaining understood in its own terms. After the middle of May any remaining stories concern the economic implications, principally for the airlines. This economic focus goes squarely against the characteristic emphasis of contemporary risk as the 'distribution of bads, not goods' (Mythen, 2005).

Another characteristic dimension to contemporary risk stories is dramatic speculation about human health impacts associated with only uncertain hazards. During the foot and mouth cattle disease crisis in 2001, for example, there was extensive media speculation that dioxins from the mass burnings of cattle would pose a major health threat. A distinctive feature of such stories is that they are advanced by 'risk entrepreneurs', i.e. alternative 'experts', three of whom were at the centre of the majority of stories linking mobile phone use with ill health, for example (Burgess, 2004). In this case there appears to be only one story on the ash cloud where such 'expert fears' were promoted. The *Mirror* (1 May) warned its readers of an 'Air con ash fear'; an expert in air conditioning systems suggesting there could be unanticipated implications. At this level, comparison stands with the one unambiguously 'happy' story about the impact of ash – on how it would be good for the gardens, so beloved of the English!

It is not that absolutely no stories appeared suggesting responsibility and blame, but that these isolated stories did not acquire any momentum, or even get widely replicated. The story that the Meteorological Office's monitoring plane was not ready for a week (*Sunday Times*, 25 April) did not become a scandal or focus. Apparent official complacency and disorganization are a long-established focus for attacks on official responses to emergencies that have acquired an even sharper focus in the 'risk society' where health and safety become paramount. Yet the *Sunday Times*' story made no further impact. There is even an unsurprising emphasis upon 'traveller misery' but surprisingly few 'moving tales' considering the missed job interviews and critical operations, for example, that inevitably occur when people remain stranded on the wrong side of the world for prolonged periods. Such was the focus for only one story, dramatically entitled: 'stranded in world of broken dreams'. The impression is that without a target for blame which can become a focus for organizing and motivating such stories, combined with a prolonged and predictable time period over which they can be pulled together, even 'moving tales' caused by the hazard do not consistently develop.

5.4 REFLECTING ON THE ASH CLOUD

Do the media play a role in emergency regulation? The answer is a conditional 'yes', but that it depends on the example and the circumstances. In some cases it has decisively shaped and sharpened responses, as in the cases of Hurricane Katrina, Brent Spar and Deepwater Horizon. In other cases, such as the ash cloud, their role has been much more limited. Above all, this appears to be because there is no plausible or consistent target for blame in an apparent 'act of God'. This is not an absolute or given attribute and it is in this context that the limited time period of the crisis is relevant, as it limited any potential for any media to develop a consistent target and a language and focus through which a wider impact might be made.

It can be considered surprising that the volcano was not somehow linked to an environmental discourse about humanity's negative impact on the earth, and how our clumsy response exposed the inadequacy of modern systems and science to anticipate or effectively manage such crises. There was scope for further speculation and suggestions of long-term, more devastating effects given the possibility of a larger eruption from Eyjafjallajökull's larger, sister volcano, Katla, which has historically always erupted soon after. The absence of this discourse confirms that the representation of hazards as significant and pervasive risks remains contingent upon the nature of the hazard and its legacy, and the context in which it becomes manifest.

The hazard posed by the ash cloud was an indirect one, to aircraft engines rather than directly to human health or insecurity and it remained shrouded in uncertainty. It was uncontrollable but not in a way that readily suggested a sustained or wider impact. It did not cause any major incident and involved no casualties, and this basic fact partially explains the limited character of the coverage. On the other hand we might also highlight the opposite issue of the number of incidents and hazards that did cause casualties in the world that generated even less coverage, as they were not 'newsworthy' (Kitzinger and Reilly, 1997): e.g. the floods in Pakistan that in the summer of 2010 affected 2.5 million people and killed at least 1,100, but only generated 200 hits on a comparable search among UK national newspapers, the same as for the ash cloud. The ash cloud was an unprecedented and novel phenomenon and this, alongside the extent of traveller inconvenience, helps explain why it generated more coverage than, for example, the British Airways cabin crew strike. Yet whilst such qualities allowed more extensive coverage than more deadly hazards, it arrived unexpectedly and the ash cloud was short-lived – too short to allow a convincing focus and language of risk to properly develop, even if there had been a will to do so. A new technology such as the mobile phone could be anticipated to become a focus for concern and journalists could plan and develop stories and angles over an extended period, something that was not possible in the ash cloud case. We might also suggest that those handling risk communication, particularly those at the CAA who bore the brunt of the media criticism that there was, might be credited with having done a good job of not encouraging further attacks.

There are also a number of factors related to the context in which the ash cloud first appeared. UK health authorities did not take the kind of precautionary line that suggested at least the possibility of significant health harms, a factor that has encouraged concern in other cases (Chakraborty, Chapter 6). Instead it was suggested that any effect was likely to be short term and advising that people remain indoors (Brandt and Krafft, 2010). Transport Minister Lord Adonis did anticipate risk-centred criticism, and repeated the mantra of 'safety is paramount' but this did not develop into a more consistent precautionary message. In other circumstances, such as ministers promising that accidents would never happen again following a train crash, even single statements along these lines have proven problematic (BRC, 2006; RRAC, 2009). But in the ash cloud case the general public imperative was to restore air travel to normal rather than seek absolute assurances of safety. There was no incident caused by the ash cloud that stimulated such demands nor created the pressure for politicians to acquiesce to it.

It must also be remembered that the ash cloud occurred during a very important and dramatic national election campaign in the UK, something that necessarily became the main focus of media attention. Further, this was an election overshadowed – like the country itself – by economic concerns that tended to displace other issues, particularly, perhaps, an esoteric 'inconvenience' like the ash cloud. In general, economic concerns have tended to be displaced in the risk society, as Beck (1992) has argued. But equally, the return of basic economic issues may tend to shift that balance back again. Following the election and as the new government's priorities have been on cutting the country's budget deficit, risk concerns have further tended to be sidelined. By contrast, the ash cloud did not coincide with heightened concern about other risks with which it might be associated and begin to form a more generalized sense of threat. We can only speculate what impact the cloud may have made had it occurred at the height of the BSE crisis, for example, or as major floods hit the country. However the fundamental 'problem' remains that the ash cloud does not readily fit into the key domains and narratives of contemporary risk. It does not relate to anxiety about child protection, food contamination, unforeseen consequences of new technology or any of the other established foci for risk-based concern in the UK. Instead it was an 'act of God' that was not easily blamed upon anyone or any institution. In so far as anyone attempted to do so – against the Meteorological Office and the CAA – these were not readily demonized targets; regulators and weather forecasters are not established villains like international corporations!

As much can potentially be learned from looking at issues put forward to be considered as risks but that 'failed' to gain momentum, as concentrating on only those that successfully demonized a risk, such as around GMOs. The ash cloud coverage falls into this category, and it is perhaps in this negative sense that reviewing the media coverage has been useful, making it clearer that no matter how easily it sometimes appears that the media are able to generate unwarranted concerns there remain clear limits on their ability to do so. These limits are given by the nature of the hazard itself, and the context in which it appears. Finally we can note that although media coverage remained largely confined to looking at the ash cloud in its own terms they singularly failed, as usual, to be able to engage with, let alone explain, the uncertainty at the heart of such issues and remain firmly wedded to making a story from conflict and certainty.

BIBLIOGRAPHY

Ahmed, M. (2006), *The Principles and Practice of Crisis Management: The Case of Brent Spar*, London: Palgrave Macmillan.

Alcabes, P. (2009). *Dread: How Fear and Fantasy Have Fuelled Epidemics from the Black Death to Avian Flu*, New York: Public Affairs.

Beck, U. (1992), *The Risk Society: Towards a New Modernity*, Oxford: Sage.

Better Regulation Commission (2006), *Risk, Responsibility and Regulation – Who's Risk is it Anyway?*, London: Better Regulation Commission.

Boin, A., A. McConnell and P. 't Hart (eds) (2008), *Governing After Crisis*, Cambridge: Cambridge University Press.

Brandt, H. and T. Krafft (2010), 'The Icelandic Ash Cloud and Other Erupting Health Threats: What Role for Syndromic Surveillance?', *European Journal of Public Health*, **20**(4), 367–8.

Burgess, A. (2004), *Cellular Phones, Public Fears and a Culture of Precaution*, New York: Cambridge University Press.

Burgess, A. (2010), 'Media Risk Campaigning: From Mobiles Phones to Baby P', *Journal of Risk Research*, **13**(1), 59–72.

Burgess, A. (2010), 'Public Inquiries in the (Risk) Regulatory State', *British Politics*, **6**(1), 3–29.

Cottle, S. (1998), 'Ulrich Beck, Risk Society and the Media', *European Journal of Communication*, 13(1), 5–32.

Dawson, C. and H. Lyons (2003), 'The Media and the Market: The Case of CJD', *British Food Journal*, **105**(6), 380–94.

Deans, J. (2010), 'TV Ratings: Channel Five's Volcano Documentary Boosts its Audience Share', *The Guardian* (21 April), available at http://www.guardian.co.uk/media/2010/apr/22/ratings-volcanic-ash-flight-terror (accessed 22 February 2011).

Douglas, M. and A. Wildavsky (1982), *Risk and Culture: An Essay on the Selection of Technical and Environmental Dangers*, Berkeley: University of California Press.

Englander, T., K. Farago, P. Slovic et al. (1986), 'A Comparative Analysis of Risk Perception in Hungary and the United States', *Social Behavior*, **1**, 55–66.

Flynn, J., P. Slovic and H. Kunreuther (2001), *Risk, Media, and Stigma: Understanding Public Challenges to Modern Science and Technology*, London: Sterling, VA: Earthscan.

Frewer, L. et al. (2002), 'The Media and GM Foods', *Risk Analysis*, **22**(4), 701–11.

Frumkin, H. (2010), *Environmental Health: From Global to Local*, New York: Jossey Bass.

Green, J. (1997), *Risk and Misfortune: A Social Construction of Accidents*, London: UCL Press.

Höijer, B., R. Lidskog and L. Thornberg (2006), 'News Media and Food Scares: The Case of Contaminated Salmon', *Journal of Integrative Environmental Sciences*, **3**(4), 273–88.

Kitzinger, J. and J. Reilly (1997), 'The Rise and Fall of Risk Reporting', *European Journal of Communication*, **12**(3), 319–50.

Marley, J. (2010), 'Volcanic Ash: Lessons from the Cloud of Unknowing?', *International Journal of Urological Nursing*, **4**(2), 51–2.

Morgan, M. et al. (2001), *Risk Communication: A Mental Models Approach*, New York: Cambridge University Press.

Mythen, G. (2005), 'From Goods to Bads: Revisiting the Political Economy of Risk', *Sociological Research Online*, **10**(3).

Olmeda, J. (2008), 'A Reversal of Fortune: Blame Games and Framing Contests after the 3/11 Terrorist Attacks in Madrid', in A. Boin, A. McConnell and P. 't Hart (eds), *Governing After Crisis*, Cambridge: Cambridge University Press, 62–84.

Pidgeon, N., R. Kasperson and P. Slovic (2003), *The Social Amplification of Risk*, Cambridge: Cambridge University Press.

Plunkett, J. (2010), Daily Star pulled from Airports over Volcano Ash Splash, *The Guardian* (21 April), available at: http://www.guardian.co.uk/media/2010/apr/21/airports-pull-daily-star (accessed 22 February 2011).

POST (2000), The Great GM Food Debate. Report 138. London: Parliamentary Office for Science and Technology, available at: http://www.parliament.uk/documents/post/report138.pdf (accessed 22 February 2011).

Preston, T. (2008), 'Weathering the Politics of Responsibility and Blame: the Bush Administration and its Response to Hurricane Katrina', in A. Boin, A. McConnell and P. 't Hart (eds), *Governing After Crisis*, Cambridge: Cambridge University Press, 33–61.

Putra, F. (2009), 'Crisis Management in Public Administration', *Planning Forum*, 13/14, 152–76.

Risk, Regulation Advisory Council (2009), *Response with Responsibility: Policy Making for Public Risk in the 21st Century*, London: BIS.

Rosenthal, U., A. Boin, and L. Comfort (2001), *Managing Crises: Threats, Dilemmas, Opportunities*, Springfield, IL: Charles C. Thomas.

Rowe, G., L. Frewer, and, L. Sjoberg (2000), 'Newspaper Reporting of Hazards in the UK and Sweden', *Public Understanding of Science*, **9**, 59–78.

Spence, L. (2006), 'The Deaths Could Have Been Prevented', Space and Culture, **9**(6), 5–6.

Tansey, J. and S. Rayner (2008), 'Cultural Theory and Risk', in R. Heath and D. O'Hair (eds), *The Handbook of Risk*, New York: Routledge.

Wallis, P. and B. Nerlich (2005), 'Disease Metaphors in New Epidemics: the UK Media Framing of the 2003 SARS Epidemic', *Social Science and Medicine*, **60**(11), 2629–39.

Washer, P. (2004), 'Representations of SARS in the British Media', *Social Science and Medicine*, **59**, 2561–71.

Washer, P. (2006), 'Representations of Mad Cow Disease', *Social Science and Medicine*, **62**(2), 457–66.

Waugh, W. (2000), *Living with Hazards, Dealing with Disasters: An Introduction to Emergency Management,* Armonk: M.E. Sharpe.

Zinn, J. (2006), *Social Theories of Risk and Uncertainty*, Oxford: Wiley.

6. The challenge of emergency risk communication: lessons learned in trust and risk communication from the volcanic ash crisis

Sweta Chakraborty

6.1 INTRODUCTION

Following the eruption of Eyjafjallajökull on 14 April 2010, the global public was faced with an onslaught of public health and safety risk communications typical of any emergency situation. Risk communications following emergency situations face specific challenges. These challenges have been addressed through the development of crisis communication paradigms following previous transnational disasters, such as pandemics and terrorists attacks. However, it is evident from analysis of the communications following the volcanic ash crisis that no such empirically founded approach towards emergency risk communication was executed. Rather the communications that were disseminated immediately following the crisis were often contradictory and stemmed from a variety of sources ranging from international organizations to private industry. Public attitudes towards these varying information sources, particularly levels of trust, and the role of the media further complicated risk communications being interpreted by the public as intended, potentially increasing public perceptions of the severity of risk.

High perceived risk events rely on effective risk communication as a critical component for effective emergency response. This chapter examines what happened in terms of risk communication following the eruption of Eyjafjallajökull and positions it within existing empirical research related to emergency risk regulation. It examines volcanic ash crisis communication activities in relation to existing disaster management paradigms. It continues on to discuss the role of public perceptions of risk, and more specifically the implications for trust in effective risk communication. Finally, this chapter concludes with lessons learned from the volcanic ash crisis that should be considered in order to deal with future challenges in emergency risk communication.

6.2 RISK COMMUNICATIONS

Emergency risk communication following a disaster such as the volcanic ash crisis must first be understood in relation to empirical research in the field of risk communication. The field of risk communication has evolved considerably since the discipline's inception in the early 1970s. The evolution of risk communication can be described through a series of developmental stages. Baruch Fischhoff, a widely revered and pioneer academic in the field, has outlined the evolution of risk communication through eight developmental stages beginning with 'all we have to do is get the numbers right' (Fischhoff, 1995, p. 138), followed by 'all we have to do is tell them the numbers' (Fischhoff, 1995, p. 139) and so on. The following table, illustrates these eight stages:

Table 6.1. Developmental stages in risk communication

1. All we [experts] have to do is get the numbers right

2. All we have to do is tell them [lay public] the numbers

3. All we have to do is explain what we mean by the numbers

4. All we have to do is show them that they've accepted similar risks in the past

5. All we have to do is show them that it's a good deal for them

6. All we have to do is treat them nice

7. All we have to do is make them partners

8. All of the above

The self-explanatory titles of the eight stages, depicted in the table above, describe the seemingly simple and straightforward skills required for a successful risk communication. Fischhoff writes, 'Simple skills are often essential to executing sophisticated plans' (Fischhoff, 1995, p. 138). These skills have been honed through empirical research and the analysis of risk communication case study outcomes. Each skill builds upon its predecessors and the eighth and final stage describes the current approach in risk communication as 'all of the above' (Fischhoff, 1995, pp.143–4). This final stage describes an approach that encompasses all the previous lessons learned as necessary for a successful and effective risk communication.

Keeping these guidelines in mind is crucial for effective risk communication, which is a critical component of effective emergency response following a high perceived risk event. The importance of these communications cannot be overstated. Clear, accurate, and timely information can be vital in preventing or reducing illness and injury, reducing anxiety levels, and facilitating relief efforts. As learned from the risk communication developmental stages (see Table 6.1), simply getting the numbers right and telling the public the accurate level of risk associated with the volcanic eruption may not be enough to quell public panic. Communicators also need to acknowledge the needs and concerns of the public and respond accordingly, as described in the later developmental stages (i.e. all we [experts] have to do is make them [lay public] partners) (see Table 6.1) (Fischhoff 2005, pp. 143–4). This approach challenges the traditional assumption that public perceptions must be brought into conformity with scientific rationality. Rather, such a technocratic view has been widely replaced by an emphasis on understanding public perceptions of risk. In accordance with this method, Baruch Fischhoff, has compiled the following empirically founded best practice principles in emergency risk communication:

• People want the truth, even if it is worrisome. They want to know what they are up against, in order to have the best chance of figuring out what to do. As a result, candour is critical in risk communications.
• People can absorb only a limited amount of new information at a time. As a result, communicators must identify the most critical facts, then organize them according to their audience's natural way of thinking.
• People have difficulty understanding some kinds of information, such as how small risks mount up through repeated exposure and how vivid instances can unduly dominate thinking. As a result, any communication must accommodate the known strengths and weaknesses of its audiences' thought processes.
• Emotions can cloud people's judgment, in predictable ways, for example when angry, people are more likely to blame other people for their problems and more optimistic about solving them. Although these effects are generally small, they interfere with decision-making. As a result, communicators must treat their audience respectfully, in order to encourage reasoned decision-making.
• Even the most experienced communicators cannot accurately predict how their messages will be interpreted, especially with novel topics (like volcanic ash or many other disaster scenarios) and unfamiliar

audiences. As a result, messages must be systematically evaluated, before they are disseminated – just the way that drugs must be. With dynamic events (like volcanic ash), that means pre-testing prototype message in advance.

- People exaggerate their ability to predict other people's behaviour. That includes experts when they predict how emergency plans will work. As a result, social scientists need to be part of the planning team, so that plans are based on science, not intuition. Failing that, citizens will receive advice that does not make sense to them, breeding distrust (like some of the hurricane evacuation messages).

- People generally make sensible decisions, if they are judged in terms of how they see their circumstances and what their goals are. Sensible decisions will not be effective decisions, though, if people do not have the right information. As a result, communicators must assume responsibility for providing relevant information in a timely fashion.

The above principles emerge from risk perception and communication literature and were compiled to be utilized in emergency risk communications following pandemic scares (Fischhoff, 2005, pp. 2–3). Even in the immediate stage following a disaster, it is evident that peoples' judgment and decision-making processes must be taken into account in order to produce effective risk communications. As evident from the bullet-pointed principles described above, the current most widely accepted best practice approach towards risk communication is to first understand how lay publics cognitively perceive risks (Fischoff et al., 1993, p. 200).

6.2.1 Risk Perceptions

Perceptions of risk following a sensational event, such as the eruption of Eyjafjallajökull, are determined by several factors. These factors include, but are not limited to whether or not a risk is familiar, voluntary, natural, and catastrophic. Based on this taxonomy of hazards, described as the psychometric paradigm (Slovic, 1987, pp. 280–5), it becomes possible to position a volcanic ash cloud in relation to other risks. This positioning is considered primarily across familiarity and dread of the risk in question. Thus, a volcanic eruption resulting in a transnational ash cloud would be considered unfamiliar, in that volcanic eruptions are relatively rare within the scope of a human lifetime (i.e. as opposed to car accidents). Additionally, perceptions of dread stem from the catastrophic potential of an ash cloud, which is far from endemic and instead conjures images of enormity of effect across a large geographic space. Sensational disasters with the perceived potential to impact large numbers of people are extremely salient in public recollections and contribute to lay assessments on the severity of a risk (Slovic et al., 2000, p. 149).

Lay publics and experts do not assess risk in the same way. Experts consider base rate statistics in assessing risk, while lay publics rarely demonstrate probabilistic risk judgments (Sunstein, 2002, p. 55). Rather, lay publics are prone to utilizing mental shortcuts known as heuristics and biases in judgment and decision-making (Kahneman and Tversky, 1974, pp. 1124–31). One example of a heuristic relevant to risk perceptions associated with a volcanic eruption is termed 'availability bias' (Tversky and Kahneman, 1973, pp. 207–32). This bias results in the over or underestimation of a risk based on how salient in may be in terms of cognitive recall. Thus, an unfamiliar event that has catastrophic potential, which has described the ash crisis, may be overestimated in terms of frequency of occurrence.

Fears of recurrence and overestimations of actual risk may be amplified by the media. This phenomenon is explained through the 'Social Amplification of Risk Framework' (SARF), which describes how both social and individual factors act to attenuate or amplify perceptions of risk, which then create ripple effects (Kasperson et al., 1988, pp. 177–87). These effects may be carried through communication channels, such as the media, to form secondary, tertiary, etc. impacts (Ragona, Chapter 3). For example, amplifying risks associated with the volcanic ash cloud can create secondary impacts such as economic losses, regulatory impacts, loss of trust and confidence in governing institutions, etc. (Kasperson et al., 2003, pp. 31–6).

Further, if the media saturates the airways with a large volume of information, it may serve as a risk amplifier. The information's symbolic connotations and volume, as well as the extent to which the information has been disputed and dramatized, can influence social amplification. Such dramatization also increases fears by exaggerating the potential consequences and abetting widespread panic (Kunreuther et al., 2001, pp. 469–84). Sensational headlines create salient messages that are easily conjured in public minds, but are not easily stifled (Mazur, 1981, pp. 113–44).

The media also tends to become a battleground for contentious viewpoints. When experts face off, it further heightens uncertainty and decreases credibility in the spokespersons. Not surprisingly, this results in an amplification of risk, perpetuating public distrust (Flynn et al., 1993 pp. 497–502; Lofstedt and Horlick-Jones, 1999, pp. 73–88). In this type of environment where confusion is rampant, trust plays a considerable role in public perceptions of the severity of risk (Siegrist and Cvetkovich, 2000, pp. 353–62). Levels of trust in sources of information can also impact how risk communications are interpreted by intended recipients. Trust plays a central role in compliance rates among message recipients; in that individuals are more likely to follow instructions given by someone they trust (Slovic, 1993, p. 677).

Trust in sources of information following the volcanic ash crisis is an example of *across groups* trust. The primary components that make up trust in such bodies include fairness, competency, and efficiency. If one or more of these characteristics is deemed as lacking in a regulatory or governing body, there is likely to be a deficiency in public trust. Therefore, a regulator perceived as unfair, incompetent, and/or inefficient may result in futile efforts towards managing and/or communicating about risks to the public (Lofstedt, 2005, p. 127). Thus, even if the best practice risk communication guidelines are executed following an emergency situation, levels of trust in the sources of information may dictate communication effectiveness outcomes. This chapter examines the levels of trust in sources of health and safety information following the volcanic ash crisis for this purpose.

Before the impact of risk perception on the interpretations of risk communications can be examined in relation to the volcanic ash crisis, this chapter considers the execution of specific crisis communication paradigms. Such paradigms have been developed following lessons learned from previous transnational disasters such as the avian flu (Fischhoff et al., 2006, pp. 131–49) or the 9/11 terrorist attacks (Fischhoff, 2003, pp. 255–8). The approaches established help to elucidate the specific needs and challenges in risk communication following an emergency situation. An example of such a method, introduced in the following section, can help to make apparent the specific challenges faced in terms of emergency communications following the volcanic ash crisis.

6.3 THE CHALLENGE OF EMERGENCY RISK COMMUNICATION

Lesson learned from disasters in the past have resulted in the development of crisis communication paradigms specifically to address the challenges of communicating to a public immediately following an emergency. The specific challenges include logistics being disrupted, victims needing care, relatives needing support, emergency responders falling victim and/or torn between professional and personal obligations, media attention, political and interest group obstacles. On the positive side, the communicator has the public's attention and there are ideally no conflicting priorities (Sandman and Lanard, 2004).

One specific paradigm to consider in regards to the volcanic ash crisis is the *Crisis Communication Lifecycle* developed by the Centers for Disease Control and Prevention following recent pandemic scares. This paradigm describes risk communication guidelines in five phases over a period of time following a high perceived risk event (Reynolds, 2002, pp. 7–10). A visual representation of the *Crisis Communication Lifecycle* is reproduced in the following diagram:

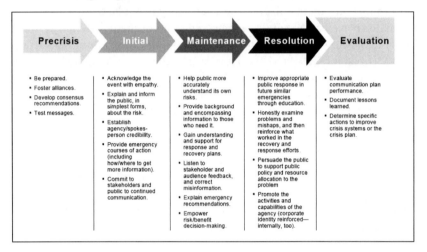

Precrisis	Initial	Maintenance	Resolution	Evaluation
• Be prepared. • Foster alliances. • Develop consensus recommendations. • Test messages.	• Acknowledge the event with empathy. • Explain and inform the public, in simplest forms, about the risk. • Establish agency/spokesperson credibility. • Provide emergency courses of action (including how/where to get more information). • Commit to stakeholders and public to continued communication.	• Help public more accurately understand its own risks. • Provide background and encompassing information to those who need it. • Gain understanding and support for response and recovery plans. • Listen to stakeholder and audience feedback, and correct misinformation. • Explain emergency recommendations. • Empower risk/benefit decision-making.	• Improve appropriate public response in future similar emergencies through education. • Honestly examine problems and mishaps, and then reinforce what worked in the recovery and response efforts. • Persuade the public to support public policy and resource allocation to the problem • Promote the activities and capabilities of the agency (corporate identity reinforced—internally, too).	• Evaluate communication plan performance. • Document lessons learned. • Determine specific actions to improve crisis systems or the crisis plan.

Figure 6.1. Crisis communication lifecycle (adapted from Reynolds, 2002, p. 7)

The above figure is an applicable communication strategy when facing a high perceived risk event. Although it has been primarily utilized in relation to public health crises, it provides an example of action measures that may be adapted to varying emergencies. Communication recommendations are described across five phases following a hazard. These phases are described as precrisis, initial, maintenance, resolution, and evaluation. Each of the phases is next examined in turn.

6.3.1 Phase 1: Precrisis

The precrisis phase can be described as the phase where all the planning and most of the work should be done. It is during this phase that types of disasters and reasonable questions should be anticipated. Initial risk communications can be drafted as blanks to be filled in later, and spokespersons, resources, etc. should be identified. It is also essential that alliances and partnerships are fostered during this phase to ensure that experts are speaking with one voice following a disaster (Reynolds, 2002, p. 7).

6.3.2 Phase 2: Initial

The initial phase of an emergency situation can be described as the phase where simplicity, credibility, verifiability, consistency and speed most count. This phase tends to be characterized by confusion and intense media interest. It is important during this phase to disperse information from a source that is credible, demonstrates sympathy, and is trusted. It is also important to convey whatever information is available, explain the state of the investigation, and finally to explain when more information will be available. The information conveyed must be checked before being released (Reynolds, 2002, p. 8).

6.3.3 Phase 3: Maintenance

The maintenance phase can be described as the phase where communicators should anticipate sustained media interest and scrutiny. This phase requires preparation for unexpected developments, rumours, or misinformation. It is during this phase following an emergency situation that experts, professionals and others will comment publicly, which can lead to contradictory messages. This can result in media amplification of risk and criticisms of how the disaster was handled. Therefore, it is most important during this phase to stay on top of the information flow and conduct ongoing assessment of the event and the allocation of resources (Reynolds, 2002, p. 9).

6.3.4 Phase 4: Resolution

The resolution phase can be characterized as having reduced public and media interest. It is during this phase that proper scrutiny may arise in retrospect on how the event was handled. Sustained interest allows for the opportunity to reinforce certain critical points, perhaps through a public education campaign or a website making updated information available. It is during this period of the crisis lifecycle that the public is most responsive to risk avoidance and future mitigation education. In the case of the volcanic ash crisis, this phase was particularly necessary in quelling public concerns over the eruption of the neighbouring volcano, Katla (Reynolds, 2002, p. 9).

6.3.5 Phase 5: Evaluation

The evaluation phase can be best described as the time during which to evaluate the communication plan performance. It is necessary during this phase to document the lessons learned from the emergency situation. Finally, it is during this last phase of the crisis communication lifecycle that specific actions are determined to improve crisis communication systems and plans (Reynolds, 2002, p. 10).

The *Crisis Communication Lifecycle* described above is an example of crisis communication management developed from empirical findings in risk communication research. It offers a protocol for risk communicators to follow before and after an emergency situation. However, neither this protocol nor an alternative paradigm was utilized in the case of the volcanic ash crisis. This is demonstrated in the following section through the examination of the risk communications following the volcanic eruption.

6.4 COMMUNICATIONS FOLLOWING THE ERUPTION OF EYJAFJALLAJÖKULL

In order to position the volcanic ash crisis in the context of risk communication research, it is necessary to analyze the communications produced and the sources from which they came. The primary sources for public health safety information following a volcanic ash crisis include public and private as well as global and local bodies and are listed as follows:

- international bodies such as the World Health Organization (WHO);
- national bodies such as the UK's Health Protection Agency (HPA);
- regulatory/advisory bodies such as the UK's Civil Aviation Authority (CAA) and the MET's office's Volcanic Ash Advisory Centre (VAAC);
- airlines industry represented through the Air Transport Association (IATA) as well as individual airlines.

Virtually all the above sources of information produced risk communications following the volcanic ash crisis. Yet there were clear inconsistencies across the varying sources in terms of the health and safety information disseminated. This will become evident upon analysis of the communications produced by the above bodies.

6.4.1 Communicating Health Issues

Two days following the eruption, the World Health Organization warned Europeans to stay indoors if ash from Iceland's volcano started to settle. WHO spokesperson Daniel Epstein stated (MSNBC.com, 16 April 2010):

'We're very concerned about it. These particles when inhaled can reach the peripheral regions of ... the lungs and can cause problems – especially for people with asthma or respiratory problems.' He described the microscopic ash as potentially dangerous for people once it reached the earth because inhaled particles could enter the lungs and cause respiratory problems. He also suggested a risk-management strategy by recommending Europeans who go outside might want to consider wearing a mask (Epstein, 2010).

In the meantime, the risk communications and advice provided to the global public by the WHO were openly contested by a number of experts. Dr Stephen Spiro, a professor of respiratory medicine and deputy chair of the British Lung Foundation, dismissed the WHO's warnings as 'over the top' and 'a bit hysterical' (MSNBC.com, 16 April 2010). Several additional experts agreed that the actual risk of inhaling volcanic ash was less than that of cigarette smoke and pollution. Ken Donaldson, a professor of respiratory toxicology at the University of Edinburgh, having studied the impact of volcanic ash in people, stated that, 'Not all particles are created equal. In the great scheme of things, volcanic ash is not all that harmful' (MSNBC.com, 16 April 2010). Donaldson stated that Europeans' exposure to volcanic ash would be negligible and that only those in the near vicinity of the Icelandic volcano, and with existing respiratory problems, would likely be most at risk.

Britain's Health Protection Agency (HPA) agreed that the volcanic ash should not cause serious harm. The agency stated that people with respiratory problems, such as bronchitis and asthma, might experience more symptoms (i.e. itchy eyes, a sore throat and dry cough) than a healthy individual. The agency advised those with such preexisting conditions to carry their inhalers or medicines to thwart what were likely to just be short-term effects (HPA, 15 April 2010). Additionally, Dr Pascal Imperato, Dean of the public health school at the State University of New York Downstate Medical Center, who worked on the response to the eruption of Mount St Helens in 1980, stated: 'People with health problems shouldn't sit around outside looking up at this cloud because there could be microscopic particles falling down. But for most people, they will not experience any major breathing or other difficulties' (MSNBC.com, 16 April 2010).

The public health related communications described above demonstrate initial contradictions and a disunited approach. Risk-perception literature discussed explains the potential for contradictory scientific information resulting in public distrust (Kasperson et al.,1988, pp. 177–87). This distrust can result in risk communications not being interpreted as intended and therefore proving futile (Fischhoff et al., 1993, pp. 201–2). For example, despite the majority of public health warnings suggesting minor health risks to the public, the initial WHO caution may have diluted public

reception of follow-up contradictory communications. This creates scope
for initial public panic and hysteria that may not necessarily be quelled
through additional communications. Such was the case of swine flu, which
took a year before being deemed to have not been an outbreak (Rubin,
2009, pp. 1–8).

6.4.2 Communicating Flight Safety

In addition to health warnings associated with the volcanic ash cloud, risk
communications in regards to flight safety were also dispersed. The CAA
applied a zero-tolerance policy in regards to aircraft operations through
volcanic ash. For relevant airspaces regulated, this translated to policy that
erred on the side of caution. Flight safety communications reflected this
policy, and therefore the public initially heard that in order to ensure public
safety, flights must not be allowed to take off. This can be compared to
regulation in Italy, where due to the limited size of the volcanic ash cloud
on its territory, air traffic was not completely halted. Professor Frank
Furedi from the University of Kent stated:

> It's very sad that in many respects the EU …finds it very difficult to do the most
> basic planning when it comes to such a major issue. I do think it's important to
> realize that many countries all over the world face volcanic eruption. For
> example, countries like Italy still manage to have air traffic just by taking sensible
> precaution. (Furedi, 19 April 2010)

In the UK, the Met Office's VAAC was responsible for releasing information in regards to flight safety. While the VAAC assured accurate and timely
information, it was alleged in the media that these warnings were not based
on empirical scientific evidence, but rather on a mathematical projection
model (Burgess, Chapter 5). Media vilification of this model ensured,
despite reassurance from the MET office, that all information communicated was based on state of the art technology (Brannigan, Chapter 7).
Scepticism of the communications stemming from the VAAC is believed to
stem from public distrust in the Met Office. This public distrust is believed
to have ensued following the 2009 'Climategate' scandal, which alleged
scientific data being manipulated and endorsed by the office. Despite its
irrelevance to information produced by the VAAC, the VAAC's affiliation
to the Met Office may have resulted in the undermining of any communication efforts (Leiserowitz et al., Working Paper, 2 July 2010). Therefore,
overarching bodies such as the Met Office must consider the importance of
public trust in terms of the effectiveness of its affiliates' communication
efforts.

6.4.3 Communication from the Airline Companies

In addition of advisory bodies, private airlines also introduced their own safety communications to the public. British Airways (BA) ran test flights and announced that they received the all clear. However, the North Atlantic Treaty Organization (NATO) reported finding ash in a jet engine, contradicting BA's reassuring claims. As previously discussed, in an environment of competing claims, public distrust perpetuates (Siegrist and Cvetkovich, 2000, pp. 353–62). Such contradictory levels of flight safety assurance therefore contributed to levels of public distrust.

6.4.4 Perceptions of Distrust in Communicators

Perpetuation of distrust through national advisory bodies such as the VAAC, and through the perceived private interest of industry (i.e. British Airways), was apparent following the volcanic ash crisis. While the scientific establishment is generally regarded as more trusted than private institutions, residual suspicion of the Met Office was evident in the wake of the 'Climategate' scandal. This suspicion can negate efforts of risk communication aiming to clarify differences between risk hazards and hype. Media in the UK following the Icelandic eruption reverberated similar sentiments. Journalist Gerald Warner of the UK newspaper *The Telegraph* asked, 'Is volcanic ash the new swine flu?' He concluded,

> We do not know. We do not know because we can no longer trust the sources from which we would normally expect to receive authoritative information. There is a complete breakdown in confidence between the public and the politico-scientific establishment. (Warner, 19 April 2010)

In order to address this alleged breakdown of trust, sources for risk communications must consider public attitudes towards their affiliated institutions. Recommendations for this, as well as other lessons learned from analysis of the risk-communication environment following the volcanic ash crisis, are discussed in the next section.

6.5 DISCUSSION AND RECOMMENDATIONS

Based on analysis of the communications produced following the volcanic ash crisis, it is evident that lessons learned in emergency communications from similar previous transnational disasters were not applied. While some of the information dissemination strategies discussed appeared to have

been acknowledged (i.e. the VAAC presenting accurate and timely information), it is evident that consideration of empirical research in the fields of
risk communication and perception were lacking. These assertions are
supported through analysis of the communications following the volcanic
ash crisis, and recommendations for the handling of similar future events
are offered in this section.

Mainly, analysis of the risk communications has made clear that a
cohesive strategy of control and coordination of the information flow was
poor to nonexistent. There was no evidence of communication across the
different bodies involved in terms of presenting a unified front or the
identification of whom or what would be responsible for the communication of risks. Thus, information was produced from various sources, and
often from irrelevant and/or independent sources. The lack of a single
uniform voice has the potential to create an information vacuum, which
can allow for unaccredited information to reach the public. This type of
landscape can lead to the propagation of rumours, misinterpretation of
messages, and the perpetuation of public distrust (Covello and Sandman,
2001, pp. 164–77).

In order to ensure against an undesirable post-crisis landscape, precrisis
planning is required. However, the lack of coordination in communicating
risks following the volcanic ash crisis described demonstrates poor precrisis
planning. Poor precrisis planning also meant that there was no accountability in terms of releasing untested risk communications, tracking risk-
communication activities or misallocating resources towards ineffective
risk communications. More specifically, releasing untested risk communications is irresponsible in an emergency situation since it is necessary to
ensure that communications are being received as intended (Morgan et al.,
2002, pp. 29–30). Otherwise communications may be unable coherently to
fulfill answers to basic post-crisis questions of the magnitude of the crisis,
the immediacy and duration of threat, and who is going to fix the problem.
Thus, untested risk communications can create confusion, provoke conflict
and cause undue alarm or complacency (Fischhoff et al., 1993, pp. 183–
203). Fischhoff states, 'One should no more release untested communications than untested pharmaceuticals' (Fischhoff, 2007, p. 190).

It is clear that communicating risks following a high perceived risk event,
such as a volcanic ash cloud, requires careful consideration prior to the
event occurring so that responsible dissemination can occur following the
event. Designing and dispensing risk communications is a careful process
that has evolved over time resulting in current guidelines (Fischhoff, 1995,
pp. 137–45) that are widely accepted among academics (see Table 6.1).
These guidelines must be taken into consideration during the preparatory
stage prior to future events. In order to ensure this, the formation of a

central communications source is recommended. This was also concluded in a report on the volcanic ash crisis from UCL Institute for Risk and Disaster Reduction. It stated as follows:

> A communications centre should be established that advises the public and which all affected bodies are required to support. This would avoid the huge expenses of individuals trying without success to contact airlines and other transport bodies. Efforts should be made to enable such a communications plan to make use of the resources available to the media in communicating advice objectively. (Sammonds et al., 2010, p. 19)

Such a source did not exist prior to the volcanic ash crisis in anticipation of this type of transnational disaster and still does not exist at the time this chapter was written. It was mainly because no such centre existed prior to the crisis that no risk communication system was in place to launch following the crisis. For this reason, it was also not possible for various information sources coherently to apply an existing crisis communication paradigm, such as the *Crisis Communication Lifecycle* (see Figure 6.1).

Risk communication paradigms suggest a coherent communication plan to be set out from a best-positioned institution or alliance as agreed in the precrisis planning stage (see Figure 6.1). It is at this stage that initial communications should be drafted with blanks to be filled in as relevant once a crisis unfolds. It is also recommended that spokespeople, resources, and resource mechanisms should be identified. Training should commence and alliances and partnerships should be fostered to ensure that all relevant scientific sources of information are consistent (Covello and Sandman, 2001, pp. 164–77). Such measures could prevent contradictory messages from being dispersed to the public, which, as previously discussed, can influence the social amplification of risk and abet public confusion, panic, and distrust (Kunreuther et al., 2001, pp. 469–84).

In order further to ensure that risk communication strategies are being appropriately developed as described, experts in the field have recommended a division of labour along four kinds of experts. These experts included subject-matter specialists, risk and decision analysts, psychologists, and communication system specialists (Fischhoff, 2005, p. 3). The combination of these experts could offer advice on how best to utilize empirical research from various fields, such as risk perception, to prepare for similar disasters in the future and to prevent against communication mishaps.

Studies in risk perception have shown that in an environment where information is incomplete and facts are disperse, such as that following an emergency situation, trust can play a vital role in effective risk communication. Trusted sources are likely to receive more credibility in terms of the information released in comparison to less trusted sources (Slovic, 1993, pp. 675–82). While the VAAC was alleged to be producing timely and accurate facts about the disaster, it appeared not to have considered its position as a credible source for information. This lack of consideration had the potential to render any communications to the public as ineffective.

Thus, in order effectively to communicate post-crisis in the future, it is necessary to understand public perceptions of risk and the factors that may influence perceptions, such as trust. It has long been established that a failure to manage trust results in failure to manage risk (Slovic, 1993, pp. 675–82). It may prove counterproductive or even harmful to communicate in such an environment of distrust. For this reason, such institutions must consider public perceptions of efficiency, competence, and fairness, which are necessary for building public trust. They must examine where they fall short in regards these dimensions in public attitudes and take steps towards addressing the issues (Lofstedt, 2005, pp. 127–32).

Finally, it is asserted that while the CAA regulations may have hindered the sovereignty of information flow, the VAAC should have made it clear to the public exactly what stage the investigation was in and when more information would be available. Increased transparency, while not always an appropriate measure (Chakraborty and Lofstedt, 2010, pp. 159–62), may have helped to reassure the public that more information would be on its way. Such reassurances are crucial in communicating risks following a crisis and were clearly lacking in the communication environment analyzed for this chapter.

6.6   CONCLUSIONS

This chapter has described the health and safety risk communications following the volcanic ash crisis in relation to existing risk communication theory, by focusing in particular on the challenge of emergency risk communication. It has illustrated how emergency communication approaches developed from previous similar borderless threats (i.e. pandemics and terrorist attacks) and how such lessons learned were not *anticipated and adapted for the type of crisis presented in this book.* This was discovered to be due to poor precrisis planning across several sources of information (i.e. WHO, national regulators, etc.). This resulted in inconsistent messages following the disaster, which had the potential to be socially amplified by the media and result in public confusion and perpetuation of distrust. Confusion in regards to whether or not risks pose an actual health and safety hazard or are just hype can be extremely detrimental to societal well-being. People need to know accurate and timely health and safety information in order to be able to make appropriate decisions. Unnecessary hype has the potential to create a public that is numb or under-reacting to serious risk communications.

Additionally, this chapter has described the importance of understanding how publics perceive and assess risks. Investing in understanding of public perceptions of risk can help to ensure that risk communications are being interpreted as intended. In particular, consideration of public trust as a factor in the shaping of risk perceptions is required for effective risk management and communication. The volcanic ash crisis discussed in this book has contributed an additional case study to the understanding of trust as integral for risk management.

Finally, this chapter has recommended that a communication protocol be put in place in anticipation for similar events to the volcanic ash crisis. Mainly, an emphasis on precrisis planning is required to ensure that risk communications guidelines are being followed and communications are being designed in accordance to best practice principles. This may be accomplished through a centralized communications centre, which includes relevant expertise in order to ensure that the appropriate measures are taken following a similar event in the future. Such a centre would not only establish accountability for faulty communications, but also allow for a single unanimous source of information to the public. Such a centre could also help to consider the factors that shape public perceptions of risk described, such as trust, and utilize the lessons learned from the volcanic ash crisis to prevent against similar communication mishaps in the future. Future challenges in emergency risk communication will have their own unique circumstances, but study of the volcanic ash crisis has resulted in lessons learned that should be applied to future communication challenges that will inevitably arise.

BIBLIOGRAPHY

Brannigan, V. (2010), 'Alice's Adventures in Volcano Land: The Use and Abuse of Expert Knowledge in Safety Regulation', *European Journal of Risk Regulation*, **1** (2), 107–14.

Burns, W. et al. (1993), 'Incorporating Structural Models into Research on the Social Amplification of Risk: Implications for Theory Construction and Decision Making', *Risk Analysis*, **13**, 611–23.

Chakraborty, S. and R. Lofstedt (2010), 'Regulatory Transparency: Forthcoming Lessons from the FDA', *European Journal of Risk Regulation*, **1**(2), 159–62.

Covello, V. and P. Sandman (2001), 'Risk communication: Evolution and Revolution', in A. Wolbarst (ed.), *Solutions to an Environment in Peril*, Baltimore: John Hopkins University Press, 164–78.

Epstein, D. (2010), 'Patients with Respiratory Conditions more Susceptible to Effects of Ash', World Health Organization, available at http://www.who.int/mediacentre/news/notes/2010/volcanic_ash_20100416/en/index.html (accessed 21 February 2011).

Fischhoff, B. (2005), *Scientifically Sound Pandemic Risk Communication*, House Science Committee Briefing: Gaps in the National Flu Preparedness Plan: Social Science Planning and Response, available at http://www.medicine.virginia.edu/clinical/departments/psychiatry/sections/cspp/ciag/conference/articles/s2006/fischhoff_pandemic_risk_communication.pdf (accessed 28 February 2011).

Fischhoff, B. et al. (1993), 'Risk Perception and Communication', *Annual Review of Public Health*, **14**, 183–203.

Fischhoff, B. et al. (2003), 'Evaluating the Success of Terrror Risk Communications', *Biosecurity and Bioterrorism: Biodefense Strategy, Practice, and Science*, **1**(4): 255–8.

Fischhoff, B. et al. (2006), 'Analyzing Disaster Risks and Plans: An Avian Flu Example', *Journal of Risk and Uncertainty*, **33**, 131–49.

Fischhoff, B. (1995), 'Risk Perception and Communication Unplugged: Twenty Years of Process', *Risk Analysis*, **15**, 137–45.

Flynn, J. et al. (1993), 'The Nevada Initiative: A Risk Communication Fiasco', *Risk Analysis*, 13, 497–502.

Furedi, F. (19 April 2010), 'This Shutdown is about More than Volcanic Ash', *Spiked*, available at http://www.frankfuredi.com/index.php/site/article/386/ (accessed 21 February 2011).

HPA (15 April 2010), 'Statement on Health Effects of Icelandic Volcanic Ash Plume', Health Protection Agency, available at www.hpa.org.uk/newscentre/ (accessed 21 February 2011).

Kahneman, D. and A. Tversky (1974), 'Judgment under Uncertainty: Heuristics and Biases', *Science*, **185**(4157), 1124–31.

Kasperson, R. et al. (1988), 'The Social Amplification of Risk: A Conceptual Framework', *Risk Analysis*, **8**, 177–87.

Kasperson, R. et al. (2003), 'The Social Amplification of Risk: Assessing Fifteen Years of Research and Theory', in N. Pidgeon et al. (eds), *The Social Amplification of Risk*, Cambridge: Cambridge University Press.

Kunreuther, H. et al. (1990), 'Public Attitudes Toward Siting a High-Level Nuclear Waste Repository in Nevada', *Risk Analysis*, **10**, 469–84.

Leiserowitz, A. et al. (2 July 2010), 'Climategate, Public Opinion, and the Loss of Trust', Working Paper, available at *SSRN* at http://ssrn.com/abstract=1633932 (accessed 18 February 2011).

Lofstedt, R. (2005), *Risk Management in Post Trust Societies*, Basingstoke: Palgrave/Macmillan.

Lofstedt, R. and T. Horlick-Jones (1999), 'Environmental Regulation in the UK: Politics, Institutional Change and Public Trust', in G. Cvetkovich and R. Lofstedt (eds), *Social Trust and the Management of Risk*, London: Earthscan, 73–88.

Mazur, A. (1981), 'Media Coverage and Scientific Communications on Public Controversies', *Journal of Communication*, 31(2), 106–15.

Morgan, G. et al. (2002), *Risk Communication: A Mental Models Approach*, Cambridge: Cambridge University Press.

MSNBC.com (16 April 2010), 'Fallen Volcano Ash Could Pose Health Risk', MSNBC.com News Services, available at http://www.msnbc.msn.com/id/ 36595264/ns/health-more_health_news/ (accessed 21 February 2011).

Reynolds, B. (2002), 'Crisis and Emergency Communication', Centers for Disease Control and Prevention, available at http://www.bt.cdc.gov/cerc/pdf/CERC-SEPT02.pdf (accessed 21 February 2011).

Rubin, J. et al. (2009), 'Public Perceptions, Anxiety, and Behaviour Change in Relation to the Swine Flu Outbreak: Cross Sectional Telephone Survey', *BMJ*, **339**, b2651.

Sammonds, P. et al. (eds) (2010), *Volcanic Hazard from Iceland: Analysis and Implications of the Eyjafjallajökull Eruption*, London: UCL Institute for Risk and Disaster Reduction.

Sandman, P. and J. Lanard (2004), 'Crisis Communication: Guidelines for Action Planning What to Say When Terrorists, Epidemics, or Other Emergencies Strike', The American Industrial Hygiene Association, available at http:// www.psandman.com/handouts/AIHA-DVD.htm (accessed 12 February 2011).

Siegrist, M. and G. Cvetkovich (2000), 'The Perception of Hazards: The Role of Social Trust and Knowledge', *Risk Analysis*, **20**, 353–62.

Slovic, P. (1987), 'Perception of Risk', *Science*, **236**(4799), 280–5.

Slovic, P. (1993), 'Perceived, Risk, Trust and Democracy', *Risk Analysis*, **13**(6), 675–82.

Slovic, P. et al. (2000), 'Facts and Fears: Understanding Perceived Risk', in P. Slovic (ed.), *The Perception of Risk*, 137–53.

Sunstein, C. (2002), *Risk and Reason: Safety, Law, and the Environment*, Cambridge: Cambridge University Press.

Tversky, A. and D. Kahneman (1973), 'Availability, A Heuristic for Judging Frequency and Probability', *Cognitive Psychology*, **4**, 207–32.

Warner, G. (19 April 2010), 'Is Volcanic Ash the New Swine Flu?', *The Telegraph*, available at http://blogs.telegraph.co.uk/news/geraldwarner/100035390/is-volcanic-ash-the-new-swine-flu/ (accessed 21 February 2011).

PART 3

Beyond the ash crisis: the many facets of emergency risk regulation

7. Paradigms lost: emergency safety regulation under scientific and technical uncertainty

Vincent Brannigan

7.1 INTRODUCTION: VOLCANIC ASH 2010

The 2010 shutdown of European airspace exposed critical failures in corporate planning and the international safety regulatory process. After 25 years of work technical regulators had developed a widely publicized regulatory response to a very predictable hazard. The official guidance from the International Civil Aviation Organization was not to fly in volcanic ash. Yet when the Icelandic eruption occurred, transport dislocations and business pressure led to a rapid abandonment of the 'no-fly' safety regime in a few days. Rapidly approved, legally permitted levels of ash were then trumpeted as 'safe levels' by the various airlines. To date there is little or no published scientific evidence justifying the claim of safety. Some members of the airline community are even proposing a covert approval process that would eliminate any public examination of future ash safety evidence.

When society regulates a technology it interacts with the technology developers to create a series of expectations and beliefs that can be described as paradigm. The entire ash event is best understood in terms of a paradigm shift in the technological frames used by the airspace safety community. The volcanic ash crisis has important lessons to all those who regulate in an environment of technological and scientific uncertainty. In a 'crisis management environment' well-connected parties can find that exploiting technological uncertainty can be an effective method to circumvent both burdensome safety requirements and avoid transparent science in the regulatory process.

7.2 TECHNICAL SAFETY REGULATION

Ordinarily, technical safety regulation is a slow process especially when multiple sovereign nations are involved. Hazards are identified, risks are calculated and the policy bureaucrats massage them into an acceptable safety regime. Regulatory processes are normally responding to relatively static hazards, where the scientific knowledge can be developed over time to a reasonably high level of confidence and the political process of negotiating sovereign interests can take place in an environment of agreement on basic scientific fact. In such an environment regulatory requirements are normally developed based on comprehensive public scientific knowledge.

But not all hazards present themselves as static and well-understood technological problems. Some hazards are new and some are poorly understood. In an emergency environment of high uncertainty there is a great deal of room for political pressure to affect the outcome, especially by shifting of burden of proof or by shifting the entire decision process to an arena where no public proof is needed. Burden of proof is critical since the party bearing the burden of proof normally has the most difficult task. The precautionary principle was designed in part at least to make it clear that those who propose a technical activity bear the burden of proof of safety. But in a crisis environment such principles can disappear under the weight of economic and political considerations. By shifting the burden of proof to a regulator the lack of evidence of hazard effectively becomes evidence of safety. Taking the entire regulatory process 'under wraps' further eliminates the need for proof.

The lack of suitable scientific evidence about the hazard is a normal problem in a crisis situation. Funding for technological research into safety hazards is often not required before products are marketed and funding is rarely provided on an international basis. International political problems with export industries may also limit the available knowledge base since countries may try to protect industries by concealing data related to hazards. Rapid development of hazards, concomitant with inadequately funded science, can result in an environment of confusion and uncertainty. Whenever possible industry can be expected to try to reverse the burden of proof and make regulators prove the hazard rather than industry prove safety. Without access to adequate research funding and/or corporate data, regulators normally cannot carry such a burden. In the volcanic ash crisis the transfer of the burden of proof from the industry to the regulators and the acceptance of substandard evidence was the paradigm shift that redefined the regulatory environment

The single factor that most affects the quality of technical regulation is the quality of evidence used in the regulatory process. Instead of the long slow transparent development of *normal* science, partisans in a crisis can use the secret and often inadequately tested approaches that are routine in *forensic* science. Particularly in an emergency situation, the use or misuse of forensic science instead of normal science can lead to undesired results. Regulatory standards can be based on inadequate understanding of the underlying phenomenon. Regulatory compliance can include 'comfortable assumptions' about the ability of various parties actually to control a hazard. The lack of transparency means that no outside person can evaluate the risks.

The European volcanic ash crisis of 2010 presented precisely such a combination of paradigm shift with the use of non-transparent forensic science to deal with uncertainties. When long-standing operational procedures based on best available science and technological understanding combined with a predictable ash eruption to produce flight chaos, affected parties scrambled to maintain operations. 'Legally accepted' levels of ash were developed in a very short period of time and routinely declared to be 'safe' by those with a vested commercial interest in flying, despite doubts by distinguished technical experts (Langston, 2010). New procedures to keep all the ash approval evidence secret are being proposed. Only time can tell whether the envelope was pushed to the edge or beyond it. However the entire process calls for a better and more fundamental understanding of the uncertainties involved in the regulatory use of forensic science, and an insistence that the regulatory treatment of the uncertainties be resolved prior to an emergency.[1]

7.3 THE 2010 ASH FLIGHT SAFETY CRISIS

The scientific problem of ash flight safety is complicated by the fundamental problem of regulating commercial transit through airspace. Airspace is largely regulated on a national basis with implications both for national security and national sovereignty. Airlines are regulated by national aviation authorities. Airports may be controlled on a national or local basis. Coordinating air traffic safety is thus a daunting task even in the best of times.

The airline industry has a massive multinational system for dealing with flight operations. Operational failures are rare but spectacular. The system depends on both reliable technology from the aircraft manufacturers and predictable and expert behaviour by flight crews and ground controllers. For the most part the problems are well understood, even if execution is complex and subject to disastrous errors. As a result most threats to air safety (such as weather) are treated as operational problems rather than public policy problems.

In the case of volcanic ash international regulators and technical specialists produced a very clear policy outcome to control flight operations. They had concurred in an international consensus always to avoid volcanic ash due to a vast number of uncertainties in the sources, measurement and effects of volcanic ash:

> 3.4.8 Unfortunately, at present there are no agreed values of ash concentration which constitute a hazard to jet aircraft engines ... In view of this, the recommended procedure in the case of volcanic ash is exactly the same as with low-level wind shear, regardless of ash concentration – AVOID AVOID AVOID. [All caps in original][2]

A regulatory consensus could hardly be clearer or more definitively stated: **Don't Fly in Ash.** This can clearly be described as the 'avoid paradigm'. As a result, when Eyjafjallajökull erupted and sent ash over Europe, national regulators began shutting down the airspace.

Airline operators were furious. Airlines erupted with charges and threats (Brannigan, 2010). It was clear that simply no one at the higher levels of airlines or airspace regulation was paying close attention to the implications of the ICAO guidance in the event of a totally predictable Icelandic eruption. In particular the senior management of the airlines either did not understand the implications of the avoid paradigm, or they simply cynically took advantage of the political weakness of technological regulators to impose a questionable safety regime. In a few short days the avoid paradigm was discarded and the safety regulators beaten into submission.

7.4 ROOT CAUSE ANALYSIS

The root cause of the ash crisis probably resides in the structure of communications and decision-making in the airline industry. Consider a list of the critical actors each aligned with their closest relative in the communication chain:

> Volcanologists <>Meteorologists <>Airspace Regulators of affected areas <> Airline operators<> National Aviation authorities (Airline and Aircraft regulators) <>Airframe builders <> Engine manufacturers.

The key regulatory interaction is among airspace regulators, airline operators and national aviation authorities. They are the ones who make sure the airline system functions at all. The two parties who knew the most about the hazard (engine designers and volcanologists), were not members of the central relevant social group that made airline policy. Engine designers were insulated by airframe manufacturers and volcanologists were not even on the radar of any of the central parties. University College London conducted a comprehensive analysis[3] and made very specific conclusions about the crisis:

- The current volcanic activity in Iceland is not unusual.
- The impact of the eruption on regional airspace could have been predicted and better prepared for as the growing problem of aircraft-ash cloud encounters has been recognized for decades.
- Similarly, the potential for ash clouds, specifically from Icelandic volcanoes, to interfere with air traffic in UK, European and North Atlantic airspace was appreciated by the aviation industry well before the start of the Eyjafjallajökull eruption.
- The response was less effective than it should have been. This was primarily a function of the failure to recognize in advance the potential threat presented by volcanic ash clouds from Iceland. The situation was made worse by the inflexible nature of existing aviation protocols and by the absence of any pre-existing agreement on safe ash levels.
- The newly defined safe limits of ash are *ad hoc* and arbitrary and cannot be scientifically justified.
- Determining a range of robust best-estimate safe levels of ash for a wide range of situations, aircraft, engine types and pilot responses will cost time and money and will require the commitment of the aviation industry.

This report clearly lays key responsibility on the aircraft operators, who clearly knew or should have known of the risk to operations and chose not to participate in the safety analysis. But the result of the crisis was a fundamental paradigm shift from protecting passenger safety to protecting airlines from disruption. 'The future will still emphasise safety but seek balance against economic costs', added Padhraic Kelleher, head of airworthiness at the UK Civil Aviation Authority (CAA).[4]

Balancing safety against costs is a traditional public policy function of regulation. The proper questions is always 'how safe' and at 'what cost'? Consider a published comment by a senior member of the ICAO staff:

Against this backdrop Eyjafjallajökull and perhaps other natural phenomena to come offer the aviation community some food for thought. A natural disaster is no one's fault, and least of all the airlines' fault. Some consideration must be given towards protecting the interests of airlines in the face of such interruptions to business. (Abeyratne, 2010)

Even in the economic arena that was the subject of the comment, natural disasters may be no one's fault but the failure to plan for and deal with natural disasters is clearly the obligation of the airlines and the regulatory authorities. Every active volcano in the world is mapped. Winds patterns are modelled. Eruptions, while difficult to predict, are not unexpected. All kinds of operations are required to take adequate precautions against natural events. That is part of running a business. Clearly the airlines were at fault for failure to plan for the crisis.

7.5 PUBLIC POLICY AND UNCERTAINTY

The balance between safety and continued operations is complex and clearly a matter of public policy. One of the most important fundamental policy decisions is the treatment of uncertainty. Uncertainty is routinely defined but is difficult to pin down. Is it a property of a system or of our knowledge about a system? There are regular disputes over the meaning of uncertainty and the nature of the uncertainty problem. In particular the concept of uncertainty varies from one technical field to another. For this chapter:

> **Uncertainty** is a lack of knowledge. In this sense uncertainty does not exist in nature, but is a human construct developed when we describe a system.

There are numerous examples of overlapping sources and types of uncertainty in any given technical system. For example:

- **epistemic** – Lack of understanding of basic rules of nature;
- **aleatory** – Lack of adequate data for use in analysis;
- **teleological** – Lack of knowledge of human intentions with regard to future actions;
- **measurement** – Problems in precision and accuracy in data development;
- **normative** – Lack of consensus as to the truly desired social course of action;
- **jurisdictional** – Lack of understanding as to who actually makes decisions;
- **regulatory** – Lack of understanding as to whether compliance with a standard will actually abate the hazard.

The effect that ash can have on engines is clear but not well quantified. The sheer number of different uncertainties in the ash problem is staggering. They include but are not limited to

- the ash content of the eruption;
- the movement of the critical ash particles in the atmosphere;
- the effectiveness of detection of the ash particles;
- the effect of the mix of particles on engines;
- the ability of inspection to detect potential long-term engine hazards.

The avoid paradigm clearly dealt with these uncertainties by putting passenger safety above airline profit, passenger convenience and national interests in flight operations. But in a few days the regulatory/scientific/ technological consensus was overthrown because there was no willingness to accept the economic consequences of the paradigm. New regulations allowing 'approved' levels of ash were developed in a matter of days and hours. The result was in fact the triumph of one worldview over another since the reversal of the burden of proof as the problem was moved from the technical to the political domain the absence of evidence of harm was considered itself evidence of safety.

7.6 REWARDING FAILURE

For a regulatory analyst the most incredible outcome of the ash crisis is that six months after, having failed utterly in planning for volcanic ash, the airlines and their national aviation authorities are now angling to get the full control over the ash problem instead of the states where the ash is in the sky. As the ICAO Draft December 2010 Guidance proposes, after a national authority approves an airline operating plan the states whose airspace is being used simply must not interfere with airline operations:

> For States whose airspace is potentially contaminated by volcanic ash, it is intended that the control measures specified in this document should be suffi- cient to satisfy their need to be confident in the ability of operators from other States to undertake operations safely into airspace that is known or forecast to be contaminated by volcanic ash; **no further action on the part of States whose airspace is potentially contaminated by volcanic ash is intended.** (ICAO, 2010)

Under the 'December Draft' affected states would be required to defer to the 'acceptance' of the operator's plan by its national aviation authority:

> The NAA should assert that it has discharged these responsibilities fully, by formally accepting the SRA of the aircraft operator, thus authorising that

operator to conduct operations into, or near, potentially contaminated areas. The guidance that follows indicates the process that the NAA should use in achieving this outcome. **NOTE:** The significance of the NAA accepting, rather than approving, the operator's SRA is that the operator clearly retains responsibility for managing the risks and mitigating measures.

And exactly what science supports the NAA approval?

Prior to committing to operations into, or near, volcanic ash contaminated areas, the operator must obtain from the OEMs (Aircraft and engine manufacturers ed.) specific information regarding the susceptibility of the aircraft they operate to volcanic cloud-related airworthiness effects, the nature of these effects and the related pre-flight, in-flight and post-flight precautions to be observed by the operator. These must be reflected in the SRA.

The critical information is 'obtained' from the OEM, but it is not required to be shared with the regulatory authorities, only 'reflected' in the SRA. If the NAA wants the information used by the airline they have to try to get it themselves: 'The NAA should solicit such information from OEMs as is necessary to confirm the airworthiness-related decisions of the operator.'

Of course the OEM may not be in any way under the jurisdiction of the NAA. Will Airbus send its information to the Chinese NAA? Which NAA will be willing to shut down a national carrier for failure to supply information? Rarely has complete pre-planning failure been so dramatically rewarded with total control over the hazard. This proposal contemplates a complete surrender of national airspace safety regulation to the operators without the slightest information going the country whose airspace is being used. There is no suggestion or requirement that any of the safety data be made public or subject to widespread technical analysis. The result is a covert approval. An analogy might be that food safety authorities in importing states would be required absolutely to accept the safety determination of the exporters without the slightest disclosure of the relevant safety analysis.

Whether this rather astonishing 'power grab' survives into the final regulatory operation is not yet known. What is known is that the uncertainties in the process remain huge and unresolved and, rather than seek transparency, 'cover up' is the name of the game. .

7.7 REGULATORY PARADIGM SHIFTS

In *Paradigms Lost* and later works Casti (1990) explores the problem of fundamental uncertainty in scientific knowledge, with a special focus on issues of public importance or controversy. Casti explores the concept of a paradigm and particularly the paradigm shift referenced by Kuhn in his structure of scientific revolutions. In the Casti formulation a paradigm is a worldview by the participants in a scientific or science related activity. In general scientific paradigms are a form of orthodoxy backed by the scientific method. Casti's contribution to the traditional Kuhn paradigm shift is to show how such shifts take place in a wide variety of areas of public, not merely scientific concern. According to Casti the concept of paradigm does not have to be limited to professional belief structures about pure scientific knowledge. The Casti/Kuhn paradigms are perhaps best described in the terms of Bijkers 'technological frame', especially when dealing with a regulated technological hazards.

> This [Technological frame] is the shared cognitive frame that defines a relevant social group and constitutes members' common interpretation of an artefact. Like a Kuhnian paradigm, a technological frame can include goals, key problems, current theories, rules of thumb, testing procedures, and exemplary artefacts that, tacitly or explicitly, structure group members' thinking, problem solving, strategy formation, and design activities. (Klein et al., 2002)

Society creates belief structures about science and technology. We use these science and technology belief structures in our regulatory systems. The concept of a paradigm shift has been a major topic of debate in the history and philosophy of science. The paradigm shift in the volcanic ash flight safety problem occurred when airline operators suddenly realized that volcanic ash disruption could be a far larger problem than they had anticipated. Since business corporations are expected to perform risk and hazard analysis as part of the business operation, the failure to understand and anticipate the risk can only be laid to deficient corporate management. Naturally these deficient corporations want to avoid any such future interruptions, hence the December draft. The issue of course is whether they or anyone else really understands the ash problem.

7.8 THERE ARE NO ACCIDENTS

The European volcanic ash crisis of 2010 involved a dramatic 'paradigm shift'. The key tool to effect the paradigm shift is the use and misuse of language and evidence. Exactly what, for example, is 'visible ash'? Especially what is it at night? Language is used to downplay both risk and responsibility. As one example, technological disasters are routinely called *accidents*, even though virtually every disaster is caused by a series of human decisions and technological structures. A frame can be used to create a belief structure that an event 'can't happen' and when it does, the event is described as an *accident* since the operators did not really intend the disaster, they only intended to operate in accordance with the belief structure.

The *Titanic* represented such a belief structure. With the company president and the builder's chief engineer on board, a highly experienced captain sailed at full speed into an enormous ice field. Numerous warnings from ships that had stopped in the ice field were ignored. After hitting an iceberg chaos ensued and hundreds of places in the inadequate number of lifeboats went unfilled. Yet many writers persist in calling this disaster an 'accident'. The goal of the language is to shift responsibility to anyone other than the creators of the disaster. Unfortunately as the *Titanic* shows, the ability to create an object (such as a ship or airplane) does not in any way automatically mean that the developers understand the risks and hazards of the object.

So how well understood is the ash safety problem? Can it be safely handled by unexamined operational approval? The current state of ash safety technical knowledge was described to Congress by General Electric's Director of aviation safety:

> On April 20th, engine manufacturers (RR, P&W, & GE) reached consensus with FAA NE office that flights in volcanic ash would be acceptable up to volcanic ash concentration levels of up to 2milligrams per cubic meter and in absence of visible volcanic ash ... This consensus was based on industry experience and engineering judgment.
>
> Much work still needs to be done to understand the effects on aircraft gas turbine engines. The quantitative flight safety risk due to volcanic ash is dependent on a number of factors, some known and some unknown. These unknowns make establishing a quantitative limit on volcanic ash a challenge. GE provided and continues to provide support to our customers and regulatory agencies to maintain safe operation in light of the recent volcanic ash threat. The current best practice for abating the volcanic ash hazard is to avoid visible volcanic ash.[5]

Against this background, confident statements of safety by airlines and regulators can be best described as disingenuous, for example: 'Flybe, the UK's Number One Domestic airline, tonight confirmed that it will be the first airline in the UK to be able to fly within the new *CAA-approved safe levels of volcanic ash.*' It should be noted how quickly the *legally approved* level of volcanic ash is transformed into a 'safe level'. The regulator did nothing to suggest otherwise. In a press release dated 17 May CAA Chief Haines stated:

I'm pleased that the huge efforts we're all making across aviation to keep flying safe whilst minimising the disruption from the volcano have resulted in further progress.

How does he know it's safe?

Unprecedented situations require new measures …

Unforeseen, but not unforeseeable.

Firstly because the standard default procedure for aircraft that encounter ash, to avoid it completely, doesn't work in our congested airspace.

The procedure does work, it just costs more money than they were willing to pay.

Secondly, the world's top scientists tell us that we must not simply assume the effects of this volcano will be the same as others elsewhere. Its proximity to the UK, the length of time it is continuously erupting and the weather patterns are all exceptional features.

Note that they do not say it makes it easier, it may make it worse.

The answer can only come, therefore, from aircraft and engine manufacturers establishing what level of ash their products can safely tolerate.

This assumes that such a safety level exists and can be known in real time.

It's the CAA's job to ensure the public is kept safe by ensuring safety decisions are based on scientific and engineering evidence; we will not listen to those who effectively say 'let's suck it and see.'

Of course a reasonable reviewer might says that is exactly what they are doing.

7.9 FORENSIC SCIENCE AND SAFETY REGULATION

The December draft guidance clearly contains a paradigm that ash is such a simple operational problem that virtually any airline can deal with it and every national aviation authority is presumed competent to supervise the airline's response to ash. That is a very comfortable set of beliefs for airlines, especially when the technical facts supporting the regulatory decisions are not disclosed, and the uncertainties are buried in the regulatory approval. This is a hallmark of regulation based on forensic science.

Any scientific enterprise whose primary market is the legal and regulatory system can be referred to as a forensic science. Forensic science is science with a legal purpose. Such purposes can range from regulatory approval to courtroom victories. Forensic science has a complex connection to normal science. Normal science is what most of the world thinks of as 'science'. Normal science can occasionally be directly used in the forensic environment but normal science is indifferent to and unaffected by the legal process. Normal science exists on its own, has its own publication track, career paths, and funding sources independent of its role in the legal system. Forensic science is sometimes based on normal science but it can also develop on its own.

The purpose of forensic science is to provide evidence for the legal and regulatory process. While political acts by public legislatures do not require any kind of reliable scientific knowledge, as soon as disputes move into the administrative, regulatory and judicial processes, the law in many, if not most, countries require the decisions to be based on evidence.

It is understandable that many scientists whose work is used directly to influence the legal and regulatory system would prefer to avoid the title of forensic scientist because of its long association both with junk science and with inappropriate advocacy instead of scientific neutrality. The practitioners would rather be thought of as doing normal science. The independence of normal science (whether actually true or not) is a cherished belief and can be very useful in persuading decision-makers. Forensic science, due its structure and influence in the legal process, may in fact have a stronger version of a Kuhnian paradigm than normal science. Casti's approach can be used to show why forensic science may have more entrenched paradigms than normal science. Industries can get very comfortable with a regulatory structure even if the regulation is irrelevant to a newly developing hazard. In the forensic environment supporting data is routinely kept secret and not exposed to competing scientific analysis. In the regulatory environment getting the science accepted by the regulator is far more important than whether it is accepted by scientific peers.

The result of such acceptance can be a form of 'ceremonial compliance'. The hazards created by technology demand a social response. A regulatory response, however flawed can be used to convince the public that the problem is well controlled. In this environment the 'facts' that support the hazard analysis are critical to the social response. But facts at the borders of our understanding of a technological process tend to be very slippery due to uncertainty. What do we do when we 'don't know what we don't know'?

7.10 CONCLUSIONS

In the emergency technological regulatory environment, such as that involved in the ash crisis, the treatment of the scientific uncertainty is crucial in defining the successful outcome of the process. Paradigm shifts can take place both within the regulatory system and by changing the system for evaluating the evidence. Competing parties try to control the process of evaluating the forensic evidence used in resolving the dispute. The availability or lack of reliable forensic evidence is a key determinant in the process, as is vital to the assignment of the burden of proof. The ash crisis is an extremely important case study in the acceptance or rejection of scientific and technological knowledge in the regulatory process. It is a particularly interesting study, in that it involves a wide variety of scientific and technological disciplines that do not routinely interact, and a variety of business and government stakeholders with a wide divergence of interests.

In the ash crisis political, economic and media power quickly overcame 25 years of regulatory science. It remains to be seen whether the scientific support for ash flight safety regulation will see the light of day, or if the controlling parties make sure it disappears into a black hole.

NOTES

1. The question of whether a particular type of knowledge is better characterized as scientific or technological is generally not relevant for the issues involved in this chapter. But it should be noted that the English word 'science' is a poor substitute for the German term '*Wissenshaft*' or organized knowledge, which was the first term used to describe the use of such knowledge in the forensic area. For example engineering and medicine are clearly *Wissenschaften* whether or not they meet the strict English definition of science.
2. ICAO (2007).
3. Sammonds et al (2010).
4. http://www.aerosocietychannel.com/aerospace-insight/2011/01/under-the-ash-cloud/ (accessed 27 February 2011).
5. Dinius (2010).

BIBLIOGRAPHY

Abeyratne, R. (2010), 'Responsibility and Liability Aspects of the Icelandic Volcanic Eruption', *Air and Space Law*, **35**, (4/5), 281–92.
Aerospace Insight (2011), 'Under the Ash Cloud', available at http://www.aerosocietychannel.com/aerospace-insight/2011/01/under-the-ash-cloud/ (accessed 27 February 2011).
Bijker, W.E (1997), *Of Bicycles, Bakelites, and Bulbs: Toward a Theory of Sociotechnical Change*, Cambridge: Cambridge, MA: The MIT Press.

Brannigan, V. (2010), 'Alice's Adventures in Volcano Land: The Use and Abuse of Expert Knowledge in Safety Regulation', *European Journal of Risk Regulation*, **1** (2), 107–14.

Brannigan, V. and E. Buc (2009), 'Forensic Fire Investigation: An Interface Of Science, Technology And Law Proc.', *Fire and Materials 2009 Conference Proceedings,* San Francisco.

Brannigan, V. and C. Smidts (1999), 'Performance Based Safety Regulation under International Uncertainty', *Fire and Materials*, **23** (6), 341–7.

Brannigan, V. and C. Smidts (1999), 'Probabilistic Risk Assessment as a Forensic Science: The Effect of Daubert and Kumho Tire on PRAs as Evidence', *Proceedings of PSA'99*, Washington, DC.

Casti, J.L. (1990), *Paradigms Lost*, New York: Harper Perennial.

Dinius, R. (2010), GE Aviation Testimony before the Space and Aeronautics Subcommittee, Committee on Science and Technology, US House of Representatives, available at http://gop.science.house.gov/Media/hearings/space10/may5/Dinius.pdf (accessed 27 February 2011).

ICAO (2007), 'Manual on Volcanic Ash, Radioactive Material and Toxic Chemical Clouds', available at http://www.paris.icao.int/news/pdf/9691.pdf (accessed 27 February 2011).

ICAO (2010), 'Management Of Flight Operations With Known Or Forecast Volcanic Cloud Contamination – Preliminary Issue – Draft Version 3.1', available at http://www.paris.icao.int/Met/Volc_Ash/docs/IVATF-AIR04-Draft%20Version%203.pdf (accessed 27 February 2011).

Josephson, J.R. (2001), 'Abductive Inference: On The Proof Dynamics Of Inference To The Best Explanation', *Cardozo L. Rev,* 22, 1621.

Klein, H.K. and D. L. Kleinman (2002), 'The Social Construction of Technology: Structural Considerations', *Science, Technology, & Human Values*, **27** (1), 28–52.

Langston, L. (2010), 'Asking for Trouble', *Mechanical Engineering*, available at http://findarticles.com/p/articles/mi_qa5325/is_201007/ai_n54716782/pg_2/ (accessed 27 February 2011).

Nyhart, J.D. and M. Carrow (1983), *Law and Science in Collaboration: Resolving Regulatory Issues of Science and Technology*, Lexington, MA: Lexington Books.

Phimister, J.R., V.M. Bier and H.C. Kunreuther (eds) (2004), *Accident Precursor Analysis and Management: Reducing Technological Risk Through Diligence*, Washington DC: National Academy of Engineering.

Sammonds, P., B. McGuire and S. Edwards (2010), 'Volcanic Hazard from Iceland: Analysis and Implications of the Eyjafjallajökull Eruption', available at http://www.ucl.ac.uk/rdr/publications/icelandreport (accessed 27 February 2011).

8. If and when: towards standard-based regulation in the reduction of catastrophic risks

Alfredo Fioritto and Marta Simoncini[1]

8.1 WHAT CAN PUBLIC AUTHORITIES DO TO REDUCE CATASTROPHIC RISKS?

Natural disasters happen. At least once in lifetime everyone can expect to be a protagonist or a spectator in a catastrophic event. The problem is that nobody can predict when calamities are going to strike. What public authorities can reasonably do is to provide regulations to prevent major impacts on population and goods as much as possible. Emergency risk regulation represents a relevant regulatory methodology that combines the risk approach with the possibility of resorting to extraordinary measures in case a disaster occurs. More precisely, it aims at mitigating the impact of a catastrophe by providing preventive instruments of protection in the immediacy of a disaster. Therefore, it combines both risk and emergency approaches to crisis, in an attempt to guarantee regulation for specific relevant cases. Since risk regulation offers protection *beforehand*, and emergency regulation generally applies *in the aftermath*, emergency risk regulation works in the immediacy with a specific preventive goal. In this way, legal orders try to fill the gap in their resilient system of protection by improving the safeguard against risks and distributing the consequences of their occurrence with the aim of mitigating the impact of disasters.

Many case studies demonstrate the significant connection between risk approach and emergency tools in the pursuit of disaster protection. By focusing on some recent catastrophic events in Europe, this chapter aims at analyzing the main issues at stake in emergency risk regulation. The first case focuses on the role played by standards in the prevention of catastrophes. By examining and contextualizing EU regulations in terms of the management of the volcanic ash crisis, this chapter investigates how standard-based regulation can provide due protection against disasters.

Indeed, in line with some other EU sector-specific models of disaster prevention and the developing European strategy against catastrophic risks, even the crisis stemming from the spread of volcanic ash in European skies has been managed through intergovernmental action aimed at establishing three different regulatory zones of increasing risk depending on the degree of ash contamination.

From this standpoint, the chapter focuses on a related aspect of standardization of protection, that is research on the effectiveness of disaster regulation. In this regard, time is considered to play a key role in the assessment of the success of standard-based regulation. To this end, the chapter compares the volcanic ash crisis with a catastrophic event that occurred in Italy in 2009: The Abruzzi earthquake. The comparison reveals that in both cases time influences the implementation of standards: As standards of protection aim at regulating human activities for very long periods (as in the case of earthquakes), the compliance with them can be affected since no catastrophic event occurs.

To prevent the dramatic effects of earthquakes, states provide special rules and standards for buildings. This means major costs for buildings and a direct impact of regulations on owners, entrepreneurs and local authorities. This is one of the reasons that determined the disastrous effects in Abruzzi: Rules established in 1960 failed to be implemented by the actors involved. As judicial and technical inquiries show, when the risk is believed to be in the distant future people are less motivated to stick to the rules (and carry their costs). From this perspective, the Abruzzi case reveals the necessity to investigate further the possibilities of resorting to market-based regulatory instruments, which can stimulate the enforcement of rules and, as a consequence, push forward the effectiveness of regulation.

Hence, the chapter is divided into two parts: The first (8.2–8.5) analyzes the volcanic ash crisis and focuses on standard-setting as a rule-making procedure that can provide sound protection against catastrophic risks. The second part (8.6–8.9) pays specific attention to the Abruzzi earthquake and the gaps in the implementation of standard-based regulation.

The final remarks underline the problems with research on regulatory solutions.

8.2 THE VOLCANIC ASH CRISIS AND THE DEVELOPMENT OF A COORDINATED AND STANDARDIZED APPROACH TO CATASTROPHES IN THE EU

The recent case of the volcanic ash spread shows the fundamental issues in the regulation of risks of catastrophic impact. It involves the necessity to identify organizational and regulatory responses that should help (but in the substance substitute) the national management of emergency situations.

Indeed, many European states followed the ICAO guidelines (section 3.4, ICAO Manual on Volcanic Ash, Radioactive Material and Toxic Chemical Clouds, 2007) and introduced emergency blocks of their airspace, placing a precautionary ban on flights regardless of the ash concentration and the economic impact of the intervention[2]. Such a national approach to a transnational issue caused significant problems for airlines and their business, as well as for the free movement of passengers and the trade in goods. Since no state could ignore international safety directives, the affected parties asked for a coordinated approach in order to contain the losses from the prolonged precautionary measures.

To this end, the European Commission proposed a coordinated European approach to the crisis that outlined the general tendency in the management of catastrophic risks, that is the elevation of the regulatory venue at a supranational level and the definition of a management model setting up progressive thresholds of alarm.

From the first standpoint, i.e. maintaining member states' competence in air traffic management and the safety of their airspaces, the proposal was discussed and endorsed by an extraordinary meeting of the ministers of transport. The regulatory solution developed on this occasion can, however, be reconstructed in the light of the more general EU approach to catastrophic risks.

This provides a subdivision of the European airspace into three zones, depending on their degree of contamination: In the first one ('located in the central nucleus of the emissions', as the declaration of the EU ministers of transport says) with the highest degree of ash concentration, the safety goal can be achieved only by maintaining the ban on flights ('a full restriction of operations'); in the second area, where there are 'still amounts of ash', the possibility of pursuing air traffic operations must be decided 'in a coordinated manner' by member states; the third zone, being 'not affected by the ash', is subject to no restrictions.[3]

This kind of risk management is not new to the European regulatory framework, since it has been applied to many sector-specific models of disaster prevention.

Consequently, the first part of this chapter aims at analyzing how such standard-based regulation works and to what extent it is a useful means to prevent catastrophes from occurring.

8.3   CATASTROPHIC RISK REGULATION FROM A COMMAND-AND-CONTROL PERSPECTIVE

Catastrophic risks are a sensitive challenge for legal orders. They carry a high level of uncertainty and have elevated consequences in terms of casualties and losses, when they occur. On the one hand, the elevated consequences call for some level of regulation; on the other hand, the uncertainty of their occurrence makes it difficult to review the evidentiary scientific justification, the assessment of costs and benefits and the means through which the goals are going to be pursued through administrative law standards familiar from the regulation of other, non-catastrophic risks.

Describing different kinds of risks that share the capability to produce disasters, these threats show the very problematic issues of risk regulation, namely the regulatory matter and the means through which the safety goals are to be pursued.

It should be pointed out that in the traditional public law approach, protection against catastrophic risks is generally achieved by resorting to the category of emergency. Such a model is based on the application of police powers in time of disaster, with the aim of restoring the legal order's ordinary route by derogating to its ordinary law (Esteve Pardo, 2003, pp. 327–8; Simoncini, 2010, pp. 17–8). Sharing the goal of maintaining security, however, emergency regulation seems to produce paradoxical effects and ends up by becoming an alternative instrument for achieving efficiency in legal systems (Dyzenhaus, 2001, p. 21). More precisely, the notion of emergency has been widening, turning from an exceptional power aimed at regulating unknown and unforeseeable events, into an ordinary method of administration for critical situations (Ophir, 2007).[4] Consequently, not only is the relationship between exceptional facts and temporary countermeasures altered, but the exercise of fundamental rights is also questioned in the attempt to prevent a further and unknown catastrophe from occurring.

Therefore, if the indelible need to prevent emergencies cannot be ignored, it must be considered as an issue in terms of risk regulation. Recognizing the necessity for anticipating the protection against those risks that are uncertain (as concerns the probability of occurrence) but can produce catastrophic effects (when they happen to impact on a legal order), the command-and-control system should avail itself of a different regulatory framework, centred on the notion of 'significant' risk, which engages in the process of mitigation only as long as the costs do not exceed the benefits, in order to provide a due level of protection only against those threats whose materialization will produce intolerable effects for the affected community: This deals with the concept of tolerable risk and identifies the kind of menace that cannot be accepted by society.

In American legal tradition it is based on an efficiency assessment, according to which given the impossibility of eliminating all risks the regulation should engage in their reduction as long as the costs do not exceed the benefits, avoiding any inefficient regulation, what Breyer called the 'tunnel vision' or 'the last 10 per cent' regulation (Breyer, 1993, pp. 10–18; see also Ricci and Molton, 1981, pp. 1096–7; Majone, 2005, pp. 133–5).[5] In the case of catastrophes, however, cost-benefit analysis cannot be the only methodology used to assess the significance of the risk, since the tolerability does not overlap with a mere mathematical or statistical analysis of probability but is a regulatory concept that relates to the effectiveness of the regulation. Therefore, the risk that cannot be accepted by society is that kind of menace that affects the ordinary management of legal, economic and political relationships and affects the resilience of the legal order.

Since research into protection against disasters collides with a double uncertainty about the probability that a disaster will take place and about the range of the effects related to its occurrence, catastrophic risk regulation aims at preserving the collective capability to make choices. Use of precautionary measures means flexibility in decision-making can be preserved for the future (Sunstein, 2005–06, pp. 856–7[6]) by the introduction of models of risk management where supportive risk assessment is sparse. Therefore, the legal aspect prevails over the scientific one and deals with the notion of significant risk and available resources.

On this basis, law should determine a right balance between the reasons for risk mitigation and the corresponding constraint of individual freedoms. To this end, if the regulation of uncertainty is based on standards of protection, liberty and authority will be balanced and this process of standardization will become a key issue in the construction of a resilient model of security. Hence, every zero-risk approach should be considered unacceptable for Western democracies, because it quashes fundamental rights in an irreversible way.

On the other hand, through standard-based risk regulation, the legal order identifies the level below which it is not willing to run a risk and therefore should introduce rules in order to preserve that degree of protection. This methodology consists in the definition of a progressive scale of standards that defines increasing levels of public attention to a threat in order to manage the period that separates the current time from a possible emergency in the attempt to preserve the legal order's ordinary route as far as possible and reduce the harm arising from the materialization of a disaster as much as possible. In this respect, by availing themselves of gradual and continuous thresholds of alarm, regulators can settle different countermeasures in correspondence with specific risk characterizations based on scientific inferences from available and updated data. Consequently it is possible to fix and gradually control the level of risk that will be considered unacceptable for the legal order, without making uncertain danger an absolute and unjustified priority (in terms of resources).

8.4 VOLCANIC ASH RESPONSE IN THE FRAME OF THE EU STANDARD-BASED APPROACH TO CATASTROPHES

Being technically and legally impossible to avoid disasters with a zero-risk approach to regulation, the EU legal system seems to focus on the regulation of significant risks by availing itself of standards of protection.

In this perspective, the EU system provides levels of protection against risks based on a case-by-case analysis of the severity of the threat to human health, the degree of reversibility of its effects, the possibility of delayed consequences and the perception of the menace based on available scientific data.[7]

In particular, the EU has already applied standard-based risk regulation in some sector-specific models of disaster prevention.[8] At the same time, thanks to this regulatory experience, the EU is going to develop a strategic approach to catastrophic risks, which is based on the recognition of the increasing vulnerability to natural as well as man-made disasters owing to technological progress and the admission that only a supranational involvement can ensure the effectiveness of protection. This means an increasing and consistent need to implement standards in the development of a multilevel approach to catastrophic issues. This is the reason why the Lisbon Treaty has allocated a fundamental function to the EU regarding protection against catastrophes, reinforcing coordination between and supplementing the action of member states.[9] To this end the EU Commission has been working on the introduction of a consistent regulation on the prevention of disasters, building an integrated approach to those risks that is based on scientific research, coordination of existing sector-based policies and, in the long run, predisposition of a framework directive for disaster prevention.[10] Moreover, through its action the Commission showed the intention of mitigating the impact of uncertain risks through the control of the whole disaster management cycle by improving the organization and procedure of both risk regulation and emergency planning.[11]

The prevention of catastrophes should therefore be pursued by integrating emergency intervention and risk management, namely by implementing their coordinated activity in the multilevel legal system. In this framework the notion of standard of protection is going to play a key role in outlining a suitable response as regards both the uncertainty of risks and the distribution of competences between the EU and its member states. Indeed, the identification of a significant risk and its possible escalation allows proportional actions and reactions against threats to be devised, contributing to the constructive enhancement of European cohesion.

From this standpoint, the volcanic ash case pointed to the need to tackle catastrophic risks at a transnational level in order to achieve a devised solution.

When we try to frame the volcanic ash regulatory response in the general EU regulatory models, a significant comparison should be made with flood risk assessment and management and pollution controls.

Regarding the first case, flood regulation is founded on the characterization and mitigation of significant flood risk through the division of the member states' territories into distinct areas matching different levels of attention to the threat; hence, the higher the risk, the more framed the management plans. To this end, flood risk is tackled by mapping the significant areas in terms of probability of the occurrence of calamities and the range of possible losses in terms of human health, environment, cultural heritage and economic activities.[12] The same methodology has also been applied in the volcanic ash case, dividing the member states' airspaces into three different areas of increasing risk according to the significance of the threat.

It is clear that given the emergency situation, in the case at issue the risk-assessment procedure was more evident to provide than in the EU regulation on floods, based on statistics, whereas the actual materialization of risk required more challenging emergency management actions.

From this perspective, the volcanic ash response was more similar to the pollution-control mechanism. Indeed, those regulations provide 'alert thresholds', namely concentration levels of polluting substances beyond which there is a risk to human health and at which immediate steps are to be taken by the member states, as public information and the arrangement of short-term action plans. Moreover, below that level an 'information threshold' is established, which is a former degree of pollution beyond which there is a risk to human health from brief exposure for particularly sensitive sections of the population and for which immediate and appropriate information is necessary; it also provides a 'margin of tolerance' related to the reference standard.[13]

Thus a system of progressive protection against pollution is carried out: It works above the limit value by setting further levels of attention and response, and below that threshold though the identification of a target value of pollution reduction.[14]

The volcanic ash crisis seems to have been managed on the same premise: According to the concentration of ash (in every area), specific and proportional countermeasures would have been taken. In particular, given the occurrence of an emergency, the concentration level matched the alert threshold and the short-term action plan consisted in the ban on flights in the worst case and for the middle zone in the arrangement of case-by-case solutions, which should have balanced the precautionary intervention with the different interests at stake.

In particular, the range of the decisions that could be taken with regard to the middle zone shows the importance of the administrative procedure in the balance of the different interests at stake in the light of the scientific evidence. Both cost-benefit analysis and precautionary principles intervene, but the proper regulatory option can be taken only by using a coherent methodology, namely regulation impact assessment.[15] In hindsight, if this standard-based model had been working from the beginning of the crisis, a great reduction in terms of economic losses for airlines and inestimable discomfort for passengers would have been achieved.

8.5 THE PROCEDURE OF STANDARDIZATION

The definition of a standard-based system of protection implies a high level of coordination in the regulatory process between science and law involving an accurate analysis of the available scientific data as well as of the different public and private interests at stake.

From the first standpoint, thresholds of alarm act as informational instruments: Through the continuous monitoring of sources of risk and the constant communication of scientific data between the interested parties, regulators can detect in advance the possible threat and promptly alert the relevant community. Therefore, they are prevention systems that can be used for both risk regulation and the arrangement of emergency plans. It is not by chance that the introduction of such instruments is favoured in the event of a serious crisis.

These more or less institutionalized procedures are based on the exchange and coordination of information about risk assessment, in the attempt to identify and keep down in advance direct and indirect risks to human health. In order to avoid improper alarms, the organization of the informative network should guarantee cross-checking of the reliability of scientific information responsible for warning and flexibility and coordination in the response.

It should be noted, however, that such systems rest upon the tacit assumption of the reliability of the risk-monitoring systems, so that continuous watching can outwit occurrences and can contain uncertainty (Hutter, 2010a, p. 3; Hutter, 2010b, pp. 6–7; Clarke and Molotch, 2010, pp. 12–3). Therefore, even chances are determined by a gap in the scientific assessment of the current situation. On the other hand, the nonlinear relationship between causes and effects that is typical of complex systems can alter the comprehension of phenomena (Goudie, 2009, pp. 605–6) and, thus, can affect the appropriateness of the response. From this perspective, the regulatory model seems to be flawed, but its rigidity can be accommodated in a more flexible understanding of the uncertainty. For instance, the administration under precise circumstances might push the level of attention to the highest degree, skipping the intermediate levels. In the end, in the face of the unforeseeable and sudden occurrence of a catastrophic risk the instruments of emergency should be employed: Although this may seem to limit the precautionary functioning of the system, the alert mechanism can make the difference in the management of the emergency situation, contributing to the reduction of harm.

As regards the counter-reaction in correspondence with a specific level of risk, the model overlaps with the traditional administrative procedure of balancing interests.

In order to fix a level of protection that can be considered an adequate expression of the risk that cannot be accepted by society, public and private parties must cooperate and their reasons for so doing, that is their legal position and even their risk analysis, weighed in the light of the regulatory interest at stake. The functioning of the model requires the participation of private interests as well as coordination among public administrations, an essential hurdle that has to be overcome in order to guarantee the coherence of public action (Merusi, 1993, pp. 22–3).[16] From this standpoint, administrative coordination assesses how different public interests (and missions) should be harmonized in the development of the administrative proceeding (Merusi, 1993, pp. 23–4).[17] Moreover, those public parties should demonstrate to some extent the necessity to implement the required level of protection. The duty to give reasons for public choices is a general instrument for promoting the accountability of risk regulation, because it embodies the grounds and the purpose of public action. Indeed, in order to shift from a lower to a higher level of alarm (and of protection) the administration is called to justify its choice. Whereas the participation of public administrations in the rule-making process is important in order to coordinate the different public interests and policies (also taking into account the settlement of regulatory priorities), the contribution of private parties has an intrinsic defensive character: As a cultural guarantee, inherent in Western tradition, any public decision that affects individual rights must respect the right to be heard or at least to have a written cross-examination.

Therefore, the regulatory administration has to show that the adopted measures are suitable and necessary for pursuing the policy goal and that they do not affect the individual legal sphere beyond the required measure: In other words, rules should comply with the proportionality principle.[18]

In this regard, regulation impact assessment (RIA) is an essential tool, aiming at verifying not only the effectiveness of provisions but also the reasonableness of the sacrifice requested of individuals: Through the consultation process, the regulator can ex ante weigh up the likely economic, environmental and social implications of action and highlight the potential trade-offs in risks and benefits.[19] The research on better outcomes and performances in regulation should inevitably absorb distributional issues in the regulatory proceeding, so that risk policies can reach a correct balance between the cost-benefit approach and the precautionary one (Wiener, 2006, pp. 33–8[20]).

Hence, the implementation of better regulation strategies can become the roadmap for the development of a standard-based model of risk regulation: Pursuing the general suitability of rules regardless of sector specificities, such methodology comes out as 'a type of meta-policy targeting the governance of the regulatory process' (Radaelli and Meuwese, 2008, pp. 1, 8, 10). Therefore, this regulatory model can contribute to fixing more fitting levels of protection and, as a consequence, organizational issues play a decisive role in its implementation. In this framework, the statement of reasons is the appropriate venue in which those limits to discretionary power should emerge.

The case of volcanic ash shows the importance of developing an apt participatory model as well as the difficulties that it involves. Indeed, underestimating the risk of catastrophe, airline companies took a small part in the scientific analysis of the hazard in ordinary times and proclaimed their expertise during the spread of the emergency. In this case RIA would have at least reduced contentions between airlines and regulatory science about the correct definition of safety thresholds in emergency conditions, because it would have pushed the airline industry to participate in risk regulation, demonstrating and contesting scientific assessments in the proper venue.

From this perspective, the costs of participation in the regulatory process of a low probability risk represent a significant limit to the effectiveness of the model itself. The institutionalization of the standard-based prevention system, however, can boost the private interest in participating in the regulatory process.

Moreover, if the standards had been in operation from the beginning of the crisis, a great reduction would have been achieved in terms of economic losses for airlines and inestimable discomfort for passengers.

8.6   EARTHQUAKES: DISASTER PREDICTABILITY AND SAFETY CONSTRUCTION

The volcanic ash crisis and the earthquake in the region of Abruzzi in Italy in 2009 were both caused by deep geological fault movements but the effects were dramatically different. Because of the earthquake more than 300 people died and the entire city of L'Aquila (70,000 inhabitants) and several villages nearby were forced to move to temporary shelter along the Adriatic Sea. Eighteen months after the earthquake, the Italian government, through its civil protection policy, built new houses for 15,000 people, and another 20,000 people returned after their houses had been repaired and strengthened. Many others provided themselves with a temporary solution (e.g. hospitality, second houses) but more than 10,000 people are still waiting for a stable solution. The entire historic centre of L'Aquila is closed by barriers under army surveillance and many experts doubt that it will ever be reconstructed. Its roots can be traced to the Roman period, but the town was effectively founded by the Emperor Frederick II during the first decades of the thirteenth century (1229), who granted permission to build a new town to 99 feudal families who built 99 palaces, churches and fountains. This is an enormous cultural heritage that risks being lost forever.

Besides their terrible toll of death and destruction, natural disasters are followed by discussions focusing on four main problems: (1) disaster predictability; (2) risk reduction; (3) promptness and effectiveness of relief activities; (4) reconstruction.

Discussions and controversy about at least two of the above-mentioned problems followed in the wake of the earthquake in L'Aquila. Conversely, everybody agreed on the promptness and effectiveness of the Civil Protection authority (that is a department of the Cabinet Office), whose outstanding organizational and practical skills in managing the emergency phase were, once again, fully proven. Therefore, it is natural to look into the reasons for such effectiveness and wonder why, if this is a positive model, it has not been adopted by other Italian agencies. The answer is of course a complex one, but all in all we can say that two main differences emerge compared with other administrations. The first one is the Civil Protection's pyramidal structure, a centralized model adopted especially in the management of emergency phases, which allows for a short and direct chain of command: A very small group of people give orders; all the others carry them out. The second difference lies in the special powers assigned to Civil Protection, which allow for derogation from ordinary law and procedures.

Therefore, Civil Protection is an effective administration whose model cannot, as a rule, be adopted in 'ordinary' situations, where special standards do not apply. In fact, we all seem ready to barter democracy for greater effectiveness in extraordinary and pressing circumstances; the same does not apply in ordinary situations when we legitimately expect the state administration to work without recourse to extraordinary measures. Conversely, in the last few years, Civil Protection has increasingly been assigned the task, sometimes going beyond remit, of replacing ineffective or inept administrations, as happened in the case of the so-called 'garbage emergency' or the G8 meeting (when, in a brilliant *coup de théatre*, the location was moved from Sardinia to the earthquake-ravaged city of L'Aquila. It has not been established whether the local population actually enjoyed the change).

As for reconstruction, discussion has not really started since, in effect, this phase is still to come; we will have to wait a few more months to evaluate whether promises of funding will be honoured.

To return to the above-named controversial aspects, discussion about earthquake predictability has been superseded, and rightly so, because today's state of scientific knowledge is such that no reliable methods are available.

Controversy about earthquake damage reduction rests, on the other hand, on a solid basis, considering that construction regulations for seismic areas, aimed at building safe and earthquake-proof buildings, were enacted a long time ago.

One of the most striking and tragic aspects of this catastrophe is the number of 'modern' buildings that were destroyed or made unfit for use. It is reasonable to expect that a seventeenth-century building may collapse as a consequence of an earthquake, although restoration and restructuring should be carried out to reinforce old structures, but how could a quake that did not rate high on the quake scale destroy public and private buildings supposedly designed and built according to safety regulations?

8.7 EARTHQUAKES: BETWEEN EMERGENCY AND RISK REGULATION

Earthquakes are natural phenomena caused by the movement of tectonic plates that make up the lithosphere, the outermost layer of the earth's crust.

Since the Italian territory covers more than one plate, most of our country has a high seismic risk.

Quakes only last a few seconds, but their highly destructive potential and unpredictability, together with the presence of massive human settlements, make accurate and widely applied preventative measures even more necessary compared with other sources of risk. That is why seismic risk was included from the very beginning in preventative system regulations based on the definition, established by the state, of seismic risk areas, and specific construction techniques aimed at ensuring the safety of buildings. In order to understand the legitimacy of criticism levelled at state administrators by many building experts, a review on the evolution of relevant regulations may prove interesting.

Seismic classifications started just after the Messina earthquake (1908) but 'down to the middle of the 1970s, Italian areas were classified as seismic only after having been struck by an earthquake' (Martelli and Forni, 2010, p. 90).

About 40 years ago a law (5 November 1971, n. 1086) was added to our national code, regulating the building of reinforced concrete structures. The use of reinforced concrete, however, became compulsory only in 1974, according to law n. 64, regarding 'Provisions on construction subject to particular directions in seismic areas'. Subsequently, however, the Public Works Minister was supposed to draft crucial ministerial decrees aimed at updating the list of seismic areas to bring the regulations into force. Without them, in fact, the law could not be implemented.

In the meantime, as normally happens in our country, various rules and regulations were approved: Law 64/1974 was reviewed and included in the 2001 Consolidated Law on Building Industry, in which a whole chapter dealt with and updated the procedures for the definition of seismic areas. These regulations, in effect, were only implemented by a ministerial decree on 14 January 2008, in which the new technical rules on construction were approved, combining all regulations previously mentioned in different ministerial decrees into a single organic text.

It was only in the wake of the emergency situation resulting from the Molise and Apulia quake of 2002 that new rules were enacted by an order of the President of the Council (OPCM n. 3274, 20 March 2003). During the earthquake a primary school in San Giuliano di Puglia collapsed and killed 27 children; the tragedy shocked the public and the government reinforced the previous regulation. On this basis, the general criteria for the classification of the national territory and the definition of technical rules for construction work in seismic areas were finally defined and subsequently implemented by decree on 21 October 2003 (Dolce, Martelli and Panza, 2005).

The provision aimed at identifying seismic-risk buildings and infrastructures under state jurisdiction in order to make them safe; it contained a list of buildings (among them hospitals, police and armed forces headquarters, Red Cross and alpine rescue premises, and railway stations and waterworks) considered of 'strategic importance' (for their institutional value) or 'relevant' (in connection with effects caused by their eventual collapse); it sets the basic criteria for the evaluation of construction risks. These rules were never brought into force, one delay following another, the last one included in the so-called '1000 prorogations decree' of 28 December 2008, which postponed their implementation further.

8.8 LESSONS LEARNED FROM THE L'AQUILA EARTHQUAKE: THE NECESSITY TO ENFORCE STANDARDS BY FINDING NEW INCENTIVES

In the meantime, on 6 April 2009, an earthquake struck L'Aquila and 300 people died. In a situation characterized by legislative confusion, delays in the implementation of the law, and removal of crimes from the statutes through prescriptive rules, where does the responsibility of the state (especially of parliament and government) end and where does individual responsibility begin? This is the unbelievably difficult judgement to be made by L'Aquila's judges, who will have to decide whether buildings were or were not built according to regulations (which ones?), and who among design engineers, construction firms and inspectors share this responsibility.

Generally speaking, in Europe building permissions are based on a declaration of conformity to the planning and building rules made by the builder. Public administrations have only limited powers to control building standards. The Abruzzi case, however, shows us the enormous cost to the public purse of the reconstruction. As a matter of fact, the Italian state supported the major costs of rebuilding the city of L'Aquila and many other villages nearby through direct and indirect grants.

As happened in other cases, the feeling is that stricter regulations will be implemented in the future (even if their entry into force is postponed), and that page upon page of rules and regulations will accumulate into a new 'paper castle' that will not collapse even under the strongest of earthquakes.

From this perspective, the current system of standard regulation seems so inefficient, at least for long-term risks. States should start to introduce a system of compulsory insurances to support the enforcement of standards by calculating the insurance premium on the degree of (non)compliance with the rules: The more you comply with standards the less you should pay for your insurance. This system could produce three benefits: (1) public authorities should introduce different scales of standards operating a distinction (e.g. from essential to incidental) so that only basic rules should be considered compulsory; (2) insurance companies would be stimulated to operate controls on the enforcement of standards so that public authorities should enforce only the basic rules; (3) last but not least, in times of public expenditure cuts, if and when disaster strikes insurances should provide extensive cover for all kinds of damage.

With regard to the evolution of regulations and prevention of the seismic risk, there has been a certain lack of awareness, at both the institutional and individual levels, that severe earthquakes occur in Italy too:

> Paradoxically, the main problem of Italy has been that severe earthquakes are not sufficiently frequent in this country and that, in any case, their return period are much longer than the duration of its governments. In the past, the consequence was that, when a severe earthquake occurred, the government in office at that time strictly limited its action to emergency management, without investing any resources in prevention, and that seismic risk was soon forgotten even in the struck areas. It has been estimated that the overall cost of this lack of prevention policies has already been almost three times larger than the overall amount of money which would have been necessary to adequate seismically upgrade all the existing Italian constructions (apart from the thousands of avoidable victims). (Martelli and Forni, 2010, p. 90)

As mentioned above, the EU is going to develop a strategic approach to catastrophic risks based on the recognition of increasing vulnerability to natural disasters. However, the regulation of the seismic risk is regulated at the state level, so that any single state can adopt different rules and approaches to the national regulation of land use. At the moment, the EU Commission is working on the introduction of a regulation for better cooperation among civil protection authorities in Europe (Fioritto, 2008, p. 183).

8.9 SEARCHING FOR RISK MITIGATION: FINAL REMARKS

This chapter aimed at investigating the methodologies of catastrophic risk regulation by comparing two different case studies, the volcanic ash crisis that occurred in 2010 and the Abruzzi earthquake the year before.

The first case reveals the necessity for a transnational coordinated approach to disaster risks, based on the shared introduction of standards of protection; the second one demonstrates that the traditional command-and-control system cannot in itself be a sufficient guarantee of the effectiveness of protection.

Actually, standards seem to represent a sound compromise between the necessity to ensure due protection against disastrous risks and their low probability of occurrence. These general rules have to tackle the costs of their implementation, which seems, however, to be more difficult the lower the probability of the risk.

From this standpoint, any legal order seeking to protect against disasters should engage in research on alternatives to the traditional command-and-control system to ensure the implementation of its standards of protection. This implies the development of market-based incentives that can match the traditional administrative enforcement by stimulating private parties to comply with the rules by themselves.

In this regulatory framework, the process of risk mitigation will be developed by the construction of a resilient system of protection that distributes the costs to reap collective benefits.

Therefore, regulation should comply with two different key issues: The process of formulation of standards and the definition of the right means of their implementation.

From the first perspective, the characterization of the risk that a legal order considers unacceptable tackles on the one hand the relation between science and law and the participation of interested parties on the other. In this respect, the chapter compared the emergency management of the volcanic ash crisis with the regulatory process that could have prevented the general embargo on flights, paying special attention to the role of public participation and the influence of regulatory science.

Moreover, as far the implementation of standards is concerned the main problematic issue is the identification of proper means, borrowed from the market, that can promote the enforcement of the protection of common goods.

The analysis of the Abruzzi earthquake suggested the need further to investigate the potential of a compulsory insurance system, as other systems have already been applied in protection against other catastrophic risks (a clear example is provided by the Kyoto Protocol, which introduced flexible mechanisms in the attempt to prevent global warming).

Three different national experiences support this suggestion. The first one is the case of the Central Park Building after the recent Chilean earthquake: In a building consisting of 150 units, approximately half of the dwellers purchased apartments with cash; having paid for their properties in full, these families did not have mortgages. Residents of the other half of the units had purchased them through bank mortgages, which required compulsory insurance. As a result, half of the owners had earthquake insurance and half did not. Those who had insurance were actively advocating for the demolition of the building and the recovery of their assets. Those without insurance opposed this solution, however, since it would mean that they would lose many if not all of their savings (Franco, Leiva and Lai, 2010).

Moreover, since 1945 a compulsory insurance system has been established in New Zealand, together with a public body called the New Zealand Earthquake Commission (EQC). The government established EQC in 1945 to provide earthquake and war damage cover for purchasers of fire insurance. Later, cover for other natural disasters was included and, later on, cover for war damage dropped. The EQC is a government-owned Crown entity regulated by the Earthquake Commission Act 1993 (supplemented in 2008). During the last 60 years EQC has collected premiums from insured people and created a substantial 'nest egg' against damage, called the Natural Disaster Fund. The Fund consists of reinsurance from overseas groups and a government guarantee that ensures that EQC will always be able to meet its obligations, regardless of the circumstances. EQC pays out on claims from New Zealand residential property owners for damage caused by earthquake, natural landslip, volcanic eruption, hydrothermal activity, and tsunami; in the case of residential land, it pays for storm or flood; and for fire caused by any of these.[21] The third case shows a different approach to the insurance problem. The California Earthquake Authority (CEA) was established in 1996 by the California legislature as a publicly managed and largely privately funded entity. After the January 1994 earthquake that struck California's San Fernando Valley it was clear that a private insurance-based system could not offer serious guarantees for major events. Policymakers and insurance companies underestimated the potential losses that would be caused even by moderate earthquakes and after the latest earthquake 'insurers and consumer groups quickly became aware that residential earthquake insurers were overexposed and would quickly exhaust their claims-paying resources if another significant earthquake occurred'.[22] In 1995, the California legislature created a reduced-coverage earthquake insurance policy designed to protect a policyholder's dwelling while excluding coverage for costly non-essential items such as swimming pools, patios, and detached structures. One year later the California legislature established the CEA, a public body that receives no money from the state budget but is financed by private insurance companies that can sell special insurance coverage affordable by the great majority of house owners. The reduced price of premiums is owed to the fact that the CEA does not pay federal income tax, and its tax status allows it to maximize the growth of its reserves.[23]

Like the New Zealand Earthquake Commission, the CEA educates residents to make informed decisions regarding earthquake preparedness and the purchase of earthquake insurance and minimizes potential earthquake damage by encouraging Californians to retrofit their homes and utilize other proven methods to mitigate loss.

All three cases highlight the need to investigate the possibility of affordable and accessible insurance solutions in Europe, constructing mechanisms of shared responsibilities between governments and communities.

NOTES

1. Dr Marta Simoncini wrote sections 2, 3, 4, 5. Professor Alfredo Fioritto wrote sections 6, 7, 8. Sections 1 and 9 were elaborated jointly.
2. Note that according to a Report of the Oxford Economics prepared for Airbus, the total impact on global GDP caused by the first week's disruption amounts to approximately US $ 4.7 billion. See Oxford Economics, *The Economic Impact of Air Travel Restrictions Due to Volcanic Ash*, available at http://www.oxfordeconomics.com/samples/volcanic%20update.pdf.
3. It is worth noting that, even before the ash crisis, the EU provided a regulation aimed at developing an integrated approach to air traffic management: see Regulation of the European Parliament and of the Council 10 March 2004, 2004/549/EC, 'laying down the framework for the creation of the single European sky (the framework Regulation)', and Regulation of the European Parliament and of the Council 21 October 2009, 2009/1070/EC, 'amending Regulations (EC) No. 549/2004, (EC) No. 550/2004, (EC) No. 551/2004 and (EC) No. 552/2004 in order to improve the performance and sustainability of the European aviation system' (second single sky package – SES II). It is worth noting that in the aftermath of the ash crisis the Commission seemed to milk the emergency in order to push forward the implementation of the SES II.
4. This kind of regulatory perspective has been termed the 'catastrophic state', in order to portray a state which resorts to the administration of disaster as 'a form of governance and a way of ruling', regularly putting at risk the ordinary system of law. From this perspective, the catastrophic state works on completely different premises from the 'providential state', based on the solidarity principle, because it rests on the management of disasters, not on their prevention.
5. See the American leading case *AFL-CIO v American Petroleum Institute*, 448 US 607 (1980), and also *Corrosion Proof Fittings v EPA*, 947 F.2d 1201 (Fifth Cir. 1991) and *United States v Ottati & Goss, Inc.*, 900 F.2d 429 (First Cir. 1990).
6. In particular, Sunstein considers the preservation of the capability to choose in terms of an option value, applying a monetary valuation to the public decision-making issue in an environmental context, which is in line with the economic analysis of law. In this perspective, he distinguishes the willingness to pay to use a pristine area (use value) from the willingness to pay for the option to use the same environmental amenity in the future (option value), basing them both on the existence value of the place.
7. See in particular CFI, *Pfizer Animal Health v Council*, Case T-13/99, [2002] ECR II-3305, paras 145–6, 153; CFI, *Alpharma v Council*, Case T-70/99, [2002] ECR II-3495, paras 157–9, 165–6; see also ECJ, *Bellio F.lli Srl*, Case C-286/02, [2004] ECR, para. 58; ECJ, *Safety High-Tech*, Case C-284/95, [1998] ECR I-4301, para. 49.
8. Similar systems have been mainly used in EU regulations in order to avoid the occurrence of health crises caused by the composition of human food (as in the case of genetically modified organisms) and by animal feed (as happened in the spreading of mad cow disease, BSE). See art. 23 Directive of the European Parliament and of the

Council 12 March 2001, 2001/18/EC, 'on the deliberate release into the environment of genetically modified organisms and repealing Council Directive 90/220/EEC' providing a safeguard clause that introduces a process aimed at restricting or prohibiting the use and the sale of GMO in the case of risk to human health and the environment; see also arts 50–52 Regulation of the European Parliament and of the Council 28 January 2002, 178/2002/EC, 'laying down the general principles and requirements of food law, establishing the European Food Law Safety Authority and laying down procedures in matters of food safety', that prescribes a rapid alert system.

9. See, in particular, art. 196 TFEU on cooperation in the field of civil protection and art. 222 TFEU for the solidarity clause between the Union and its member states. Moreover, due reference is to be made to art. 4 and art. 6 TFEU on the principal areas of shared competence between the Union and the member states.

10. See Communication from the Commission to the European Parliament, the Council, the European Economic and Social Committee and the Committee of the Regions 23 February 2009, COM (2009) 82, 'a Community approach on the prevention of natural and man-made disasters'. In particular, this strategy 'outlines specific measures to boost disaster prevention in the short term' (para. 5), providing the creation of an inventory of information on disasters (para. 3.1.1), the spreading of best practices (3.1.2), the development of guidelines on hazard/risk mapping (para. 3.1.3) and promoting coordination among the actors and the policies involved in 'the disaster management cycle' (paras 3.2 and 3.3). Moreover, a previous report from the European Commission DG-Environment, focusing on a long-term approach to catastrophic risk regulation, suggests the introduction of a new framework directive aimed at addressing prevention of national as well as cross-border disaster impacts. See European Commission DG Environment, *Assessing the Potential for a Comprehensive Community Strategy for the Prevention of Natural and Manmade Disasters*, Final Report, March 2008, pp. 18–9, 85–90.

11. In this regard it should be pointed out that in accordance with the principle of subsidiarity, the EU has also strengthened the emergency cooperation between the Community and its member states in case of major crisis and imminent threats, in order to meet emergencies in a more appropriate manner. See Council Resolution 8 July 1991, 91/C198/01, 'on improving mutual aid between Member States in the event of natural and technological disaster'; Council decision 9 December 1999, 1999/847/EC, 'establishing a Community action program in the field of civil protection'; Council decision 23 October 2001, 2001/792/EC, 'establishing a Community mechanism to facilitate reinforced cooperation in civil protection assistance interventions'.

12. See Recitals 3 and 11 and art. 2(2) of the Directive of the European Parliament and of the Council 23 October 2007, 2007/60/EC, 'on the assessment and management of flood risks'. More precisely, the risk assessment stage is based on the arrangement of flood hazard maps and flood risk maps (art. 6) for those areas where a potentially significant flood risk is likely to occur after a preliminary flood risk assessment founded on the available information (arts 4–5). On this ground, flood risk management plans, focused on prevention, protection, preparedness and early warning systems, are established (arts 7–8).

13. See Directive of the European Parliament and of the Council 21 May 2008, 2008/50/EC, 'on ambient air quality and cleaner air for Europe', which provides that at the 'informational threshold' (art. 2, point 11) and the 'alert threshold' (art. 2, point 10, and art. 3, para. 2) immediate information is given to the public and to the Commission (art. 13), and short-term action plans (art. 24) are arranged in order to reinstate the standard level of risk. The Directive also defines the 'margin of tolerance' (art. 2, para. 7) that is the acceptable percentage of the limit value (the guaranteed standard of protection, regulated in art. 2, para. 5) by which that value may be exceeded (arts 22–23). It is worth noting that this regulation represents a rationalization and an updating of the principles and the requirements already laid down in the Directive of the

Council 27 September 1996, 1996/62/EC, 'on ambient air quality assessment and management', in the Directive of the Council 22 April 1999, 1999/30/EC, 'relating to limit values for sulphur dioxide, nitrogen dioxide and oxides of nitrogen, particulate matter and lead in ambient air', in the Directive of the European Parliament and of the Council 16 November 2000, 2000/69/EC, 'relating to limit values for benzene and carbon monoxide in ambient air', and in the Directive of the European Parliament and of the Council 12 February 2002, 2002/3/EC, 'relating to ozone in ambient air'. In a similar way, the Directive of the European Parliament and of the Council 25 June 2002, 2002/49/CE, 'relating to the assessment and management of environmental noise', defines at art. 3, letter *s*), the 'limit value' as the noise tolerability's standard, the exceeding of which causes competent authorities to consider or enforce mitigation measures (art. 8, para. 2) and to inform the public about the arrangement of strategic noise maps and action plans (art. 9).

14. The target value is a concentration level fixed with the aim of avoiding, preventing or reducing harmful effects on human health and the environment as a whole, to be attained where possible over a given period; on air quality: see art. 2, point 9, and Directive 16, 2008/50/EC. By availing itself of another specific language, the environmental noise regulation states a target value in the 'strategic noise map', a plan aimed at determining the global assessment of noise exposure in a given area; see art. 3, letter *r*), and art. 7, Directive 2002/49/EC.

15. In this case RIA would have at least reduced contentions between airlines and regulatory science about the correct definition of safety thresholds in emergency conditions, because it would have pushed the airline industry to participate in risk regulation, demonstrating and contesting scientific assessments in the proper venue.

16. The author considers that the requirement for coordination of public administration derives from the interaction between the pluralism of public interests and the constitutional uniqueness of the executive power exercised by public administration.

17. On this point, Merusi identified three distinct roles played by other public interests in an administrative proceeding developed around a principal public interest, namely (1) mere factual assumptions with regard to the decision-making process; (2) elements of the fact-finding stage, which allow the individuation of other public interests and the definition of a consistent relation between them and the principal public interest (pursued in the administrative process); and (3) dialectic factors in administrative decision-making.

18. In this regard see COM (2000) 1, cit., paras 6.3.1 and 6.3.4, which temper the precautionary approach with the assessment of the proportionality of the regulatory action and the cost-benefit analysis.

19. Making the RIA a systemic part of the regulatory process requires rationalisation in the allocation of the public resources. To this end, in 2005 the European Commission introduced a proportionality requirement in impact analysis, so that its depth (and, in particular, the level of public participation and the accuracy of its findings) was commensurate with the significance of the regulatory action and the range of the expected effects. RIA is therefore strictly tied to the other main goal of better regulation, administrative simplification. See Communication from the Commission to the Council and the European Parliament 16 March 2005, COM (2005) 97, 'Better Regulation for Growth and Jobs in the European Union', para. 2A and Annex I; European Commission, *Impact Assessment Guidelines*, 15 June 2005, SEC (2005) 791, para. 5. Moreover, the proportionality requirement has been implemented by Impact Assessment (IA) Guidelines, 15 January 2009, SEC (2009) 92, which bases the significance of impacts on the type and the content of regulatory initiative (see para. 3.2).

20. Wiener defines this approach to regulation as a 'warm analysis', because it focuses on regulatory impacts and tradeoffs, mitigating possible overreaction to risks and at the same time not being tied to rigid measurements of cost and benefits.

21. This and other information can be found at http://www.eqc.govt.nz. At a time of major disaster, such as a large earthquake, EQC works through its Catastrophe Response

Programme (CRP), which includes an alternative operations site and the provision of additional staff and equipment. EQC also encourages and funds research about matters relevant to natural disaster damage and it educates and otherwise informs people about what can be done to prevent and mitigate damage caused by natural disasters.
22. See http://www.earthquakeauthority.com.
23. For further information see the website of the authority: http://www. earthquake authority.com.

BIBLIOGRAPHY

Alemanno, A. (2008), 'The Shaping of European Risk Regulation by Community Courts', Jean Monnet Working Paper n. 18, available at http://papers.ssrn.com/sol3/papers.cfm?abstract_id=1325770 (accessed 11 March 2011).

Alemanno, A. (2009), 'The Better Regulation Initiative at the Judicial Gate: A Trojan Horse within the Commission's Walls or the Way Forward?', *European Law Journal*, 15, 3, available at http://papers.ssrn.com/sol3/papers.cfm?abstract_id=1297170 (accessed 11 March 2011).

Alemanno, A. (2010), 'The European Regulatory Response to the Volcanic Ash Crisis between Fragmentation and Integration', *European Journal of Risk Regulation*, 1 (2), 101–6.

Allio, L. (2007), 'Better Regulation and Impact Assessment in the European Commission', in C. Kirkpatrick and D. Parker (eds), *Regulatory Impact Assessment. Towards Better Regulation?*, Cheltenham, UK and Northampton, MA, USA: Edward Elgar.

Baldwin, R. and M. Cave (1999), *Understanding Regulation. Theory, Strategy and Practice*, Oxford: Oxford University Press.

Black, J. (2007), 'Tensions in the Regulatory State', *Public Law*, (Spr), 58–73.

Branningan, V.M. (2010), 'Alice's Adventures in Volcano Land: The Use and Abuse of Expert Knowledge in Safety Regulation', *European Journal of Risk Regulation*, 1 (2), 107–13.

Breyer, S. (1993), *Breaking the Vicious Circle. Toward Effective Risk Regulation*, Cambridge, Ma.: Harvard University Press.

Clarke, L. and H. Molotch (2010), 'Scientists as Disaster Warning Systems', *Risk & Regulation*, (19), 12–3.

Dolce, M., A. Martelli and G. Panza (2005), *Proteggersi dal terremoto: le moderne tecnologie e metodologie e la nuova normativa tecnica*, Milan: 21° secolo.

Dyzenhaus, D. (2001), 'The Permanence of the Temporary: Can Emergency Powers Be Normalized?', in R.J. Daniels, P. Macklem and K. Roach (eds), *The Security of Freedom: Essays on Canada's Anti-Terrorism Bill*, Toronto: University of Toronto Press, 21–37.

Esteve Pardo, J. (2003), 'De la policía administrativa a la gestión de riesgos', *Revista española de derecho administrativo*, (119), 323–46.

Fioritto, A. (2008), *L'amministrazione dell'emergenza tra autorità e garanzie*, Bologna: Il Mulino.

Franco, G., G. Leiva and T. Lai (2010), 'Post-Disaster Survey Findings from the M8.8 Chile Earthquake', available at http://www.air-worldwide.com/PublicationsItem.aspx?id=19125 (accessed 20 March 2011)

Goudie, A.S. (2009), 'Uncertainty', in D.J. Cuff and A.S. Goudie (eds), *Global Change*, Oxford: Oxford University Press.

Hutter, B. (2010a), 'In Catastrophe's Shadow', *Risk & Regulation*, (19), 3.
Hutter, B. (2010b), 'Risk Regulation and the Anticipation of Natural Disasters', *Risk & Regulation*, (19), 6–7.
Majone, G. (2005), *Dilemmas of European Integration*, Oxford: Oxford University Press.
Martelli, A. and M. Forni (2010), 'Seismic Isolation and Protection Systems', *The Journal of The Anti Seismic Systems International Society*, **1** (1), 75–123.
Meuwese, A.C.M. (2008), *Impact Assessment in EU Lawmaking*, The Netherlands: Kluwer Law International BV.
Merusi, F. (1993), 'Il coordinamento e la collaborazione degli interessi pubblici e privati dopo le recenti riforme', *Diritto amministrativo*, (1), 21–39.
Ophir, A. (2007), 'The Two-State Solution: Providence and Catastrophe', *Theoretical Inquiries in Law*, **8** (1), 117–60.
Oxford Economics, *The Economic Impact of Air Travel Restrictions Due to Volcanic Ash*, available at http://www.oxfordeconomics.com/samples/volcanic%20update.pdf (accessed 20 March 2011).
Radaelli, C.M. (2007), 'Whither Better Regulation for the Lisbon Agenda?', *Journal of European Public Policy*, **14** (2), 190–207.
Radaelli, C.M. and F. De Francesco (2007), *Regulatory Quality in Europe: Concepts, Measures, and Policy Processes*, Manchester: Manchester University Press.
Radaelli, C.M. and A.C.M. Meuwese (2008), 'Better Regulation in the European Union. The Political Economy of Impact Assessment', available at http://centres.exeter.ac.uk/ceg/research/riacp/documents/The%20Political%20Economy%20of%20Impact%20Assessment.pdf (accessed 20 March 2011).
Renda, A. (2006), *Impact Assessment in the EU. The State of the Art and the Art of the State*, Brussels: CEPS.
Ricci, P.F. and L.S. Molton (1981), 'Risk and Benefit in Environmental Law', *Science*, 214 (4525), 1096–100.
Simoncini, M. (2010), *La regolazione del rischio e il sistema degli standard. Elementi per una teoria dell'azione amministrativa attraverso i casi del terrorismo e dell'ambiente*, Naples: Edizioni Scientifiche.
Sunstein, C.R (2005–06), 'Irreversible and Catastrophic', *Cornell Law Review*, 91 (4), 841–98.
Weatherill, S. (ed.) (2007), *Better Regulation*, Oxford: Hart Publishing.
Wiener, J. (2006), 'Better Regulation in Europe', Duke Law School Legal Studies Paper No. 130, available at http://papers.ssrn.com/sol3/papers.cfm?abstract_id=937927 (accessed 11 March 2011).

9. Normative uncertainty and ethics in emergency risk regulation

A.M. Viens

Risks are a pervasive and inescapable aspect of modern society. Indeed, risks are endemic to our daily lives, with particular sources and levels of risk contributing to what constitutes normalcy for most individuals and populations. The significant risk of harm, loss or burden associated with emergencies is different from what we typically experience in times of normalcy and presents pressing challenges to risk regulation. The significant risk of harm, loss or burden is, however, only one feature of emergency. There are numerous events or activities that have significant risks associated with them to which we do not justifiably apply the label of 'emergency'. It would be a mistake to differentiate times of normalcy and emergency on the basis of the magnitude or seriousness of risk alone.

In this chapter, I focus on another feature of emergency: normative uncertainty.[1] It is a feature of emergency that risk regulation often, if not exclusively, neglects to take into account. This neglect can have some important justificatory and explanatory implications for what individuals and groups ought or ought not to do – as well as what we ought and ought not to do to individuals and groups being regulated – during times of emergency. Different regulatory responses to emergency circumstances may yield a different set of morally optimal outcomes, and risk regulation can benefit from a greater understanding of how normative uncertainty contributes to why normative standards can change in times of emergency, and how this possibility affects the ethics of emergency risk regulation.

While much of the work on emergency risk regulation is descriptive in nature – even with some attention being given to evaluative considerations concerning which risk models or accounts of probability are better than others – this contribution will be firmly normative in nature. More precisely, its focus is on the contribution of moral philosophy to emergency risk regulation. While it is not typical to view risk regulation through the lens of moral philosophy, such an approach is gaining more attention.[2] As John Oberdiek (2004, p. 200) notes, 'Moral theory has much to offer regulatory policy-making; not by falsely promising to systematize it in accordance with a comprehensive philosophical theory, but, rather, by clarifying the core assumptions of policy making, exposing any flaws in them, and replacing the faulty assumptions with a sound foundation.' This chapter is a small attempt to make such a contribution.

The chapter proceeds in two parts. In the first part, I distinguish between different types of uncertainty and argue that normative uncertainty should be understood as a distinct type of uncertainty that risk regulation should take into account. I explicate some of the main considerations for taking normative uncertainty seriously, especially in the context of regulation for emergencies. In the second part, I briefly touch on the changing nature of moral standards in emergency, and how understanding normative uncertainty as a feature of emergency can help to account for how our normative and motivational reasons to conform to moral standards might influence the shape of some risk regulation. Taken together, these considerations should motivate the importance of taking the issue of normative uncertainty seriously in the development, implementation and enforcement of emergency risk regulation.

9.1   NORMATIVE UNCERTAINTY

Uncertainty, as with risk, is not only a pervasive and inescapable aspect of our everyday lives, it is also intensified during times of emergency. Emergencies are circumstances that are plagued with a higher prevalence and level of uncertainty. When focusing on the uncertainties relevant for emergency risk regulation, uncertainty is often distinguished as either being epistemic, aleatory or intentional uncertainty.

Before going on to say something about different types of uncertainty, it is worth setting out how I understand the concept of uncertainty itself. Uncertainty is established when there is discordance between facts and beliefs.[3] To be uncertain is to have an absence of, or a limited, knowledge requisite to form, a belief about some particular fact(s). This discordance may exist by virtue of facts about the types of entities or phenomena under consideration or by virtue of our inability to access such facts. That is to say, being in a state of uncertainty makes it the case that either we are unable to describe some present state of the world or predict some future state of the world. We may do particular things as a response to the existence of uncertainty. We could adopt a sceptical posture about the entity or phenomena in question. We could seek to diminish the level of uncertainty that exists by seeking to acquire further evidence or knowledge, which may take the form of direct empirical investigation or constructing physical or mathematical models. Regardless of our response to uncertainty, it is possible to ask a number of questions in relation to the relevance of uncertainty for risk regulation.

First, what is the content of the belief in relation to the facts, i.e., what is the uncertainty *about*? Second, how does this uncertainty affect how people *actually* deliberate and act? Third, how does this uncertainty affect how people *ought* to deliberate and act? My focus shall be primarily on the last question. As I shall argue, it is a question to which epistemic, aleatory nor intentional uncertainty can provide an answer. Moreover, we will require clarity about what kinds of answers are provided to the question about how people *ought* to deliberate and act in order to justify what kind of regulatory regimes and responses are needed. Not only in relation to understanding how regulation should guide action and deliberation, but also in relation to establishing normative standards against which we can assess how people *actually* deliberated and acted in times of emergency.

While risk regulation is concerned with both persons and their environment, the purpose of regulation is to guide the action of *persons*, individually or collectively. It does not make sense to speak of regulating an earthquake or hurricane. Of course, we seek to control environmental factors that are harmful to persons or to objects deemed valuable to persons, but this is accomplished through regulating human actions in some way or another. Thus, while risk regulation is naturally concerned with physical, biological and social phenomena that affect the well-being of persons, ultimately, the most pressing and interesting matters that arise from uncertainty concern human behaviour.

In the case of *epistemic uncertainty*, it is ignorance about what makes particular propositions true as a result of incomplete knowledge or human deficiencies. In the case of *aleatory uncertainty*, it is ignorance about the existence of data as a result of the stochastic features of a situation. In the case of *intentional (or teleological) uncertainty*, it is ignorance about what facts will allow us to predict how people will actually deliberate and act.[4] Epistemic, aleatory and intentional uncertainty are all forms of non-normative uncertainty. That is to say, they are forms of uncertainty concerning descriptive considerations. There is, however, also a normative form of uncertainty. *Normative uncertainty* is a kind of uncertainty that arises about the normative reasons we have to act in virtue of particular non-normative facts.

Consider, for example, a risk regulator who may be uncertain about the permissibility of separating and confining individuals or groups with signs, symptoms or laboratory evidence of infection during an infectious disease pandemic. She might be uncertain about the justifiability of putting people into isolation, even if she is certain about the non-normative facts of the natural history and transmissibility of the infectious agent, seroresponse to vaccination, effectiveness of containment measures, availability of anti-viral medication, etcetera. While there are a number of normative reasons that count in favour of isolating infected individuals in a pandemic, as well as normative reasons that count against isolating infected individuals, these conflicting reasons are not fully explained by her uncertainty about the non-normative facts. It is this kind of uncertainty about what ought to be done that is relevant for risk regulation.

Risk regulation has recognized that there will be circumstances where one may need to make moral decisions when one is uncertain about various non-normative facts. It is this kind of non-normative uncertainty, for example, that has led a number of people to advocate that we should adopt the pre-cautionary principle when it comes to regulating certain emergency and non-emergency events.[5] Normative uncertainty, however, is different from this kind of non-normative uncertainty. In cases where regulators advocate the use of the pre-cautionary principle, there is no normative uncertainty – the regulators believe that while particular non-normative facts are uncertain, the normative reasons we have to act in virtue of this non-normative uncertainty are clear, i.e., we ought to adopt a regulatory position of precaution and actions that reflect this precaution are justified. When one is normatively uncertain, one is making moral decisions when one is uncertain about the various normative reasons that are relevant in the circumstance. If someone is normatively uncertain, they are not in a position to be able to say if a regulatory position of precaution is what is, ultimately, morally justified.

So why should risk regulators worry about normative uncertainty? There are, I suggest, two main considerations. The first concerns the risk regula-tor. In so far as any regulator takes their regulations to be morally justified, there is some moral standard that the regulations are taken to meet. In being justified in advancing a particular set of regulations, there are normative reasons that support the particular regulations chosen. How-ever, when one is normatively uncertain, one is uncertain about the various normative reasons that would justify a particular set of regulations. If this normative uncertainty persists, then risk regulators will never be able to obtain moral justification for their regulations. The second concerns the regulatees the risk regulator seeks to guide with regulation. If regulatees are normatively uncertain about what they ought to do, this could be problem-atic for the regulator because having regulatees in this state could hinder the deliberative and co-operative action many regulatory systems presume. If regulatees are uncertain whether the normative reasons that apply to them are reflected in regulations that purport to guide them, regulators run the risk of regulatees viewing the regulation as lacking moral justification. A growing body of quantitative and qualitative research is beginning to show that a perceived lack of moral justification in standards that seek to guide behaviour can, and often does, result in non-compliance with such standards.[6] In an emergency situation this could also serve to prolong the intensity or duration of the emergency, since the diminished ability of the regulation to coordinate and regulate the behaviour of the regulatees means regulators will have less time and resources to devote to source of the emergency itself.

The recognition of the existence and relevance of normative uncertainty, then, should lead us to reject the view that, according to Tannert et al. (2008, p. 893), 'Uncertainty itself has no ethical quality – it is an inherent attribute of a situation.' Features of a situation are what provide us with normative reasons to act. If features of a situation, or characteristics of these features, change then the balance of our normative reasons will change. In rejecting this claim, this is not to say that uncertainty should be considered a moral property of some sort, merely that, as in inherent attribute of a situation, it can have relevance for our understanding of moral concepts (e.g. obligations) and the deontic properties of actions (e.g. permissibility).[7]

Philosophers have different views on the extent to which uncertainty has moral significance. According to some views, it has a direct impact on how we ought to act.[8] That is to say, being ignorant of particular facts – both normative and non-normative facts – can change what morally ought to be done in a situation. In terms of risk regulation, this would mean that the moral justification of what regulatory policy should be undertaken can depend on the level of normative uncertainty that exists. According to other views, uncertainty only has an indirect significance in relation to how we ought to judge people in light of the actions undertaken while ignorant of particular facts. In terms of risk regulation, this could mean that for those areas or issues that the regulator allows the regulatee to handle on their own, the level of moral responsibility for any unjustifiable harm, loss or burden resulting from the action (or inaction) of the regulatee must take into account ignorance of particular facts.

Uncertainty, to some extent or other, does have moral significance, and scholars and practitioners of risk regulation should take this into account. Since normative uncertainty exists to a much higher degree in times of emergency, I also suggest that normative uncertainty will also have significance for emergency risk regulation.

9.2 THE ETHICS OF EMERGENCY

Moral theories elucidate various moral standards that tell us what to do – what our normative reasons for action are. Morality provides both normative and motivational reasons for action. Normative reasons are those considerations that *justify* why acting (or failing to act) in a particular situation is right or wrong, just or unjust, obligatory or permissible, blameworthy or praiseworthy. Motivational reasons are those considerations that *explain* why individuals were motivated to act as they did. While it is certainly possible to be motivated to act in a way that we have no normative reason to do, moral theories tell us what normative reasons *should* become our motivational reasons.

As I said before, normative reasons are facts – i.e. features of a situation. It is these features of a situation that favour, justify or require action. It is these features of a situation that comprise the balance of normative reasons, and are, when considered in totality, determinative of what one ought to do. Emergencies are circumstances in which the features of a situation will significantly change and can produce a corresponding change to the balance of normative reasons – i.e. compared to balance of reasons in normal circumstances.[9] When the balance of reasons changes in this way, it could potentially affect what one ought to do. The philosophically interesting question is how this will be so and whether it will always be the same. What is uncertain is how and to what extent the modification of the balance of reasons will take place in these non-normal circumstances, and whether the modification is such that what one ought to do in these circumstances differs from what one ought to do in normal circumstances.

Moral theory is typically concerned with telling us what ought to be done in normal circumstances. However, recently greater attention has been brought to bear on the issue of the nature and status of morality in times of emergency and whether, and if so in what ways, moral standards might change during emergencies.[10] I believe, and argue elsewhere, that moral standards can indeed change in particular and noteworthy ways during emergencies – but I shall not have time to present such arguments here.[11] Instead, I want to say something about how normative uncertainty plays a part in accounting for how morality can differ in times of emergency, and why this should be understood as a general problem for emergency risk regulation.

Normative uncertainty, as a feature of emergency, increases the possibility that conventional moral standards may or may not hold up in the same way. For instance, Tom Sorell (2002, pp. 31, 32) claims that emergencies are '… occasions for serious rupture of moral conventions' and 'can undermine everyday morality itself at a place and time'. Others talk about the possibility of 'moral black holes' developing as a consequence of an emergency, whereby the applicability and binding of morality no longer hold.[12] This claim could be understood in two ways – often it is unclear how some writers are deploying the claim. Descriptively, it could be understood as the claim that the nature of an emergency is such that in these circumstances individuals turn to immoral actions – lying, cheating, stealing, promise-breaking, manipulation, price-gouging, assaults, killing – and, as such, behave *as if* morality is not applicable or binding in the circumstance. Conceptually, it could be understood as the claim that the nature of emergency is such that in these circumstances the structure and substance of morality *may actually transform* such that previously respected rights, obligations and responsibilities lose their applicable or fail to carry the same normative force as they did in normal circumstances.[13]

The worry that morality may not hold up in the same way can be understood both in terms of our normative and motivational reasons. In terms of normative considerations, the normative uncertainty associated with emergency might make it the case that what was a moral right in times of normalcy will no longer be a right in times of emergency, or, if still exists, it has new exceptions or loopholes that previously did not exist. This possibility can have significant implications for risk regulation. Consider, for instance, the moral right persons have against others that they not impose high risk of harms on others. If this right could not be justifiably overridden in times of emergency, this would severely limit a number of options thought morally appropriate in regulating the risk inherent in emergencies. In terms of motivational considerations, even if the higher level of normative uncertainty of the situation does not end up leading to a change in moral standards, the extent to which persons are motivated to do what they morally ought to do remains an important concern. Sorell (2002, p. 31) maintains that, in times of emergency, 'it is easy to feel deeply cut off from the world, with all connections to people and things that are dear or familiar lost or at risk. In these circumstances, it is natural to distrust others and to keep what one has for those one knows best'. If persons have a psychological propensity in emergencies to not view moral standards as motivationally efficacious as they are in times of normalcy, then this again has significant implications for risk regulation: not only in terms of trying to predict people's behaviour, but also in terms of determining what actions or policies will be ultimately justifiable in the face of the possibility of non-compliance with the regulations that are aimed to mitigate or eliminate the consequences of emergency.[14]

9.3 CONCLUSION

While normative uncertainty can exist in our everyday lives, it is even more
pressing during times of emergency. This is directly relevant for emergency
regulation because normative uncertainty will have a direct impact on how
we deliberate (and should deliberate) about what we ought to do, as well as
the justificatory basis on which we need to co-operate under emergency
circumstances. Given the level and extent of normative uncertainty during
times of emergency, risk regulation should devote more attention – both
from the point of view of the regulator and the regulatee – to the question,
'what ought one do when one does not know what to do?'[15] The relationship between regulator and regulatee is a complex one informed by a
number of inputs. In this short chapter, I have attempted to call attention to
the importance of moral considerations as an input. Not only in terms of
the moral justification of emergency risk regulation, but in relation to how
viewing risk regulation as being morally justified can have an effect on
compliance with regulation.

NOTES

1. For an argument concerning why normative uncertainty should be taken as a feature of
    emergency, see Viens (manuscript).
2. For example, see Adler (2003, 2005) and Oberdiek (2004).
3. It is popular within the risk regulation literature to speak of uncertainty as a relation
    between facts (or reality) and models. See Morgan and Henrion (1990). Not much
    hangs on this though; one could easily adapt what I have to say if one merely just
    changes the wording to 'beliefs about models' or 'beliefs given by models'.
4. Brannigan and Smidts (1999).
5. See, for example, Raffensberger and Tickner (1999); Commission of the European
    Communities (2000); Sandin (2004); Fisher, Jones and von Schomberg (2006). For an
    important critique of the pre-cautionary principle in risk regulation: see Sunstein
    (2005).
6. See, for instance, Tyler (2006, 2010). In relation to how this issue is of relevance to
    emergency risk regulation concerning pandemics, cf. Viens et al. (2009).
7. Tannert et al. (2008, p. 893) do go on to say, in citing the use of the precautionary
    principle, that '... in a potentially dangerous situation, uncertainty can trigger ethically
    adjusted behaviour that aims to avoid dangers and diminishes risks'. While this is
    certainly also possible, it should not lead us think that uncertainty itself does not have
    moral significance.
8. See Zimmerman (2008).
9. By modifying the balance of reasons, I mean giving rise to new reasons, defeating
    reasons or modifying one's undefeated reasons.
10. Cf. Sorell (2002); Zack (2006, 2009); Sandin and Wester (2009).
11. See Viens (manuscript).
12. Sorell (2002).
13. This claim often underpins arguments justifying extraordinary measures and powers in
    an emergency and it is important to examine both descriptive and conceptual claims in
    such arguments.

14. A further concern for regulatory regimes will be the question of how we ought to hold people responsible for not complying with regulations during times of emergency. As a result of features, such as urgency, necessity and epistemic uncertainty, emergencies will be circumstances in which we will be ignorant of a number of facts, and this ignorance is morally significant with respect to how we are held responsible for our subsequent actions. This has been recognized to be an issue within ethical theory in normal circumstances, so it should be clear that it is certainly one, *a fortiori*, in emergency circumstances. Cf. Lockhart (2000); Zimmerman (2008).

15. For more on practical rationality and normative uncertainty, see Sepielli (2009).

BIBLIOGRAPHY

Adler, M.D. (2003), 'Risk, Death, and Harm: The Normative Foundations of Risk Regulation', *Minnesota Law Review*, **87** (5), 1293–418.

Adler, M.D. (2005), 'Against Individual Risk: A Sympathetic Critique of Risk Assessment', *University of Pennsylvania Law Review*, **153** (4), 1121–49.

Brannigan, V. and C. Smidts (1999), 'Performance Based Fire Safety Regulation under Intentional Uncertainty', *Fire and Materials*, **23** (6), 341–7.

Commission of the European Communities (2000), *Communication from the Commission on the Precautionary Principle*. Brussels, COM (2000).

Fisher, E., J. Jones and R. von Schomberg (eds) (2006), *Implementing the Precautionary Principle: Perspectives and Prospects*, Cheltenham, UK and Northampton, MA, USA: Edward Elgar.

Lockhart, T. (2000), *Moral Uncertainty and Its Consequences*, Oxford: Oxford University Press.

Morgan, M.G. and M. Henrion (1990), *Uncertainty: A Guide to Dealing with Uncertainty in Risk and Policy Analysis*, Cambridge: Cambridge University Press.

Oberdiek, O. (2004), 'The Ethics in Risk Regulation: Towards a Contractualist Re-Orientation', *Rutgers Law Journal*, **36** (1), 199–204.

Raffensberger, C. and J. Tickner (eds) (1999), *Protecting Public Health and the Environment: Implementing the Precautionary Principle*, Washington, DC: Island Press.

Sandin, P. (2004), 'The Precautionary Principle and the Concept of Precaution', *Environmental Values* **13** (4), 461–75.

Sepielli, A. (2009), 'What to Do When You Don't Know What to Do', in R. Shafer-Landau (ed.), *Oxford Studies in Metaethics*, Vol. 4, Oxford: Oxford University Press, 5–28.

Sorell, T. (2002), 'Morality and Emergency', *Proceedings of Aristotelian Society*, **103** (1), 21–37.

Sunstein, C.R. (2005), *Laws of Fear: Beyond the Precautionary Principle*, Cambridge, Cambridge University Press.

Tannert, C., H.D. Elvers and B. Jandrig (2007), 'The Ethics of Uncertainty', *EMBO Reports*, **8** (10), 892–6.

Tyler, T.R. (2006), *Why People Obey the Law: Procedural Justice, Legitimacy, and Compliance,* Princeton: Princeton University Press.

Tyler, T.R. (2010), *Why People Cooperate: The Role of Social Motivations*, Princeton: Princeton University Press.

Viens, A.M. (manuscript), *In Extremis: Morality and Law in Times of Emergency.*

Viens, A.M., C.M. Besimon and R.E.G. Upshur (2009), 'Your Liberty or Your Life: Reciprocity in the Use of Restrictive Measures in Contexts of Contagion', *Journal of Bioethical Inquiry*, **6** (2), 207–17.

Zack, N. (2006), 'Philosophy and Disaster,' *Homeland Security Affairs*, **2** (1), 1–13, available at: http://www.hsaj.org/hsa/volII/iss1/art5 (accessed 19 February 2011).

Zack, N. (2009), *Ethics for Disasters*, Lanham, MD: Rowman & Littlefield.

Zimmerman, M.J. (2008), *Living with Uncertainty: The Moral Significance of Ignorance*, Cambridge: Cambridge University Press.

PART 4

The organizational mechanisms of
emergency risk regulation

10. Effective regulatory processes for crisis management: an analysis of codified crisis management in Europe[1]

Lorenza Jachia and Valentin Nikonov

It was the best of times, it was the worst of times. (Charles Dickens, *A Tale of Two Cities*, 1859)

10.1 INTRODUCTION

This chapter aims at identifying issues that regulators should consider when designing, testing, implementing and maintaining crisis management plans and developing legislation that covers situations of emergency.

Using the 2010 volcanic ash crisis as a case study of regulatory actions during emergency, we introduce a holistic model for managing risks within regulatory systems. We present contingency planning and emergency regulation as functions of well-designed regulatory systems and part of codified risk management. We argue that actions taken by the regulator in the immediacy of crisis will only be effective if the regulatory system embraces all functions of the risk-management process.

The model provides insight into the research questions that this volume addresses; in particular determining a proportionate response to risks, assigning responsibility for risk-management functions to different stakeholders, involving the industry into preparing and responding to the situations of emergency. Also, the model is a tool to assess the gaps in legislation in different fields with regard to risk-management best practice. In the chapter, we analyze how environmental, food safety, financial and aviation laws or regulations address crisis management and situations of emergency. Finally, we present our conclusions and recommendations on incorporating crisis management into regulatory processes.

10.2 COULD CRISES BE THE BEST OF TIMES?

The closing of the European airspace following the eruption of the Icelandic volcano was an extraordinary event. More than 100,000 flights were cancelled, the estimate of losses by airlines, airports and tour operators 'ranged from $2 billion to $3.3 billion' (Kanter and Clark, 2010; Ragona, Chapter 3). The full range of the consequences of the events of April 2010 will never be fully grasped. Some were certainly very mundane, like Whitney Houston opting for 'a slightly unglamorous ferry ride across the Irish Sea' (Mirror.co.uk, 2010). Other disruptions, though less visible, were of a quite different scale, like the cancellation of medical operations due to delays in the dispatch of vitally needed organs for transplant.

Yet, the eruption caused no accidents, no casualties, and no immediate damage to the environment. It has even been calculated that the release of CO_2 into the atmosphere by the volcano was partially offset by the flight cancellations, making this the first 'carbon neutral volcanic eruption' in history (The Independent, 2010).

The ash cloud crisis – in contrast to other major hazards that are before us today – had a clear beginning and end. This makes it well suited as a case study of how regulations allow society to manage risks, the costs these regulations have, and the efficiency of crisis-management processes that different stakeholders (consumers, economic operators, regulators) have or do not have in place.

Crises for regulators can be 'the best of times'. In times of crisis, regulators have access to resources and enjoy broad power and media exposure. And the public clearly expects that they meet their expectations; which are that costs be minimized, unnecessary damage avoided, and that operators and citizens can quickly return to 'business as usual'.

We will focus on the fact that many crises happen in the same way, leading to similar consequences, even if caused by different risks. The ash cloud crisis was not the first event that left thousands of people stranded. So, if a risk that causes a crisis is an emerging risk (which is very often the case), and therefore unknown and missed, as was the case here, we argue that a contingency plan developed by a regulator for another risk can sometimes be used (Briggs, Chapter 11). We will therefore deal with more general aspects of developing regulatory processes for crisis management.

The Global Risk Report of the World Economic Forum (WEF, 2010) identified many emerging risks that may become systemic risks. The fact that a volcanic eruption was not identified there as a systemic risk is not surprising and does not lower the value of the report; it is another confirmation that there will always be an element of the unknown, and that a regulator should put processes in place for dealing with all crises. The report urges for 'a holistic approach to risk management at country level' to be developed.

We aim at using the experience gained from the ash cloud crisis and other recent crises to provide guidance to regulators on how to increase the capacity of regulatory systems to respond effectively to emergencies. For this purpose, we will do the following:

- show how crisis management can only work in the context of a well-functioning risk-management system involving all stakeholders, including regulators, business operators and surveillance authorities;
- analyze how crisis management is addressed in existing legislation in different fields (aviation, environment, food safety, finance);
- review current standards and reference models on crisis management;
- identify issues that regulators should focus on when designing, testing, implementing and maintaining crisis-management plans and developing respective legislation.

10.3　RISK-MANAGEMENT TOOLS AT THE CENTRE OF REGULATORY SYSTEMS

10.3.1　Optimal Balance between Regulations and Risks

A fundamental goal of European and national aviation policy is to ensure the safety of passengers. In the press statement by the European Commission, Vice-President of the European Commission Siim Kallas, responsible for transport, said that 'there can be no compromise on safety' (EC, 2010a). This makes this policy no different from other regulatory systems that apply in other sectors, ranging from consumer products to food safety. Authorities and standardization bodies – with the goal of guiding and changing our behaviour, at home, in our cars, at our jobs – draw up laws, administrative measures and technical regulations, complemented by voluntary standards and norms. Taken collectively, all of these help to make products safe, organizations' processes stable and consumers better protected from hazards.

Regulations have always been used to manage risks. The code of Hammurabi – perhaps the oldest recorded set of laws – had a provision that if a builder did not construct a house properly, and the house were to kill its owner, the builder should be put to death. In modern times, the World Trade Organization, in its Agreement on the Application of Sanitary and

Phytosanitary Measures, requires that trade restrictions be based on scientific evidence of a risk to the life or the health of humans, animals or plants.

These two references, antique and modern, are also two interesting cornerstones. On the one hand, a limit is set, based on an assessment of risks, to protect citizens from possible harm. On the other, there is the realization that regulations are costly, for trade and for business in general, and should only be introduced if there is a need. Taken together, they point to the use of risk management as a tool to minimize failures of two kinds: failure to regulate when there is a need, and failure by regulating when there is no need.

10.3.2   How Safe is Safe Enough?

All regulators, in principle, would agree that regulation should strike a balance between safety and cost. Some risks are particularly difficult to regulate: those that we cannot control by our actions, those that pertain to phenomena that we can only partially understand with our senses, and those that can result in fatal outcomes. Not surprisingly, the hazards that were at the centre of the ash cloud crisis had elements of all these. Passengers cannot influence the ash concentration, they cannot measure it themselves as this requires sophisticated tools, and the potential consequences of an accident in the sky can in no way be compared even to the very high estimated costs.

Weighing costs against safety is nonetheless something that lies at the heart of all regulatory and management systems, and this can only be done when the regulator has enough information to evaluate potential losses against potential benefits.

In the following pages, we present the UNECE Model of Risk Management in Regulatory Systems. The model systemizes the outcome of the UNECE International Conference on Risk Assessment and Management[2] and serves as a reference model for the work of the newly established UNECE Group of Experts on Risk Management and Regulatory Systems.

One of the main features of a risk-management methodology is the guidance it offers on dealing with hazards of all types. Regardless of the scope any piece of legislation, 'the engine' for decision-making that should be included in the legislation remains the same. The following are the seven main functions of a risk-management process (UNECE, 2010a) (for a regulatory system):

(1)   Setting the objectives.
(2)   Identifying and managing the assets being protected.
(3)   Identifying the risks to the assets.

(4) Prioritizing the risks.
(5) Choosing risk-management strategies, starting with the most important risks.
(6) Putting risk-management strategies in place.
(7) Developing a 'crisis management' plan.

When these processes operate efficiently within a regulatory system, the system strikes an optimal balance between safety and cost.

10.3.3 Responsibility for Risks

This model not only systemizes the functions that are typical of all regulatory systems but also assigns specific roles to the different stakeholders in the regulatory system (e.g. regulators, conformity-assessment bodies, surveillance authorities). Among regulatory systems, these functions are carried out by different bodies, but functions themselves remain similar.

For example, in aviation policy, the absence of conformity assessment function was highlighted in the report, prepared by the EU services in the aftermath of the volcanic ash crisis (EC, 2010b). Since 'in the absence of a defined certification standard for volcanic ashes, it has been difficult to obtain full information on the performance of aircraft and engines operated in airspace contaminated by volcanic ashes', the European Aviation Safety Agency (EASA) 'has developed an action plan to overcome the current absence of adequate certification of aircraft and engines in relation to volcanic ashes' (EC, 2010b).

The report on the UNECE International Conference on Risk Assessment and Management (UNECE, 2010b) states that 'regulatory goals for appropriately addressing and mitigating risks cannot be met unless all stakeholders are actively involved. These include business operators, conformity-assessment bodies, market-surveillance authorities and consumers'. The risk-management process should serve as a basis for cooperation among all stakeholders within a regulatory system.

It is the job of the regulator to create a framework that involves all stakeholders in mitigating risks effectively. The regulator can only be considered responsible for a risk that occurred due to some inefficiency in the process. If a driver's mistake leads to a car accident, it is the driver's fault; if the accident occurs as a result of incorrect road signs, it is the regulator's fault. Common risk-mitigation tools include efficient standardization systems, appropriate conformity assessment procedures, market surveillance infrastructures, etc.

The UNECE report (UNECE, 2010b) also states that in many countries regulators are 'moving towards goal-setting regulations'. This approach

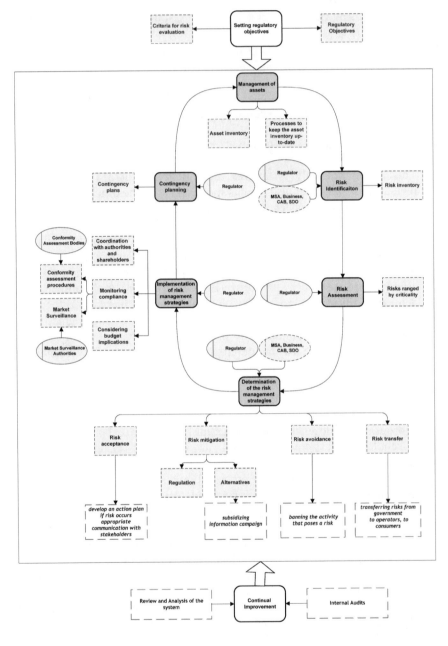

Figure 10.1. UNECE Model for Risk Management in Regulatory Systems

offers economic operators more freedom in choosing tools and methods for achieving the goals. At the same time, it implies that operators bear the primary responsibility in case a risk occurs.

The model also provides insight on integrating a crisis-management function into the regulatory system. We will now focus on models that regulators can use to manage crises efficiently. The models come from a number of different sectors.

10.4 REGULATORY FRAMEWORK FOR CRISIS MANAGEMENT

Crisis management is only one building block in the risk-management process. To be effective, it needs input from other steps of the process.

In particular, the regulator needs criteria to decide which risks should be considered acceptable (the result of the first function ('setting the objectives').

Other inputs are also needed. An important thing to do is to identify the assets. In the ash cloud crisis, and more generally regarding the aviation policy, these include passenger safety and passenger rights, as well as airline industry assets (such as airplanes, slot times, etc.).

In deciding whether or not the planes could fly though the ash, the regulator was in fact protecting these assets against the risks that had been identified to them. This required transparent interfaces among stakeholders performing different risk-management functions, so it depended on optimal communication tools, common risk management methodologies, and a solid legislative basis.

The next step in managing the crisis was choosing a risk-management strategy. During the ash crisis, the regulators chose to avoid potential risks to passengers by closing down the European airspace. But as one risk is avoided, others may be created. In choosing a risk-management strategy, the regulator has not only to balance costs and safety, but also to do so across the interests of different groups.

Choosing a strategy also involves an understanding of the choices available and full cooperation of all stakeholders in putting the strategy in place.

We, therefore, cannot separate crisis management from the other functions of risk management. To be effective it requires coherent approaches to managing risks within the regulatory system as a whole. This is reflected in the European Commission report on the actions undertaken in the context of the impact of the volcanic ash crisis (EC, 2010b). The report refers to the need for 'an improvement of the risk assessment and risk management in such crises' and also recommends a 'definition of a new European methodology and a coherent approach for safety risks assessment and risk management' (EC, 2010b).

To apply coherent approaches to crisis management, legislative documents for establishing regulatory systems should:

- describe all functions of the risk-management process;
- assign responsibility and authority for performing these functions to well-identified stakeholders (including the responsibility for crisis management);
- put in place an effective risk-communication process that will be operational even in case of a crisis.

The management of risks is at the core of a number of legislative documents and regulatory systems. Most importantly, risk management is applied in the following areas:

- food safety (e.g. US, European Union);
- technical regulation (e.g. EU, New Zealand);
- environment (e.g. EU, US);
- energy efficiency (EU);
- public health (e.g. Australia, EU).

In regulatory systems across various sectors, the crisis-management function is described:

- In regulations and directives:
    - as one of the logical steps of the risk-management process, such as in the Food Safety Regulation of the European Union (EC Regulation 178/2002);
    - as a separate function, without any links to other steps of the risk-management process, such as risk identification, etc. (as in the environment legislation, like Directive 2004/35 on environmental liability (with regard to the prevention and remedying of environmental damage);
- In documents of other type such as post-crisis reports (aviation and finance).

10.4.1   Aviation Crisis-management Plan

The report on actions undertaken in the context of the impact of the volcanic ash cloud crisis on the air transport industry (EU, 2010b) is the only comprehensive description of the crisis-management framework for the aviation sector. Unfortunately, for the stranded passengers all over Europe, this document was developed after the crisis. It describes measures undertaken during the crisis (the system of zones that 'allowed the greater access to the European airspace while fully guaranteeing the highest level of safety') and proposes an action plan ('establishment by the relevant authorities […] of binding limit values', developing new certification schemes, ensuring the applicability of the passenger rights regulation, etc.).

The framework establishes the authority responsible for crisis management – 'Immediate creation of a crisis coordination cell' – EACCC, with 'the main role of the EACCC to facilitate the management of crisis situations affecting aviation in the European region'. The group is to be 'activated when unexpected circumstances would affect significantly the environment of operations'. The report urges the development of a coherent risk-assessment and risk-management methodology.

In describing the crisis-management framework, the report mostly covers immediate measures related to the ash crisis. It does not establish a crisis-management system as a part of the overall risk-management framework; though the need to develop coherent risk-management methodologies is mentioned.

10.4.2 Financial Sector

The recent financial crisis led to a 'new framework for crisis management in the financial sector' ('An EU framework for Crisis Management in the Financial Sector', EC, 2010c). The need for developing a new crisis-management framework as it is presented in the text ('in the case of a failure of a large bank, those functions could not be shut down without significant systemic damage') is not sector specific and can be easily generalized to other areas.

The objectives of the new framework can also be applied to other regulatory fields and include:

- put this prevention and preparation first;
- enabling fast and decisive actions;
- reducing moral hazard;
- limiting distortions of competition.

This underscores how fundamental principles on risk regulation can be applied across regulatory systems.

The framework establishes the authorities responsible for crisis management and requires 'each Member State to identify a resolution authority to exercise the resolution powers'. It also establishes 'the group level resolution authority' that 'would be responsible for crisis planning and the preparation of resolution plans'.

What makes this framework sophisticated is that it provides specific tools to increase the chances that developing problems will be identified and addressed at an early stage, including 'reinforced supervision' and requirements for 'all credit institutions to [...] prepare and keep updated recovery plans setting out measures the institution or group would take in different scenarios'.

The framework defines the process and states that 'these plans are prepared by resolution authorities and supervisors, in close cooperation with the firms which would be required to supply the necessary information'. One of the policy actions is a 'Proposal for a Directive on crisis management to include a cross border coordination framework'. This document has many similarities with the report of the aviation sector:

- It was developed *after* the crisis.
- It emphasizes the need for developing coherent frameworks for managing crises.

10.4.3 Environmental Legislation

Within the European environmental regulatory system, EU Directive 2004/35 on environmental liability with regard to the prevention and remedying of environmental damage sets out the basic tenets of crisis management. Although the environmental legislation does not use the risk terminology presented here, the decision-making process can be aligned with the fundamentals of risk management.

The legislation is built around the terms 'environmental damage' ('damage to protected species and natural habitats, which is any damage that has significant adverse effects on reaching or maintaining the favourable conservation status of such habitats or species') and 'imminent threat of damage' ('a sufficient likelihood that environmental damage will occur in the near future'). The term 'preventive measure', which is a risk-mitigation strategy, is referred to in the legislation as 'any measures taken in response to an event, act or omission that has created an imminent threat of environmental damage, with a view to preventing or minimizing that damage'.

The environmental legislation contains a detailed description of crisis-management procedures. Any environmental risk that occurs becomes subject to these provisions. The crisis-management process is described as follows. Economic operators shall 'inform the competent authority of all relevant aspects of the situation and take: all practicable steps to immediately control, contain, remove or otherwise manage the relevant contaminants and/or any other damage factors […]'.

This legislation also provides advice on choosing remedial measures: 'Operators shall identify … potential remedial measures') and a set of criteria for choosing the measures: 'the cost of implementing the option' and 'the likelihood of success of each option'. Operators can, therefore, use this list to develop internal procedures in advance. The measures chosen must then be sent for approval to the competent authority.

While the legislative text quoted above may create the impression of dual responsibility for determining and putting in place the crisis management plan, other sections highlight the primary responsibility of the competent authority in a crisis.[3]

The legislation defines how EU member states should cooperate in the event of an environmental risk:

> where environmental damage affects or is likely to affect several Member States, those Member States shall cooperate, including through the appropriate exchange of information, with a view to ensuring that preventive action and, where necessary, remedial action is taken in respect of any such environmental damage.

Having analyzed the EU environmental legislation, we can conclude as follows:

- The crisis management function is described in legislation that establishes a crisis-management system that is not related to any particular crisis. For example, there was no crisis-management framework for the aviation sector before the ash cloud crisis. However this crisis highlighted the need for such a framework, which has subsequently been developed.
- While this legislation does not use the most common risk-management terminology that is referred to in this chapter, it does address all the functions of risk management.
- The legislation establishes a European agency, which plays a major coordinating role in cross-border environmental crisis management.

10.4.4 Food Safety Regulation

The Food Safety Regulation (EC Regulation 178/2002) is another example
of legislation that presents crisis management as a logical step in the overall
risk-management process. More generally, it bases the food regulatory
system on a well-structured and well-defined risk-management process.
The system – which was developed, as stated on the EFSA website[4]
'following a series of food crises in the late 1990s' – assigns the main
functions to stakeholders and serves as a basis for harmonizing national
legislation in this sector.

This Regulation shows all aspects of how risk-management concepts can
be used by legislators.

- It establishes 'a risk-based decision-making' mechanism within the
  system for developing measures proportionate to hazards, and
  requires that 'measures adopted by the Member States and the
  Community governing food and feed … be based on risk analysis
  except where this is not appropriate to the circumstances or the nature
  of the measure' and also has provisions for these measures to be
  'effective, proportionate and targeted'.
- It builds a common legislative framework for all EU member states. It
  explicitly aims at 'forming a common basis for measures governing
  food and feed' and provides that 'food law[5] shall be based on risk
  analysis except where this is not appropriate to the circumstances or
  the nature of the measure'.
- It provides that the main functions of the risk-management process,
  including risk assessment, risk management and risk communication,
  be performed when making a decision aimed at reducing, eliminating
  or avoiding a risk to health.
- It establishes the European Food Agency (EFA), which is also
  responsible for risk-management processes and methodologies.

To summarize, we see that the food safety legislation contains all the
elements that we identified above:

- It sets out the objectives of the system.
- It establishes processes for assets management (traceability requirements complemented by a database maintained by the EFA).
- It establishes mechanisms for stakeholders to participate in risk
  identification (business operators, advisory council, rapid alert system, etc.).

- It assigns responsibility for risk-assessment methodologies (to the EFA).
- It designs a process for choosing risk-management strategies and managing crises.

The Regulation defines a crisis[6] and assigns to the Commission the responsibility for drawing up the general plan for crisis management.[7] It says that in the event of a crisis, the Commission will 'notify the Member States and the Authority' and 'set up a crisis unit immediately, in which the Authority shall participate, and provide scientific and technical assistance if necessary'.

The food safety regulatory system and respective legislation:

- is built on the basis of the risk-management process;
- uses risk-management terminology and describes all functions necessary for effective risk management;
- presents crisis management as a step in the overall risk-management process.

10.4.5 Conclusions from the Analysis of Crisis-management Frameworks

The above analysis allows us to conclude that contingency planning takes a similar form across different sectors. Perhaps the three most important recommendations that can be made are as follows. First, that risk-management provisions should be laid out before a crisis occurs, and integrated in the main legislative texts. Second, that crisis management will not function effectively unless it is a function of the risk-management process with transparent interfaces among functions. Third, the general conclusion that can be drawn is that harmonizing crisis-management approaches and developing a common structure will make the entire regulatory system more efficient. Each framework described in the chapter has strong points that can be utilized when designing crisis-management processes, such as:

- determining the crisis-management objectives (as in financial crisis-management framework);
- establishing a central cross-border authority responsible for crisis management;
- providing guidance on tools used to build an early-warning system;
- requiring business operators to develop contingency plans (finance);
- introducing crisis management as a part of the risk-management process of the regulatory system (as in food).

The model presented in (UNECE, 2010a) can be used as a basis for harmonizing legislation across various sectors and for providing consistency in addressing risks within regulatory systems.

10.5 DEVELOPING AND IMPLEMENTING CRISIS-MANAGEMENT PLANS: HOW THE UNECE MODEL CAN BE USED

Within a regulatory system, the crisis-management function needs to be implemented along with other steps of the risk-management process. The UNECE model presents crisis management as a part of this process and shows its interaction with other functions and respective stakeholders. Crisis-management tools are referred to in many of the standards related to risk management (see Box 10.1), which also can be used in emergency regulation.

BOX 10.1. CONTINGENCY PLANNING IN STANDARDS

Crisis-management tools are referred to in the following standards:

- ISO 31000:2009, Risk management – principles and guidelines on implementation. Recommends that establishing external communication and reporting mechanisms should involve 'communicating with stakeholders in the event of a crisis or contingency'.
- ISO 27001:2005, Information security management systems – Requirements. Describes the risk-management process as applied to information-security risks and requires organizations to: identify 'events that may cause interruptions to business processes'; 'develop and implement continuity plans' that would allow to 'maintain and restore operations ... following an interruption to, or failure of, critical business processes'. An important requirement of this standard is that 'business continuity plans shall be tested and updated regularly to ensure that they are up to date and effective'.
- BS 25999, a business continuity management standard developed by British Standards Institution, describes 'a management process that identifies potential impacts that threaten an organisation and provides a framework for building resilience and the capability for an effective response

---

> which safeguards the interests of its key stake holders, reputation, brand and value creating activities'.
>
> The concept for developing, testing, implementing and maintaining business continuity plans and respective recommendation given in the above-mentioned standards could be easily applied to the design of the crisis-management function of the regulatory system.

Some specific issues to examine when developing crisis-management systems include the following:

The legislation establishing a regulatory system should define what is a risk to the system, and what represents a crisis situation (the Food Safety Regulation determines it as 'a serious risk to health').

- The regulator should determine the objectives of the regulatory system and use them as criteria in its risk-management processes.
- The legislation should contain a description of the responsibilities for performing all of the risk-management functions presented in the model.
- Stakeholders should be required to use stress-testing and scenario-analysis tools when identifying risks. Responsibility should be assigned for the identification of low-probability risks.
- For these risks, the regulator should develop crisis-management plans. Crisis-management planning includes:
  - making reserves (buffers);
  - developing precise plans of action in case a risk occurs;
  - developing communication processes. Authorities need to communicate effectively, so as to enable economic and social operators, as well as citizens, to take the right decisions in the event of a crisis. Communication is critical to getting back to business as usual, which is the regulator's ultimate goal.
- A crisis-management plan should include 'consultation'. During a crisis, problems are compounded by the diversity of interests among stakeholders and even within a single group of stakeholders. For example, there is no such person as 'the consumer', there are consumer women, men and children, rural, urban, educated or not, working or unemployed, etc. Not only should all the stakeholders be represented, but representatives should be sensitive to the diversity of interests that they represent. For the regulator, making decisions in a crisis is not easy because of the need to balance different perceptions

of risks, which vary substantially across individuals as well as across societal and political groups.

10.6 CONCLUSION

In analysing existing crisis-management frameworks, we can see that many of them were developed after a crisis and are crisis-specific. These frameworks should be a compulsory part of any regulatory system and be described in the related legislation. The structure of legislation, and of regulatory processes, should be consistent with the risk-management methodology used. A set of models could be used, including the UNECE one, together with specific crisis-management standards.

NOTES

1. The views and opinions expressed in the chapter are those of the authors, and do not reflect the views of the organization and its member states.
2. Information on speakers, background documents, presentations and the conference outcome are available at: http://www.unece.org/trade/wp6/documents/2009/2009_ConferenceRisk.htm (accessed 11 March 2011).
3. In 'those situations where several instances of environmental damage have occurred in such a manner that the competent authority cannot ensure that all the necessary remedial measures are taken at the same time, [...], the competent authority should be entitled to decide which instance of environmental damage is to be remedied first'. In making [...] decision, the competent authority shall have regard, inter alia, to the nature, extent and gravity of the various instances of environmental damage concerned, and to the possibility of natural recovery. Risks to human health shall also be taken into account'.
4. http://www.efsa.europa.eu/en/aboutefsa.htm (accessed 11 March 2011).
5. Of the member states.
6. A situation involving a serious direct or indirect risk to human health deriving from food and feed, and the risk cannot be prevented, eliminated or reduced by existing provisions.
7. The Commission shall draw up, in close cooperation with the Authority and the Member States, a general plan for crisis management in the field of the safety of food and feed. The general plan shall specify the types of situation involving direct or indirect risks to human health, ... and practical procedures necessary to manage a crisis, including the principles of transparency to be applied and a communication strategy.

BIBLIOGRAPHY

BSI (2006), British Standard 'Business continuity management – Part 1: Code of practice', Directive 2004/35/EC of the European Parliament and of the Council of 21 April 2004 on environmental liability with regard to the prevention and remedying of environmental damage, available at http://eur-lex.europa.eu/

smartapi/cgi/sga_doc?smartapi!celexplus!prod!DocNumber&lg=en&type_doc=
Directive&an_doc=2004&nu_doc=35 (accessed 11 March 2011).

EC (2010a), 'Volcanic Ash Cloud', press statement by Commission Vice-President
Siim Kallas, responsible for transport (19 April 2010), available at http://
ec.europa.eu/commission_2010–2014/kallas/headlines/news/2010/04/20100419_
volcanic_ash_cloud_statement_de.htm (accessed 11 March 2011).

EC (2010b), Report on Actions Undertaken in the Context of the Impact of the
Volcanic Ash Cloud Crisis on the Air Transport Industry, available at http://
ec.europa.eu/transport/doc/ash-cloud-crisis/2010_06_30_volcano-crisis-report.
pdf (accessed 11 March 2011).

EC (2010c), Communication on a New EU Framework for Crisis Management in
the Financial Sector, 20 October 2010, available at http://ec.europa.eu/internal_
market/bank/crisis_management/index_en.htm (accessed 11 March 2011).

EC Regulation 178/2002 Laying Down the General Principles and Requirements of
Food Law, Establishing the European Food Safety Authority and Laying Down
Procedures in Matters of Food Safety.

The Independent (2010), 'Volcano Emitting 150–300,000 Tonnes of CO2 Daily:
Experts' available at http://www.independent.co.uk/environment/volcano-
emitting-150300000-tonnes-of-co2-daily-experts-1948708.html (accessed 11
March 2011).

ISO (2005), International Standard 'ISO 27001:2005. Information Technology –
Security Techniques – Information Security Management Systems – Requirements'.

ISO (2009), International Standard 'ISO 31000:2009. Risk Management – Principles and Guidelines'.

Kanter, J. and N. Clark (2010), 'European Countries Are Cautioned to Be Even-
Handed in Assisting Airlines', *The New York Times*, 27 April.

Mirror.co.uk (2010), 'Iceland Volcano Crisis: Stuck Stars – Sir Paul McCartney,
Robert Downey Jr, Mika and the Celebs Caught up in the Chaos', 19 April 2010,
available at http://www.mirror.co.uk/celebs/news/2010/04/19/iceland-volcano-
crisis-stuck-stars-sir-paul-mccartney-robert-downey-jr-mika-and-the-celebs-
caught-up-in-the-chaos-115875–22196634/ (accessed 11 March 2011).

UNECE (2010a), Risk Management in Regulatory Systems. A Proposed Reference
Model. UN Doc., ECE/TRADE/C/WP.6/2010/3, 23 August 2010.

UNECE (2010b), Risk Assessment and Management in the Activities of the
Working Party. UN Doc, ECE/TRADE/C/WP.6/2010/2, 7 April 2010.

World Economic Forum (2010), 'Global Risks 2010. A Global Risk Network
Report', available at http://www3.weforum.org/docs/WEF_GlobalRisks_
Report_2010.pdf (accessed 11 March 2011).

11. Abrupt environmental changes: scenario planning for catastrophic security risks

Chad Michael Briggs

Environment risk assessment was originally developed largely for controlled situations, and despite significant advances in methodologies over the years, still reflects limitations inherent both in our scientific understandings of events, and psychological limitations when dealing with catastrophes. The risks to operational and strategic planning often stem from a lack of experience with new or novel conditions, and proceed with assumptions that future projections will look very much like the present (March, 1988).

It is therefore not surprising that when confronted with abrupt changes in operating assumptions, organizations operating under standardized methodologies and assumptions are often unable to respond effectively. Common reactions tend to be inadequate, and those who are responsible often suffer from paralysis until more information can be made available. It is not widely understood that complex systems often contain specific vulnerabilities to change, particularly if such changes are unanticipated and appear suddenly.

The Eyjafjallajökull eruption of 2010 introduced abrupt environmental changes to European airspace, forcing large-scale cancellations of operations and disruption of international transport (Peterson, 2010). The indirect impacts of the volcanic ash plumes were also significant, resulting in economic damages to economies and financial stresses on specific industries. Responses from multiple affected stakeholders were disjointed, resulting from a lack of advanced planning, adequate communication channels between those in a position to respond, and the much needed trust (among empowered decision-makers) to deliberate adequately upon which risk values to consider in responding (Alemanno, Chapter 1; Brannigan, Chapter 7; Macrae, Chapter 2).

Emergency regulation is the immediate response to sudden and often unforeseen disasters, meant to prevent recurrence in the future or to mitigate continuing effects (Alemanno, Chapter 1) The suddenness of certain events leaves little time for detailed reflection on available options, while competing claims for action (e.g. passenger safety versus economic viability) place pressures on policymakers and regulators to act quickly. Emergency regulation also tends to occur in cases where little historical experience can act as a suitable guide, or where what experience exists is not considered applicable to a new situation. Militaries and security organizations have attempted to avoid such situations, recognizing that strategic surprise can invalidate well-established plans and procedures. As predictions are never as exact as public expectations, methods such as scenario planning are used to foresee potential risks in advance of their emergence. Effective foresight allows better regulatory response in the case of emergencies, as potential problems and responses are discussed in advance, and not as *ad hoc* responses to new situations.

This chapter examines recent developments in scenario planning with a focus on abrupt environmental risks, and how advanced planning can be accomplished even in emergency situations characterized by unknown probability risks. Employing complex networks of experts and adapted methods of cumulative risk assessment, contingency planning for major environmental changes/events can be taken well in advance. A proper risk frame can escape the often-made false juxtaposition between science and safety, whereby expectations demand either full safety or full certainty. As neither can be reasonably achieved, deliberations must be made in order to determine which values (including safety and economic considerations, for example) should be prioritized, and how much risk is therefore considered acceptable among all considered variables.

At a macro level, this reflects organizational conflict over core values, and often exposes distrust between relevant decision-makers over how to prioritize such values in assessing risks. A key question to ask, therefore, is in whom to trust, meaning that these deliberations are likely to occur successfully only if prior work has been done to establish reliable networks of communication and response.

11.1 UNBOUNDED UNCERTAINTY

Large-scale environmental changes are too often considered external and disconnected events, and systems are considered within themselves rather than tracing potential cascading effects across systems. For example, researchers identifying drought conditions in Australia are not communicating with energy planners in the same region, while scientists warning of glacial melt in Peru have no mechanism for telegraphing such warnings to security planners in a coherent fashion (Briggs, 2009). The excuse has been that under conditions of uncertainty, one should wait until more information is available before acting (Shrader-Frechette, 1985). In contrast, scenario planning accepts that uncertainty exists, that more information can increase uncertainty ranges, and that the only sensible reaction is to embrace the nature of uncertainty and explore it further. Changing scenario environments under plausible conditions can provide better understanding of systemic tolerances and acceptable risk.

Aeronautic and aerospace engineering use such system tolerance tests, both to determine potential component failures under various conditions, but also to prioritize upgrades and maintenance schedules (Willsky, 1976, Wang et al., 2004). These tests are based upon engineering approaches to component interaction, where earlier works focused on stochastic failure in a linear system. The probabilities of failure were largely determined according to the performance of individual components and relations with components in closest proximity. The weakness inherent in such approaches is that they are sometimes difficult to apply in cases where key risks were unacknowledged among components across systems considered unrelated (for example, flammable insulation in Swiss Air flight 111 in 1998) (Masys, 2004). The potential for underestimating the complex interactions often leads to an underestimation of total risks due to lower-level failures. This second point has been explored in some depth not only in aerospace literature, but in criticisms of nuclear power plant safety, where the unrecognized failure of a single dial can spark a cascade of events leading to much greater risks and an overall more vulnerable system (Wilkinson and Kelly, 1998).

A more general concern is that such systemic risks do not occur in isolation. Systems do not only operate according to internal rules in isolation, but within a larger environment that serves as a background 'steady state' for all other operations. Should designs and operations not take into account such conditions, or fail to foresee future changes in environmental variation, internal risks within the system can be underestimated. With nuclear power plants, for example, earlier designs (especially Soviet models such as the RBMK-1000) did not include adequate failsafe systems, which in turn meant that in a larger sense planners failed to recognize that geophysical factors could create new risks or impede operations. Similarly, the 2003 summer heat wave that hit Europe forced the shutdown of one-third of France's nuclear reactors, as coolant water exceeded design specifications for temperature. The extreme heat was unforeseen on a number of levels, and response from authorities was inadequate, especially at a time when demand for electricity was at its highest (Lagadec, 2005, Sacchetti, 2008).

Likewise, the 2010 Icelandic volcano eruption at Eyjafjallajökull posed new challenges and risks to commercial air traffic. The risks posed by volcanic ash particles has been recognized for decades and remediation plans were put into effect, especially after several high-visibility events occurred in the early 1980s, damaging windscreens of aircraft and forcing emergency shutdown of engines. And yet despite these risk-mitigation efforts, military training flights were grounded in April 2010, after UK and Finnish jet engines were damaged by ash particle ingestion (The Independent, 2010).

In response to the volcanic eruptions in the 1980s, the safety procedures first developed for dealing with ash clouds, were based upon standard flight training techniques in North America as mentioned above. Alaska Airlines instructed its pilots to follow four basic rules (Boeing, 2000):

(1) When in doubt, don't fly.
(2) Use facts and data.
(3) Identify the location of both the ash and clear areas.
(4) Stay focused.

Although hardly more technically sophisticated as rules than those given to postal service pilots of the 1930s, these rules reflected both caution on the part of the airline, and the relatively isolated nature of volcanoes in areas of Alaska and the Pacific Northwest. Curiously, the fourth point suggested that small teams worked better in responding to ash risks than larger groups. Although true from a group psychology standpoint, this reflected a technical approach to risks where identification and avoidance were the primary objectives. Similar work by the International Civil Aviation Organization (ICAO) starting in 1982 reflected these priorities in which identification and avoidance were the primary goals (Swanson and Streett, 2003).

The 2010 Icelandic eruptions were not entirely different in length and size of eruption than previous events, although there was relatively high silica content in the ash, which increased the risk of engine failure. The real problem was location, and the potential second- and third-order impacts that resulted from large-scale reactions. While avoidance of ash plumes was a workable solution to eruptions in less densely populated areas or regions where air travel is not so common, Europe relies heavily upon air travel and transport for tourism, military operations, business, and cargo. This reliance has increased significantly in recent years, with the UK reporting a four-fold increase in air passengers since 1980 (Greenair, 2009). The emergence of low-cost carriers in the late 1990s and shift from rail travel in some sectors left Europe particularly vulnerable to disruption in air travel, as substitute networks deteriorated in capacity.

What is striking is that such disruptions to air traffic within Europe were not without precedent, and yet the response was so poorly handled. The impacts from cancelled flights has been well documented over the years from a variety of causes ranging from the aftermath of the 9/11 attacks, to the periodic disruptions from labour strikes and bankrupted carriers. And yet, no contingency plans for large-scale cancellations from geo-physical events had been developed as part of the panoply of potentially large events to affect air traffic on a large scale, thus leaving travellers at the mercy of individual carriers, the carriers financially liable for otherwise insurable events, and alternative transportation systems overburdened (Castellano, Chapter 16)

Many of the affected sectors had not been consulted about safety issues earlier, as the risks associated with ash had been considered a technically isolated concern that was not assumed to warrant wider planning or preparation. There is little evidence that such scenarios had been considered by anyone outside a limited scientific community of volcanologists (Brooker, 2010). The lack of planning presented several notable conditions:

- *Public distrust over risk:* the lack of historical experience associated with infrequent, outlying environmental conditions. While disruptions may be acceptable when associated with risks of terrorism, the public had not been primed to consider volcanic risks a substantive concern. This might have led to an underestimation of related risks.
- *No consensus over values:* related to the above point, public discussion over potential impacts of long-term disruption to air travel was a necessary prior condition to determining where to place the weight in risk assessments. For instance, do we focus on absolute safety, or allow some risks in order to alleviate economic risks given the shaky financial conditions in the airline industry?
- *No redundant systems:* disruptions to air travel were considered isolated and infrequent, ultimately leading to systems unable to cope (insurance, alternative travel bookings) with the scale and longevity of the ash cloud risk. Advanced planning may have identified financial and transport mechanisms that would suitably address a similar situation, and identified key transport 'choke points' where more attention to pre-determining alternative travel routes is necessary.

It is possible to approach potential risks such as the volcanic eruptions from a scenario methodology, but proper integration with environmental risks requires further refining of the approaches. The following sections describe work that has been done to date on filling this gap.

11.2 SCENARIOS AND PLANNING

Scenario planning has been used for many years, beginning with the work of Herman Kahn and others at the RAND Corporation in the early Cold War years. Kahn was interested in creating more systematic and 'scientific' approaches to war-gaming, where decisions could be made in advance concerning potential contingencies and disasters. By constructing such war games in advance, policies could be constructed and officers trained to deal with a variety of situations, improving both preparation for conflict and the ability of officers to make decisions under conditions of uncertainty. Since the situations they would encounter would not be entirely new or unique to them, paralysis in decision-making could be avoided (Kahn and Weiner, 1967). In essence, the idea was to move beyond assumptions of 'business as usual' planning assumptions, where current conditions are simply projected into the future. A simple example is that if the weather has been calm and fair for the past 30 days, plan for much of the same in the future. Adaptive planning scenarios are meant to introduce uncertainty into planning for the unexpected.

These adaptive planning methods were adopted into standard pilot training in North America. Understanding that risk is not only a function of impact and probability, but also a function of uncertainty, a great deal of time is spent in pilot training dealing with events that may never happen. As one instructor's adage went, 'A superior pilot is one who uses his superior judgment to avoid situations requiring the use of his superior skills.' But when such situations do occur or are unavoidable, pilots cannot afford to hesitate or react improperly (Cohen et al., 2000). In many ways these approaches were quite the opposite of more formalized risk-assessment methodologies developed for engineering (or similar assessment in epidemiology), as they are focused on plausible events rather than on the probabilities associated with them. The focus tended to remain on the probability of a given situation to occur.

In the 1970s, scenario planners began to realize that a fundamental problem existed with the construction of such scenarios. In order to be used systematically, variations on conditions were introduced while keeping the 'environment' constant, a reference not to ecological conditions, but rather to the background assumptions that underlay other operations (DeWeerd, 1973). In the Cold War, for example, war-game scenarios simply assumed as a matter of course that any European conflicts would occur between

NATO and the Warsaw Pact, assumed that East and West Germany were divided, and assumed a particular order of battle, etc. By 1989, however, it became evident that the environment itself was changing as the political landscape of European security shifted with the fall of the Berlin Wall and subsequent collapse of the Soviet Union. How is operational and strategic planning possible under conditions of such great instability and uncertainty?

A group at Royal Dutch Shell, led by Pierre Wack, applied questions involving uncertainty, probability, risk mitigation and assessment to assumptions about investments and operations in the energy sector. In the early 1970s, all oil companies were investing heavily in new capacity and expanding operations. Such assumptions made sense under contemporary economic and political conditions, but what if, Wack asked, oil supplies were to become constrained? The rise of OPEC as a power bloc was a plausible scenario at the time, but it was ultimately an unknown risk that challenged assumptions of standard operations procedures among oil executives. It was not an easy process to shift assumptions about possible futures, but by engaging senior managers, rather than simply handing them a report warning of potential risks, they bought in the potential for environmental shifts (Wack, 1985).

By constructing a process whereby relatively unexamined assumptions about environmental conditions were challenged, Shell was able to reduce its vulnerabilities with respect to capital outlays, and was thus less negatively impacted by the oil shocks that did ultimately hit, and were ultimately better prepared to react when OPEC embargos were put into place (Wack, 1985). These were essentially Dickensian *Christmas Carol* scenarios: essentially, go over *past* operations, point out *current* conditions that are not well monitored, and describe what the *future* may well look like if nothing is done to prevent it. Imagery of potentially negative futures can be a strong motivator to avoid just such occurrences.

Yet visionary as Wack's work was, Shell (and subsequent work by Global Business Network – GBN – associates) diverged from Kahn's original desire to create a robust and methodologically sound process (Schwartz, 1991). Although suitable to business outlooks, Wack's approach was largely defined by a narrative style that had enormous difficulty integrating complex data or environmental conditions. The approach was intended to open up discussion for new ideas and ways of thinking, to examine assumptions of worldviews held by executives that could prevent effective planning. A number of complex issues, however, tend to go beyond cognitive boundaries, and involve the necessary inclusion of other experts and integration of their knowledge into potential scenarios. Environmental scenarios too often focus on tertiary issues of political response or technology, rather than the underlying assumptions of the system itself.

Partly, this is a cultural artefact of how we see environmental systems. People largely assume environmental conditions to be static and fairly predictable, while any changes are external events that work on the edges of important considerations of a scenario (Robison, 1994). For example, Booz Allen Hamilton designed scenarios for energy companies to address the impacts of global warming, but focused the scenarios on political forces and the possibilities of 'cap and trade' restrictions on carbon emissions. Although an important consideration for energy companies, changes in environmental conditions themselves were described as 'fairly gradual' and only had an impact because of pressures from environmentalists (Herman et al., 2008, pp. 138–41). Likewise, the SECURENV program in the European Union, intended to examine potential security vulnerabilities due to environmental change, tended to focus on the potential impacts of environmentally-related technological developments, rather than environmental changes themselves (https://www.securenv.eu/) In contrast, environmental security scenarios run with the US Department of Energy and US Department of Defense suggested that changing environmental conditions could negatively impact (at times quite severely) the technological systems and adaptation strategies of multiple systems (Briggs, 2009). It was too easy to focus on technologies instead of how vulnerable technologies are themselves.

A scenario with narrow focus is often the result of historical and experiential bias. Energy companies have experiences with fighting tax reform, while permanent environmental shifts that cripple production would be fairly novel. Likewise, airlines were aware of periodic risks to volcanic eruptions in places like south-east Asia and the Pacific Northwest of the US and Canada, but widespread and prolonged disruption of European air networks due to environmental factors was unknown. Even in the winter of 2010–11, European airports failed to anticipate potentially colder and wetter winters, resulting in airports in Paris and Berlin running out of deicing fluid (BBC, 2011; Chakraborty, 2011).

An additional and most significant obstacle has been the reliance upon linear thinking in planning scenarios. By 'linear' we refer to the assumptions that future change will be relatively gradual and will proceed from a fixed starting point. This allows the future to be considered relatively predictable, as future conditions will be very much like the present, only more so. Environmental futures have used linear models since at least the 1960s, with popular representations of population/resource lines depicted by Paul Ehrlich and the Club of Rome (although these ideas can be traced back to Thomas Malthus in the 1700s) (Hartmann, 1995, pp. 93–113). This is related to the earlier points raised concerning the environment as a static, external system, but is distinct in the sense that there persists a belief that trends move in one direction, toward a predictable point in the future; time and again such simplistic modelling has proven to be inadequate.

Capturing the complexity of cascading effects, where relevant risks are not those most directly observable, is admittedly difficult to put into practice. An example of this was the 2003 Schwartz and Randall report for the US Defense Department, entitled, *An Abrupt Climate Change Scenario and Its Implications for United States National Security* (Schwartz and Randall, 2003). Although the report garnered headlines for its emphasis of a topic that was largely silenced by the Bush Administration, its approach was largely linear, and had little ability to trace cascading impacts or feedback effects. Its approach to security was also quite narrow, resulting in a disconnect between physical plausibility and belief, and leaving the report open to criticism from the very scientists it referenced. In short, the report took summary climate change data, and applied it to existing threats and risks in a national security framework (i.e. risk of violent conflict, or what the military refers to as 'kinetic operations') under the assumption that simply adding more information to existing worldviews would be sufficient. Evidence suggests that applications such as these have been insufficient for most purposes, for although they highlight potential risks and environmental factors in a general sense, most planners are left wondering 'what now?'

11.3   NEW HORIZONS

In 2007, the US Department of Energy (DOE) created a new intelligence office devoted to assessing long-term risks from energy and environmental systems. The logic behind the effort was that waiting for conditions to change left no room for effective response, and that effective warning systems could help to increase resilience in the short and long term. Only by identifying risks in advance could adequate mitigation and adaptation measures be put into place. Rather than relying upon the standard strategic intelligence approach, which was to gather information in one central office for analysis by a select few, it was postulated that a distributed system could be created that engaged experts from different fields and in various geographic locations (GlobalEESE, 2007, Bray et al., 2009).

The intention of designing this different approach was to create an emergent early warning capability, which was the impetus for creation of the foresight project, Global Energy and Environmental Strategic Ecosystem (GlobalEESE), which went online in early 2009. The system relied upon interpreting 'weak signals' in a system, or the ability to detect patterns of emergent behaviour in a complex system that indicated the possibility of greater risks. Using weak signals takes information from one area of risk and applies it to similar vulnerabilities, as a structured way of asking 'what if this gets worse'? GlobalEESE relied on a risk framework discussion where evidence from one field (e.g. volcanology) could be interpreted and assessed by those dealing with the impacts (e.g. pilots) (Mead and Snider, 2011).

A challenge to implementing this process, however, was how to engage different fields of expertise in a meaningful way. It is easy enough to claim that 'silos must be broken' and to speak of interdisciplinarity, but in practice this rarely works effectively, even within single university campuses. DOE recognized that scientists did not want simply to hand over data and allow others to interpret their meaning, that researchers had a stake in their research and (like at universities) wished to remain involved in reviews and similar activities. Input from different fields could be invaluable in eliciting critical questions concerning scope and unexamined assumptions, but only if everyone were speaking within the same basic framework. A major problem with the 2003 Schwartz and Randall report was that neither security specialists nor climate scientists could recognize where their contributions could contribute to the larger debate – it was both a static 'deliverable' (not a process), and ultimately the relevant climate and security experts were isolated without a common risk/research framework.

The abrupt climate change team at DOE recognized this cognitive disconnect between critical expert fields, and as a result began development of a refined scenario process, with a focus on abrupt environmental changes and their security implications. Building on concepts of distributed knowledge and networks, the new process refined existing approaches, and created a multi-step assessment methodology for translating complex risks. Underlying the scenario process is the assumption that work should be transparent and participatory. Only by engaging relevant experts can potential surprises be found and identified in advance, and legitimacy of the process considered more acceptable by those involved.

The result of the disconnect within the risk and environmental security communities has been that the two steps (geophysical risks, impacts) described above have been largely approached as separate issues. Abrupt geophysical risks have been assessed in isolation to affected systems, resulting in a reactive risk response that does not address key vulnerabilities. Climate systems have been studied by various scientific fields, with little translation to regional and functional impacts until quite recently. Framing risk as a network stability issue can provide a common language for researchers and assessors from climate science, ecology, sociology, engineering, and other areas, who in a cooperative scenario assessment can provide 'peripheral' vision of previously unacknowledged risks. By mapping out boundaries of what is not known or recognized as a risk with a diverse network of experts, it is possible to avoid tunnel thinking that leaves key system components vulnerable (Briggs, 2009).

11.4 APPLICATION TO AIR TRANSPORT

Air transport consists of multiple-layered complex systems, which in the need to mitigate risk may create unacknowledged, cascading risks onto dependent systems. Although individual aircraft are themselves systems in need of risk assessment, they operate within larger systems that interact in sometimes unforeseen ways. By addressing plausible scenarios in advance, reactions can be better adjusted and certain resources mustered in advance. There are three techniques that can be used to identify and explore geophysical risks, particularly in air transport operations.

(1) The first is the use of scenario-creation workshops, a process designed by DOE/GlobalEESE to allow expert groups to create 'scenario clusters' of potential risks. By engaging a process where experts from different fields are forced to explore interconnections with various aspects of air transport (e.g. climatic or weather changes, energy shortages, design failures, government policies, disease outbreaks), experts can collectively create new clusters of potential risk scenarios that exist outside normal operations. Often these workshops are useful for creating stakeholder involvement and opening lines of communication between groups that normally would not sit at the same table (Wack's first stage). Our experience confirmed the argument that ideas for new scenarios can be drawn from the collective wisdom of groups. Individual scenarios can be drawn from the clusters and explored more fully through either war games or complex scenario development.

(2) War games are the technique used in the military to practice operations in a learning environment, and have been applied to commercial operations as well. Generally war games ask the question of how business-as-usual operations can continue given changes in either the operating environment or the behaviour of rival firms/militaries. A successful example of this, in the case of the 2010 eruptions in Iceland, was United Parcel Service (UPS). UPS had previously undertaken a war-game scenario which involved asking how it could continue operating should an outbreak of avian influenza shut down airport access in Europe. When the eruption occurred in 2010, there

was enough institutional memory to draw upon the obvious connections between the two events and enabled UPS to draw upon the lessons learned during their war-gaming experience. By successfully finding alternatives to an event analogous to the war game, the institutional learning from this exercise provided UPS decision-makers with the tools to mitigate what would have otherwise resulted in significant financial losses. UPS rerouted its flights to Turkey, and then distributed its packages to mainland Europe via road and rail connections (Schwartz and Babington, 2010). The US Air Force is now inserting 'layers' of environmental change into its war games, in order to examine how shifts in energy and environmental security risks affect its operations and strategic planning.

(3) Complex scenarios are meant to examine the longer-term implications of environmental or energy changes across complex systems. As war games are necessarily constrained in scope, they cannot explore cascading effects, including reactions of associated groups and feedback effects. The GlobalEESE abrupt climate change team had to face the challenge of assessing geophysical risks where probabilities could not be established, regional impacts where models alone could not provide adequate resolution, response of multiple groups and systems (regarding social, economic and environmental factors) to events they had not experienced before, and the need to scale back to a global level to examine global impacts from regional risks. In the 2010 volcanic eruption case, this would have meant moving beyond the experience of UPS alone, to tracing the complex economic impacts from the disruption of European air transport.

Another complex scenario could be initiated taking into account shifting climatic conditions in Europe, and the potential risks of increased variability/severity of winter storms to airport infrastructure and operations. The complex scenarios allow greater visibility of 'peripheral risks', where events or conditions occur outside of the normal field of view or monitoring systems. However, complex scenarios require a two-step process of expert engagement, and require the use of communication channels outside normal organizations.

The first step, which itself is still being refined in cooperation with climate scientists and the IPCC, is to take a multidimensional approach to environmental futures and scenarios. In contrast to the opaque approach of most environmental change scenarios (including the IPCC), interactions of variables can be mapped out, establishing what the boundaries of the system are, and finding optimum distance between potential phase states of a complex system. Certain factors could be established as too unlikely or implausible, while other risks could be identified as potential outcomes to keep within ones vision for the future (Carlsen, 2009).

The same method can be applied to environmental systems, in general, and simplified versions (usually three-dimensional) can be useful for training purposes. The task is to see if potential environmental changes may occur in a given geographical region, particularly ones where little research has been done previously or where little monitoring exists. Volcanic eruptions are relatively simple to include in such scenarios, but complex interactions in environmental systems, such as acutely severe winters in Europe, are far more difficult. In fact, the winter disruptions to air travel in 2010–11 are an example of where establishing linear trends (warming air) can blind planners to extreme variability.

Under greater complex systemic risk situations, potential geophysical changes must be transferred to an interactive network analysis, which visually maps out first, second and third order impacts (Horizon 1–3), reactions, and feedback loops. This step involves input from a diverse set of experts working either together or remotely, who identify relationships between impacts, and from these interactions can identify critical nodes. In network analyses, critical nodes are those areas where failure of one component seriously undermines overall function of the system, and where alternative relationships are not possible. These nodes can represent either key pieces of equipment in a system (e.g. vulnerable fan blades from jet engines), critical members of a society, communication nodes, transport routes, etc. By identifying these nodes in advance, redundant systems can be developed or greater monitoring/protection can be put into place. Similar systems engineering approaches are used in complex operations, and USAF has used such assessment teams in assessing potential equipment failures to the B-2 bomber, for example (Briggs, 2010).

The other advantage of recognizing the existence of and designing planning around complex systems is that, like the smaller scenario creation workshops, lines of communication are already established with groups that will need to be engaged should disaster strike. And by identifying risks in advance, it creates stakeholder involvement at an earlier stage, allowing for the realization that a volcanic eruption in Iceland involves not only aeronautical engineers and pilots, but rail operators, insurance executives, and Dutch flower merchants.

This advance communication is crucial not only for technical resolution of how to maintain air and related operations, but to allow discussion of associated values and normative dimensions of the risks themselves. In advance of the Icelandic eruption in 2010, this would have allowed prior debate on questions concerning:

- Is it more valuable to protect lives or to maintain economic viability of the airlines?
- What responsibilities do airline and insurance companies have toward travellers?
- What responsibilities do other transport sectors (road, rail, sea) have to assist?
- Are regulations necessary to ensure that redundant transport systems exist efficiently and fairly?

USAF is implementing further development of such risk-scenario methodologies under the Minerva programme, with the intent of providing greater foresight and planning capabilities for both its airmen and planning staff. Inclusion of geophysical risks into operational and strategic planning can be done with the correct risk frameworks, and can avoid costly, *ad hoc* reactions to problems that might otherwise have been dealt with proactively in the future.

11.5 CONCLUSION

Although application of scenario methods is not a cure-all to potential risks, they do provide valuable tools for addressing risks in advance of their emergence. Risk regulations, whether formal or informal, are often based upon past experience and the hope that future risks can be mitigated. But in the case of risks that have never occurred before, and in a world where both complex, vulnerable systems expand and environmental conditions increasingly shift, new planning techniques may be required. The past may not be prologue, as things that have never happened before happen every day.

BIBLIOGRAPHY

BBC News (2011), 'EU Demands Airports Get Ready for Winter', http://www.bbc.co.uk/news/world-europe-12229735 (accessed 20 January 2011).

Boeing Aero, No. 9. January 2000, http://www.boeing.com/commercial/aero magazine/aero_09/volcanic_story.html (accessed 20 February 2011).

Bray, D., S. Costigan, K. A. Daum, H. Lavoix, E. L. Malone, C. Pallaris (2009), 'Cultivating Strategic Foresight for Energy and Environmental Security', *Environmental Practice*, **11**(3), 209–11.

Briggs, C. (2009), Environmental Security, Strategic Intelligence and Abrupt Climate Change. *US Department of Energy briefing paper*, May 2009.

Briggs, C. (2010), 'Environmental Change, Strategic Foresight, and Impacts on Military Power', *Parameters*, **40**(4), 1–15.

Brooker, P. (2010), 'Fear in a Handful of Dust: Aviation and the Icelandic Volcano', *Significance*, 7(4), 112–5.

Carlsen, H. (2009), 'Climate Change and the Construction of Scenario Sets that Span the Range of Societal Uncertainties', Paper presented at the annual meeting of the ISA's 50th Annual Convention 'Exploring the Past, Anticipating the Future', New York, NY, 16 February 2009, http://www.allacademic.com/meta/p313532_index.html (accessed 20 February 2011).

Chakraborty, S. (2011), '2010 Meltdown –Airport Closure Risk Communications in London and NYC', *European Journal of Risk Regulation*, 2 (1), 108–10.

Cohen, M. S., L. Adelman, and B. B. Thompson (2000), 'Experimental Investigation of Uncertainty, Stakes, and Time in Pilot Decision Making', Report prepared for NASA Ames Research Center, Contract NAS2–14075.

DeWeerd, H. A. (1973), *A Contextual Approach to Scenario Construction*. Santa Monica, CA: RAND Corporation, (P-5084).

GlobalEESE (2007), 'Enabling Strategic Intelligence on Energy and Environmental Security Impacts and Consequences', Summary report of the Glasgow Group, October 2007 available at www.climateactionproject.com/docs/GlasgowFinal.pdf (accessed 20 September 2010).

Greenair, UK statistics report a quadrupling of passengers and trebling of aviation emissions since 1980, 24 February 2009, http://www.greenaironline.com/news.php?viewStory=381 (accessed 20 February 2011).

Hartmann, B. (1995), *Reproductive Rights and Wrongs: The Global Politics of Population Control*, Boston: West End Press.

Herman, M., M. Frost, and R. Kurz (2008), *Wargaming for Leaders: Strategic Decision Making from the Battlefield to the Boardroom*, New Tork: McGraw-Hill. 138–41.

The Independent (2010), 'RAF Grounds Fighter Jets after Volcanic Dust is Found in Engines', 23 April 2010, http://www.independent.co.uk/news/uk/home-news/raf-grounds-fighter-jets-after-volcanic-dust-is-found-in-engines-1951953.html (accessed 20 February 2011).

Kahn, H. and A. J. Wiener (1967), 'The Next Thirty-Three Years: A Framework for Speculation', *Daedalus*, 96 (3), 705–32.

Lagadec, P. (2005), 'Understanding the French 2003 Heat Wave Experience: Beyond the Heat, a Multi-Layered Challenge', *Journal of Contingencies and Crisis Management*, 12 (4), 160–69.

March, J. G. (1988), 'Bounded Rationality, Ambiguity, and the Engineering of Choice', in J. March (ed.), *Decisions and Organizations*, Oxford: Blackwell Publishing, 266–93.

Masys, A. J. (2004), 'Aviation Accident aetiology: Catastrophe Theory Perspective', *Disaster Prevention and Management*, 13 (1), 33–8.

Mead, C. and A. Snider (2011), 'Why the CIA is Spying on a Changing Climate', McClatchy, 10 January 2011, http://www.mcclatchydc.com/ 2011/01/10/106406/why-the-cia-is-spying-on-a-changing.html (accessed 20 February 2011).

Petersen, G. N. (2010), 'A Short Meteorological Overview of the Eyjafjallajökull Eruption 14 April–23 May 2010', *Weather (Royal Meteorological Society)*, 65 (8), 203–7.

Robison, W. (1994), *Decisions in Doubt: The Environment and Public Policy*, Dartmouth: University Press of New England.

Sacchetti, D. (2008), 'Earth, Wind and Fire. Preparing Nuclear Power Plants for Nature's Fury', *IAEA Bulletin*, **50**(1), http://www.iaea.org/Publications/Magazines/Bulletin/Bull501/Earth_Wind_Fire.html (accessed 20 February 2011).

Schwartz, P. (1991), *Art of the Long View*, New York: Doubleday.

Schwartz, P. and D. Babington (2010), 'Getting Ahead of the Curve in a World of Cascading Crises', *Technology Review*, December 2010, http://www.techreview.com/printer_friendly_article.aspx?id=26797 (accessed 20 February 2011).

Schwartz, P. and D. Randall (2003), 'An Abrupt Climate Change Scenario and Its Implications for United States National Security', *Global Business Network report*, http://www.gbn.com/articles/pdfs/Abrupt%20Climate%20Change%20February%202004.pdf (accessed 20 February 2011).

Shrader-Frechette, K. S. (1985), *Science Policy, Ethics, and Economic Methodology: Some Problems of Technology Assessment and Environmental Impact Analysis*, Dordrecht: D. Reidel Publishers.

Swanson, G. and D. Streett (2003), 'Ultimate Goal of Volcano Watch is Complete Avoidance of Ash Encounters', *ICAO Journal*. **58** (2), 10–12.

Wack, P. (1985), 'Scenarios: Shooting the Rapids', *Harvard Business Review* **63** (6), 139–50.

Wang, W., J. Loman, P. Vassiliou (2004), 'Reliability Importance of Components in a Complex System', *Reliability and Maintainability*, 2004 Annual Symposium, RAMS, 6–11.

Wilkinson, P. J. and T. P. Kelly (1998), 'Functional Hazard Analysis for Highly Integrated Aerospace Systems', *Certification of Ground/Air Systems Seminar* (Ref. No. 1998/255), IEE, 4/1–4/6.

Willsky, A. S. (1976), 'A Survey of Design Methods for Failure Detection in Dynamic Systems', *Automatica*, **12** (6), 601–11.

12. Systemic risks and the reformation of European Union law concerning network industries

Francisco B. López-Jurado[*]

12.1 INTRODUCTION

The volcanic ash crisis and the structural measures proposed by the European Commission when the calm came after the storm stress an important characteristic of air transport: its vulnerability to systemic risks. That feature is common to other network industries providing services of general economic interest such as electricity and gas. European Union law concerning network industries has focused on facilitating competition while achieving effectiveness and high levels of performance. Those provisions are changing the structure of the industries and as a side-effect their exposure to systemic risks. This chapter explores some common characteristics shared by network industries, and how the recent regulatory restructure of those industries affects their exposure to systemic risks. The need for an increase in the robustness and resilience of those industries recommend the approval and implementation of adequate regulatory provisions aimed to fill the gap between the new structures and the old security of supply approach, specially in the field of 'emergency risk regulation' as defined by Alemanno in the Introduction to this book. The volcanic ash crisis operated as a wake-up call stressing the need to review, under a systemic risks-prevention and management perspective, EU law related to network industries.

12.2 AIR TRAFFIC, ELECTRICITY AND NATURAL GAS AS NETWORK INDUSTRIES: COMMON FEATURES

12.2.1 Network-based Industries

The concept of network industry or network-based industry is not a legal concept. It refers to branches of the economy providing services when:

(1) the end supply relies upon a network, (2) the networks or some of its parts are natural monopolies, and (3) services provided by the industry are potentially competitive. Network industries provide some of the most important services of general economic interest such as transport, postal services, energy and communications (EU Commission 2004, 2003, n. 17). The expression 'services of general economic interest' can be found in the Treaty on the Functioning of the European Union (TFEU) articles 14 and 106.2, and in secondary EU legislation. Yet EU law does not foresee any definition of it. Nevertheless in EU practice there is a broad agreement that such concept refers to services of an economic nature subject to specific public service obligations by virtue of a general interest criterion. Public service obligations can be considered specific requirements imposed by public authorities on the providers of the services in order to ensure that certain public interest objectives are met (EU Commission 2004, 2003, n. 17). Examples of public service obligations are: universal service, continuity, quality of service, affordability, and consumer protection.

Network industries are subject to specific regulation in order to introduce and preserve competition as well as guarantee the fulfillment of a common set of public service obligations. It is not always easy to harmonize the imposition of public service obligations with the rules on competition. Article 106.2 TFEU (previously 86.2 of the Treaty European Community), as construed by the Court of Justice of the EU in its case-law (see Lopez-Jurado, 2009, pp. 789–91), constitutes the normative base that should permit harmonization. The services of general economic interest also occupy a special place in the shared values of the EU and have an important role in promoting social and territorial cohesion as article 14 TFEU provides '... A high level of quality, safety and affordability, equal treatment and the promotion of universal access and of user rights' are part of those shared values of the EU' (see article 1 of Protocol to the Treaties on European Union, no. 26 on 'Services of General Interest').

Air transport, electricity and natural gas are network industries highly dependent on network infrastructure: nodes and edges. From the point of view of European Union law, those industries should be considered as performing services of general economic interest. Their regulatory situation was described by the EU Commission (2007, p. 4) as follows:

> the provision and organisation of these services are subject to internal market and competition rules of the EC Treaty [now TFUE] since their activities are economic in nature. In the case of large network industries having a clear European-wide dimension, such as telecommunications, electricity, gas, transport and postal services, the services are regulated by a specific EU legislative framework.

The institutional reform of the EU due to the Lisbon Treaty (2007–09) enhances the powers of the EU institutions regarding some important network industries such as electricity and natural gas. Energy and transport are considered areas of shared competence (article 4.2 g) and i) in relation to article 2.2 TFEU) between the Union and the member states. Both are subject to specific provisions under articles 100.2 (air transport) and 194 (energy) of the TFEU. According to those articles the European Parliament and the Council, acting in accordance with the ordinary legislative procedure, after consulting the Economic and Social Committee and the Committee of the Regions, shall establish the measures necessary to achieve the objectives of Union policy on energy established in article 194 paragraph 1 and may lay down, according to article 100. 2, appropriate provisions for air transport.

12.2.2 Natural Monopolies

Network industries performing services of general economic interest carry out economic activities for the public, subject to public service obligations. To fulfill their duties those industries require a network infrastructure, some of its elements coincide with natural monopolies. Artificial monopolies can be considered a barrier to entry into a market imposed or enforced by regulators; natural monopolies, on the other hand, exist when the most efficient mechanism for providing a service or for performing a commercial activity is achieved by the existence of a single firm in the market, i.e. a monopoly (see Kahn [1971] 1998, p. 117). As Alfred E. Kahn suggested, the potential economies of scale are so great that only a single firm, capable of supplying the entire market, can take the fullest possible advantage of them. According to Christopher D. Foster (1992, pp. 19, 23–4), the origin of the idea of natural monopoly is linked with nineteenth century British railway regulation. As he explains, at the time geographical reasons, the need to get a bill and raise substantial capital, were important barriers to entry. Duplication of the incumbent facilities was then and is now – almost 200 years later – an unrealistic alternative, because competition in provision of network services entails grossly inefficient duplication of facilities (Laporta and Moselle ,1999, p. 455). Where a natural monopoly exists, and there will always remain an unavoidable element of natural monopoly in some industries (Foster, 1992, p. 187), effective regulation is necessary to make competition possible by bettering the conditions for access to the networks. Energy grids as well as air traffic control are examples of natural monopolies in the sense described. The presence of a natural monopoly beyond its economic consequences affects the vulnerability of the whole industry to systemic risks.

12.2.3 Common Patterns of Regulatory Restructure

Common features shared by network industries performing the above mentioned services determine the existence of common regulatory characteristics. Those industries were subject to and are still undergoing a deep regulatory restructure. The liberalization of European network industries, whatever its effective outcomes has been, has followed some common patterns suggested by Mehmet Ugur (2009, p. 3): (1) unbundling of upstream and downstream operators, necessary to prevent cross-subsidization and to reduce the ability of incumbents to control markets, (2) non-discriminatory third-party access to networks, to make market contestability through new entry possible, (3) supply of transparent information on access charges and tariffs, necessary to prevent discrimination against new entrants.

Third-party access, common carriage impositions, an adequate public price policy for the use of the networks, independent regulators, unbundling, etc. are well-known mechanisms, to cope with the limits that natural monopoly poses over competition in sectors such as energy supply, transport, postal services or communications. The idea of essential facilities, itself subject to controversy,[1] has its origin in the same phenomenon: the existence of economical, technological, geographical, or environmental factors that make the proliferation of key installations, usually networks with their nodes and edges, unreasonable. Those unavoidable factors are relevant for economic regulation and for regulation aimed to prevent or manage systemic risks. The economic regulation passed to cope with those factors changes the structure of the industries and, at the same time, modifies its exposure to systemic risks.

12.3 SYSTEMIC RISK

12.3.1 Concept of Systemic Risk

The field of financial regulation has nourished several definitions of systemic risk. A common factor in those various definitions is, as Steven L. Schwarcz (2008, pp. 198 and 204) suggests, 'that a trigger event, such as an economic shock or institutional failure, causes a chain of bad economic consequences – sometimes referred to as a domino effect. These consequences could include (a chain of) financial institution and/or market failures.'

The concept of 'systemic risk' rapidly exceeded the boundaries of the financial sector, as a 'side-effect' of globalization,[2] or as an intrinsic consequence of the multiplication of highly complex interconnected systems.[3] Nevertheless, the concept should be applied to different fields with some degree of precaution.

According to Kaufman and Scott (2003, pp. 371–2) the contrast between the probabilities of an individual component breakdown and that of an entire system is made evident by the co-movements (correlation) amongst most if not all parts; this is at the heart of systemic risk. As George G. Kaufman (1995, p. 47) previously suggested, systemic risk is therefore the risk of a chain reaction, like that of falling interconnected dominos.

In the characterization of Duncan Watts (2009, p. 16), systemic risk results from the unpredictable interplay of various parts in the system but is not related in any simple way to the risk profiles of the system's parts. His example for electricity supply illustrates such interplay.

> In 1996 a single power-line failure in Oregon led to a massive cascade of power outages that spread across all the states west of the Rocky Mountains, leaving tens of millions of people without electricity ... Engineers can reliably assess the risk that any single power generator in the network will fail under some given set of conditions. But once a cascade starts, they can no longer know what those conditions will be for each generator – because conditions could change dramatically depending on what else happens in the network. (Watts, 2009, p. 16)

Similar cascades of negative effects and interplays were present in the January 2009 gas supply disruption to Europe, and in the 2010 volcanic ash crisis.

Some systems are more complex than others; some rely more on technical assets (nodes, edges, grids, different kinds of facilities), and the risk-transmission mechanisms differ from one system to another. However, amongst all systems a common ground of analysis exists. In all cases of systemic risk the fundamental problem is the same. According to Watts (2009, p. 16) risk managers (regulators, CEOs, etc.) are only able to assess their own institutions' exposure on the assumption that conditions in other parts of the system remain predictable, but in a crisis these conditions change unpredictably. Emergency regulation encompasses regulatory actions undertaken in the immediacy of a disaster in order to mitigate its impact (see Alemanno in the Introduction to this book). The systemic nature of a crisis influences the three-part characterization (sudden, significant and natural) of such events and should be taken into account by regulators in their attempt to reduce the severity of such disasters.

12.3.2 Behavioural and Structural Factors

Three circumstances influence the emergence and contagion of systemic risks: social contagion, some kind of tragedy of the commons and structural factors such as the interconnection needed to create a system.

Social contagion has been described by Watts (2004, p. 260) as a contagion that applies to a class of models that deal with collective decision-making: 'The aggregation of individual to collective decision making can be understood in terms of social contagion, where decisions are "transmitted" from one individual to another in a manner reminiscent of disease'. Social contagion flows through social networks and is important for financial system dynamics, because as Hammond (2009, p. 5) affirms individual decision-makers pay attention to the actions, decisions, and even beliefs of others to whom they are socially related. In network industries such as air transport, electricity or natural gas, social contagion is less relevant because the decision-making process is much more centralized. Public authorities can also be subject of contagion. As the volcano ash crisis shows vividly, no public authority would depart from the ICAO (2009–10) guidelines unless a common decision was taken by the public authorities of all or most of the states involved in the crisis (Alemanno, Chapter 1). The coordinated departure from ICAO guidelines was a response to the public authorities' contagion due to the initial zero-risk threshold suggested by those guidelines.[4]

A tragedy of the commons affects the financial system but also displays influence over network industries. We face a tragedy of the commons as Schwarcz (2008, pp. 198, 206 and 238) suggests when no individual market participant has sufficient incentive, and when there is an absence of regulation to limit its risk-taking, in order to reduce the systemic danger to other participants or third parties. According to Beville (2009, p. 246) in the financial system firms tend to price only internal costs and benefits and not risks to the entire system; therefore, individual firms find it profitable to take on more risk and leverage than is socially optimal. That kind of tragedy of the commons is at the heart of the emergence of a crisis and also influences the way systemic risk crisis propagate.[5] Creating the right incentives to limit risk-taking is relevant for financial welfare and for security of supply in network industries; as well as for emergency risk-regulation. For example, it is important in order to put in place regulatory measures to maintain the investments needed for an adequate development of the transmission and distribution grids in electricity and gas industries; as it is to lay down common rules on air traffic flow to manage the restrictions in the availability of routes and airspace due to critical events.

However the structure of the system determines the way systemic risks emerge and propagate and has a decisive impact on network-based industries. Physical, technological, geographical, economic and legal conditions of the networks are decisive in the way systemic risk appears within network industries. The presence of natural monopolies and key facilities, the role played by regulatory oversight bodies in the decision-making processes and the regulation applicable to introduce competition, give a specific weight to the structural element in the analysis of systemic risk applicable to network industries.

12.3.3   External Threats, Internal Structures

The vulnerability of air transport, energy supply, public health, the financial system, the environment, etc., depend on the nature of the menace as well as on the features of the phenomenon, activities and interests to be protected. Both aspects are intrinsically encroached.[6] With network industries the systemic dimension of risk depends more on the intrinsic features of the threatened phenomenon than on the source of probable harm. The network structure catalyzes external factors in action making possible the chain of adverse effects that are at the core of what are considered systemic risks.

The sources of threat for network industries vary in nature and consequences; in addition, some are better known than others. New forms of threat develop throughout the years. Long-time latent risks suddenly become actual threats as the volcanic ash crisis shows vividly.[7] Terrorists look for new ways of damaging the society as a whole.

The difference between well-known and less well-known risks is an important issue for regulation. Public authorities should, through regulation, prevent well-known risks, if these are evitable. The lack of effective regulation by well-known avoidable risks can have specific consequences in the field of liability. Highly unpredictable sources of risk recall the application of the controversial precautionary principle that, in its strongest versions, is considered by Sunstein (2006, pp. 853 and 856) to offer little guidance and could lead to expensive regulations with unfortunate distributional effects. To focus the risk regulation on the source of risk is most of the time necessary, but it should not diminish the importance of risk regulation centred on the intrinsic characteristics present in the phenomenon at risk. Goldin and Vogel (2010, p. 5) see systemic risk as a whole 'as reflecting endogenous structural weakness that can be predicted and better understood through network theory'.

The dynamics of contagion of systemic risks across a network as well as the extent of the damage can be, according to Hammond (2009, p. 5), strongly shaped by the network's structure. The networks are indispensable to the performance of the services involved, they are also the chains used by shocks to expand and propagate the damage. The intrinsic features of the threatened systems nourish the probabilities and the extent of harm. The regulatory response to systemic risks cannot avoid giving a hard look at the characteristics of the industry. Those features are highly dependent from the regulatory processes that air transport, electricity and natural gas industries are undergoing in order to create a Single European Sky for air transport and an Internal Energy Market for electricity and for gas.

12.4 THE REFORMATION OF EU LAW CONCERNING ENERGY AND AIR TRANSPORT

12.4.1 The Internal Energy Market for Electricity and Natural Gas

For the past 20 years the European Communities, Community and now Union have developed prolonged and intense efforts to introduce competition in energy markets, particularly in electricity and natural gas. A breakdown of national monopolies, to open up member state borders, and by that creating an effective internal energy market, has been the focus of the Commission's proposals since 1988. Creating well-functioning natural gas and electricity markets in Europe would augment European competitiveness in an increasingly globalized and delocalized world. Although the powers of European institutions in the energy sector are limited, three important legislative packages[8] have been adopted in order to achieve competitive, secure and environmentally sustainable markets for natural gas and electricity.

The latter package (Third Energy Package)[9] encompasses measures aimed to support successful liberalization by a profound restructure of the industries. The attaining of a fully interconnected European energy network is a need for an effective internal energy market. The provisions related to trans-European networks in the treaties (now articles 170–172 TFEU) made additional actions possible from the EU in order to promote interconnections in the areas of transport, telecommunications and energy infrastructures.[10] The combined effect of the Third Energy Package and the provisions stated to promote interconnections are drastically changing and will increasingly modify those industries. European electricity and natural gas industries, as heavy regulated sectors, undergo a deep liberalization programme that includes as Joskow (2009, p. xvi) suggests: industry restructuring along both horizontal and vertical dimensions and deep regulatory reform. Such a major shift has consequences for the exposure of the affected industries to systemic risks. One of the problems is that safeguard and security of supply provisions are still centred on the avoidance of individual risks by the member states and lack of a systemic risk perspective.

Besides the internal market and the cross-border provisions of the Third Energy Package, two specific directives were passed to face security of supply.[11] The scope of both directives is to establish measures to safeguard adequate levels of security of supply, which includes in the case of electricity an adequate level of generation capacity, an adequate balance between supply and demand, and an appropriate level of interconnection between member states. However both directives adopt a predominant non-systemic perspective, mainly centred on member states' decisions as if electricity and natural gas industries were only slightly connected. On the other hand, the Third Energy Package includes decisive measures in order to improve market integration, cross-border exchanges, and EU dimension of both natural gas and electricity industries. The gap between those two regulatory frameworks reduces the capacity of public authorities to respond to the challenges posed by systemic risk.

The insufficiency of those provisions and the need to adopt a systemic perspective within EU law concerning the security of energy supply was made clear by the January 2009 gas supply disruption to Europe.[12] Recent proposals concerning measures to safeguard security of natural gas supply,[13] made in the aftermath of that crisis, follow a more systemic path in response to major supply disruptions. The proposal includes provisions such as: (1) competence of the Commission to coordinate capable national authorities at the EU level, (2) establishment of preventive action plans and of emergency plans at national or regional level (the Commission has the power to amend those plans), (3) the Commission can declare community emergencies that temporarily increases its executive powers.

12.4.2 The Single European Sky

Four basic EC regulations concerning air traffic flow management, interoperability, air navigation services and a framework regulation were approved in 2004.[14] Those regulations are known as the Single European Sky (SES) package. The SES initiative was aimed at enhancing safety and efficiency of air transport in Europe, improving services and reducing costs by lessening fragmentation of the air traffic management and decreasing delays by improving the use of limited airspace and airport resources. The Commission (2008, 1) and Eurocontrol (2010) considered that the SES package had not delivered the expected results in important areas such as, for example, the efficiency of the design and use of the European air network. A second legislative package known as Single Sky Package (SES II) was adopted in order to sharpen the regulatory tools already in place and to face environmental challenges such as the reductions of noise and emissions by rationalizing the routes and optimizing the flight profiles (Alemanno, Chapter 1).[15]

Similar to the energy legislative packages, the SES packages affect the industry by reshaping many aspects of how the different services within air traffic are performed, but are not directly aimed at air safety. Those provisions have an air safety dimension and affect air safety by restructuring the industry and, thus, by changing its vulnerability to systemic risks. An example is the promotion of the integration of airspace in Functional Airspace Blocks (FAB).[16] By defragmenting the actual EU airspace, the nine FAB should allow substantial economies of scale. At the same time, changing the level of fragmentation has consequences for exposure to systemic risk: it facilitates crisis spreading but it also supports a coordinated reply when crisis emerge. By extending the competence of the European Aviation Safety Agency (EASA) to key safety fields of air traffic management and air navigation services, SES II makes possible a more integrated response to crisis emerging from systemic risks.

12.5 INCREASING ROBUSTNESS AND RESILIENCE

Robustness is considered the ability of a system to continue working even when some of its parts fail to perform their tasks or are damaged. Resilience as Hammond (2009, pp. 1 and 5) considers it, is the ability of a system to restore functionality after suffering damages. It is a kind of 'self-healing' adaptation that permits quick recovery. Better interconnections should increase the strength of a system as a whole as the electricity or natural gas industries show vividly. But as Goldin and Vogel (2010, p. 5) suggest, connectivity can also amplify and spread risk instead of sharing it; at the same time, greater connectivity decrease individual risk but increase the severity of systemic risks. However, improving the number and capacity of nodes and edges (links between nodes within a network) of a previously connected system augments its capacity to endure severe crisis if the right fire-walls are in place. In that sense, better connectivity increases the robustness of a system.

The Third Energy Package and the Single Sky Package (SES) II provide measures to augment the connectivity of energy and air transport industries giving a new dimension to industries that have had a predominant

national character. Network industries providing services of general economic interest are, as previously seen, facility dependent so that the risks
they are exposed to should not be as complex as those of the financial
system that is global in some of its elements. However some of the risks
affecting network industries are also systemic and crises involving systemic
risks are by definition difficult to confine to a specific country or region.
The 2010 volcanic ash crisis and the 2009 disruption of gas supply to
Europe pointed this out. The scope of systemic crisis is not necessarily
determined by national boundaries, and is usually not confined to those
limits.

Decision-making in the financial system is highly dispersed and decen-
tralized. Regulatory oversight was traditionally seen as an external framework for the development of individual or entrepreneurial freedom.
Markets would correct wrong decisions. But as Watts (2009, p. 16) states,
the present financial crisis has made visible that 'markets do not automatically control systemic risk, any more than they automatically create competition'. Even though, the status of regulators within the financial system
differs from the position of public authorities by network industries performing services of general economic interest such as air transport, electricity or gas, the latter has been from its origin subject to a heavy regulation
due to the characteristics of the services involved and to the social impact
of those services. Therefore the decision-making, key to cope with systemic
crisis affecting network industries, relies on public authorities from different levels (local, regional, national, supranational). To be effective, the
response to systemic crisis has to be adequate to the dimension of the crisis,
making it necessary to coordinate authorities or to empower supranational
authorities.

The Third Energy Package, although it augments the competences of the
Commission and creates an Agency for the Cooperation of Energy Regulators, fails to cope with those new challenges. It tries to restructure the
industries, changing drastically the exposure to systemic risks but does not
encompass the right allocation of competencies in case of crisis. Nor does it
provide the establishment of plans for preventive action and emergency
situations. The Directives aimed to deal with the security of supply also
respond to an insufficient non-systemic perspective, as previously shown.

The SES II legislative package includes provisions mainly aimed at
increasing flight efficiency, environment protection and cost-efficiency. But
provisions aimed at improving air safety, a quick and adequate reaction to
the emergence of crisis with a systemic component are also present in the
SES II. Those 'emergency risk regulatory provisions' are, for example: the
EASA's competences in air traffic safety to ensure the safety oversight of
the European network in support of the network manager and the creation

of a crisis coordination cell able to react in case of sudden crisis and take appropriate initiatives. Some of the most important regulatory measures recommended just after the 2010 volcanic ash crisis were already foreseen in SES II but not yet implemented.[17] The rationale of economic efficiency and risk prevention perspective encroach as the crisis made salient. On the other hand, building alternative key facilities, such as power or gas grids, could increase the robustness of the system under a risk-mitigating perspective, but could be economically inefficient. Increasing the integration of functional airspace blocks can have divergent effects: it can facilitate the spreading of a crisis as well as making possible an adequate management of the crisis.

In this context, the volcanic ash crisis has operated as a 'wake-up call'. To create the political momentum for the acceleration of the full implementation of the SES is one of the most important consequences of the 2010 crisis, as Alberto Alemanno emphasizes in his chapter. In particular, the crisis showed the need for the introduction and implementation of clear and effective integrated risk-management regulatory tools in air transport. Other network industries affected by the same kind of vulnerability should follow the same path. Those tools, some of them already present in the regulatory packages of the EU, should be adjusted and implemented in the near future.

12.6 STRENGTHENING THE EUROPEAN DIMENSION

With the evolution of network industries due to regulation and technological development, the European dimension is becoming more and more important. It also justifies a greater involvement of the EU institutions, in particular the Commission. Major changes in the industries involved should lead to readapt the competences of the different public authorities. The principles of subsidiarity and proportionality can be construed to uphold that conclusion.[18] The increased powers of EU institutions in these fields enable them to be more ambitious in the search for an integrated regulatory response to economic and social challenges, including those derived from the presence of risk.

12.7 CONCLUSION

The regulation of network industries providing services of general economic interest deeply shapes the structure of the sectors involved. The same factors determining the existence of natural monopolies augment the vulnerability of those industries to systemic risk. An integrated risk-management perspective is called upon to heavily and increasingly influence the network industries' regulation in a more integrated regulatory approach. The characterization of systemic crisis emphasizes the need for an emergency risk regulation adequate to mitigate its impact. Risk perception has changed as more interconnection can determine more capacity of risk to spread; external factors out of the control of national authorities recommend a supranational approach. The new institutional framework of the EU makes possible a more daring approach to systemic risk prevention.

The volcanic ash crisis as well as the previous gas supply disruption increase the visibility of systemic risks affecting network industries and impose the need for an integrated regulatory approach. Such a regulatory shift should include mechanisms of response adopted by authorities at the adequate level to cope with supranational threats. For air transport regulation as well as for energy regulation, the legal provisions establishing the structure of the industry and the powers conferred to regulators influence not only how the industry behaves and performs its services, but also affects its strength to cope with systemic risks. The balkanized structure of EU law concerning air transport and energy, in addition to the balance of power between EU institutions and the member states, should be reexamined in order to provide better responses to systemic risks affecting network industries.

NOTES

*   Research Project DER 2008–4154/JURI *Governance and Risk Management Administrative Procedures* funded by the Spanish Ministry for Science and Innovation.

1. The scope and limits of the doctrine of essential facilities is analyzed by Cocker (2005, p. 242). For the import of the essential facilities doctrine by the Court of Justice of the EU, see Villar (2004, pp. 44–77) and Evrard (2004, p. 491).

2. As Goldin and Vogel (2010, p. 5) suggest. See also OECD (2003, pp. 30–47) with a wide idea of systemic risk as hazards or potential damages to and vulnerability of vital systems such as health services, transport, energy, food and water supplies, on which highly organized modern societies increasingly depend (at p. 33).

3. See Kambhu, Weidman and Krishnan (2007, pp. 6–7, 43–4).

4. For the response to the volcanic ash crisis in depth see Macrae (Chapter 2) and Johnson and Jeunemaitre (Chapter 4).

5. Anabtawi and Schwarcz (2010, pp. 13–29) explore how economic shocks produce systemic consequences.

6. See Briggs (Chapter 11).

7. Chapter 1 by Alemanno illustrates that those threats were already known due to previous major problems caused by volcanic ash to civil aviation. There were also Protocols and Manuals of the International Civil Aviation Organization (ICAO) to guide the decisions of the civil aviation authorities in the case of volcanic ash crisis. See ICAO (2009–10).

8.   After an initial Directive on Transmission Grids (1990) came the First Energy Package of 1996, followed by the Cross-border Regulations and Internal Market Directives of 2003. The Third Energy Package includes the 2009 Regulations and Directives. See below.

9.   EC Regulations 13.7.2009 published in the OJ 211 14.8.2009: 713/2009 of the European Parliament and the Council establishing an Agency for the Cooperation of Energy Regulators, 714/2009 of the European Parliament and the Council on conditions for access to the network for cross-border exchanges in electricity, and 715/2009 of the European Parliament and the Council on conditions for access to the natural gas transmission networks. Directives 13.7.2009 published in the OJ 211 14.8.2009: 2009/72/EC of the European Parliament and the Council concerning common rules for the internal market in electricity, and 2009/73/EC of the European Parliament and the Council concerning common rules for the internal market in natural gas. Member States shall bring into force the laws, regulations and administrative provisions necessary to comply with those Directives by 3 March 2011.

10.   See EC Regulation 67/2010 of the European Parliament and of the Council laying down general rules for the granting of Community financial aid in the field of trans-European networks, 30.11.2009 OJ L27/20 30.1.2010. See also Commission of the European Communities (2008, 2).

11.   Council Directive 2004/67/EC 26.4.2004 concerning measures to safeguard security of natural gas supply, OJ L127/92, 29.4.2004, and Directive 2005/89/EC of the European Parliament and of the Council 18.1.2006 concerning measures to safeguard security of electricity supply and infrastructure investment, OJ L33/32, 4.2.2006.

12.   See Commission of the European Communities (2009, 1).

13.   See Commission of the European Communities (2009, 2).

14.   EC Regulation 549/2004, laying down the framework for the creation of the single European sky (the framework Regulation); EC Regulation 550/2004 on the provision of air navigation services in the single European sky (the service provision Regulation); EC Regulation 551/2004 on the organisation and use of the airspace in the single European sky (the airspace Regulation); EC Regulation 552/2004 on the interoperability of the European Air Traffic Management network (the interoperability Regulation). All of them of the European Parliament and of the Council, of 10.3.2004 OJ L 96.

15.   EC Regulation 1070/2009 of the European Parliament and of the Council of 21.10.2009 amending EC Regulations 549/2004, 550/2004, 551/2004 and 552/2004 in order to improve the performance and sustainability of the European aviation system OJ L 300.

16.   Article 8 of the Framework Regulation.

17.   See, European Commission (2010).

18.   Both principles are established in art. 5 of the Treaty on European Union. Specific provisions for the application of those principles within the EU could be found in Protocol (No. 2) On the Application of the Principles of Subsidiarity and Proportionality, OJ C83/206 30.3.2010.

BIBLIOGRAPHY

Alemanno, A. (2010), 'The European Regulatory Response to the Volcanic Ash Crisis: Between Fragmentation and Integration', *European Journal of Risk Regulation,* **1** (2), 101–6.

Anabtawi, I. and S. L. Schwarcz (2011), 'Regulating Systemic Risk: Towards an Analytical Framework', UCLA School of Law, Law-Econ Research Paper 10–11, available at SSRN http://ssrn.com/abstract=1670017 (accessed 20 February 2011).

Areeda, P. (1990), 'Essential Facilities: an Epithet in Need of Limiting Principles' *Antitrust L. Journal*, **58**, 841–53.

Beville, M. (2009), 'Financial Pollution: Systemic Risk and Market Stability', *Florida State University L. Rev.*, **36**, 245–74.

Cocker, J. R. (2005), 'Saving *Otter Tail*: The Essential Facilities Doctrine and Electric Power Post-*Trinko*', *Florida State University L. Rev.*, **33**, 231–58.

Eurocontrol (2010), *Report on the SES Legislation Implementation (reporting period January/09 – December/09)*, produced on request of the European Commission, 31 May 2010.

European Commission (previously: Commission of the European Communities):

—   (2010), *Consequences du nuage de cendres genere par l'eruption volcanique sur venue en Islande sur le trafic aerien- etat de la situation*, Note d'information M. Kallas, en accord avec M. Almunia et M. Rehm, 27 April 2010 SEC(2010) 533.

—   (2009, 1), *The January 2009 Gas Supply Disruption to the EU: an Assessment*, Commission Staff Working Document accompanying the *Proposal for a Regulation of the European Parliament and of the Council concerning measures to safeguard security of gas supply*, 16 July 2009, COM(2009) 363 final, SEC(2009) 977 final.

—   (2009, 2), *Proposal for a Regulation of the European Parliament and of the Council concerning measures to safeguard security of gas supply*, 16 July 2009, COM(2009) 363 final.

—   (2008, 1), *Single European Sky II: towards more sustainable and better performing aviation*, Communication from the Commission, 25 June 2008, COM(2008) 389 final.

—   (2008, 2), *Green Paper Towards a Secure, Sustainable and Competitive European Energy Network*, 13 November 2008 COM(2008) 782 final.

—   (2007, 1), *Evaluation of the Performance of Network Industries Providing Services of General Economic Interest*, Commission Staff Working Document 12 July 2007, SEC (2007) 1024

—   (2007, 2), *Services of general interest, including social services of general interest: a new European commitment*, Communication from the Commission to the European Parliament, the Council, the European Economic and Social Committee and the Committee of the Regions, 20 November 2007, COM(2007) final.

—   (2004), *White Paper on Services of General Interest*, 12 May 2004, COM(2004) 374 final.

—   (2003), *Green Paper on Services of General Economic Interest*, 21 May 2003 COM(2003) 270 final.

Evrard, S. J. (2004), 'Essential Facilities in the European Union: *Bronner* and Beyond', *Columbia Journal of European Law*, **10**, 491–526.

Foster, C. D. (1992), *Privatization, Public Ownership and the Regulation of Natural Monopoly*, Oxford: Blackwell.

Goldin, I. and T. Vogel (2010), 'Global Governance and Systemic Risk in the 21st Century: Lessons from the Financial Crisis' *Global Policy*, **1**, 4–15.

Kahn, A. E. (1971, 1998), *The Economics of Regulation. Principles and Institutions*, vol. II, Cambridge, MA: The MIT Press.

Kambhu, J., S. Weidman and N. Krishnan (*Rapporteurs*) (2007), *New Directions for Understanding Systemic Risk: A Conference Cosponsored by the Federal Reserve*

Bank of New York and the National Academy of Sciences, available at http://www.nap.edu/catalog/11914.html (accessed 20 February 2011).

Kaufman, G. G. (1995), 'Comment on Systemic Risk' in G.G. Kaufman (ed.), *Research in Financial Services: Banking, Financial Markets, and Systemic Risk*, Greenwich, Conn: JAI, 47–52.

Kaufman, G. G. and K. E. Scott (2003), 'What Is Systemic Risk, and Do Bank Regulators Retard or Contribute to It?', *The Independent Review*, 7 (3), 371–91.

Hammond, R. A. (2009), 'Systemic Risk in the Financial System: Insights from Network Science', *Insights from Network Science*, The Pew Charitable Trust, Financial Reform Project, Briefing Paper 12., available at http://www.pewfr.org/project_reports_detail?id=0026 (accessed 20 February 2011).

ICAO (2009–10), *Volcanic Ash Contingency Plan* EUR Region, 2nd edn, issued by the ICAO EUR/NAT Office, Paris, September 2009, EUR Doc 019. Modified in important aspects through a new *Volcanic Ash Contingency Plan* EUR Doc 019 NAT Doc 006, Part II, July 2010.

Joskow, P. L. (2009), 'Foreword: US vs. EU Electricity Reforms Achievement', in J.-M. Glachant and F. Lévêque (eds), *Electricity Reform in Europe: Towards a Single Energy Market*, Cheltenham, UK and Northampton, MA, USA: Edward Elgar, xiii–xxx.

Lapuerta, C. and B. Moselle (1999), 'Network Industries, Third Party Access and Competition Law in the European Union', *Northwestern Journal of International Law and Business*, **19**, 454–78.

Lopez-Jurado, F. B. (2009), 'Técnicas específicas de los servicios en red', in S. Muñoz Machado and J. Esteve (eds), *Fundamentos e Instituciones de la Regulación Económica*, Madrid: IUSTEL, 759–825.

OECD (2003), *Emerging Risks in the 21st Century: an Agenda for Action*.

Schwarcz, S. L. (2008), 'Systemic Risk', *The Georgetown L. Journal*, **97**, 193–249.

Sunstein, C. R. (2006), 'Irreversible and Catastrophic', *Cornell L. Review*, **91**, 841–97.

Ugur, M. (2009), *Liberalisation in a World of Second Best: Evidence on European Network Industries*, MPRA, online at http://mpra.ub.uni-muenchen.de/17873/ (accessed 20 February 2011).

Villar, F. J. (2004), *Las instalaciones esenciales para la competencia*, Granada (Spain): FERE/Comares.

Watts, D. (2009), 'Too Big to Fail? How About Too Big to Exist?', *Harvard Business Review*, **87**, 16.

Watts, D. J. (2004), 'The 'New' Science of Networks', *Annual Rev. Sociology*, **30**, 243–70.

PART 5

An example of codified emergency risk
regulation: the EU Passengers'
Rights Regulation

13. Unexpected turbulence: on the application of the Denied Boarding Regulation to exceptional situations

Morten Broberg

13.1 WHEN REALITY EXCEEDS IMAGINATION

On 20 March 2010 the Icelandic volcano Eyjafjallajökull began to erupt. The first eruption was followed by a second on 14 April 2010. Due to favourable winds, ash from the new eruption began to spread across Europe and, as there was fear that the volcanic ash could pose a danger to air traffic, the authorities on 15 April 2010 began to close down European airspace. The ash cloud spread over great parts of Europe and so did the closure of airspace. The flight ban was only lifted several days later (Eurocontrol, 2010).

In particular European air carriers were severely affected by the ban. Thus, according to the *Financial Times* (2010) the no-fly zone, which had been imposed over much of Europe, was threatening the livelihood of a number of carriers. The air carriers lost money due to much reduced revenue following the grounding of their planes and as a consequence of significant costs flowing from their obligations *vis-à-vis* the stranded passengers (BBC 2010a; European Commission, 2010, paras 2, 7 and 13ff) – not least obligations imposed by Regulation 261/2004,[1] or the Denied Boarding Regulation as it is generally known. This Regulation lays down passengers' minimum rights where they are denied boarding or where a flight is cancelled or delayed.[2]

When drafting the Denied Boarding Regulation the drafters unambiguously had the Regulation cover both ordinary and extraordinary circumstances. However, the Icelandic ash cloud was not merely extraordinary; rather it brought about exceptional circumstances, or, to be more precise, it produced an emergency situation. The present chapter proposes to examine the application of the Denied Boarding Regulation in emergency situations like the one experienced during the ash cloud.

First, in section 13.2, I will set the stage by providing a brief presentation of the Denied Boarding Regulation as well as identifying the problems caused by the ash cloud. Next, in section 13.3, I will examine the Regulation's application to 'extraordinary circumstances'. In section 13.4 I will go on to discuss whether the Denied Boarding Regulation provides an adequate legal basis for dealing with exceptional situations like the one experienced during the 2010 ash cloud. Finally, in section 13.5, I will sum up my findings and provide specific suggestions for how the Regulation may be improved.

13.2 SETTING THE STAGE

The Denied Boarding Regulation, which entered into force on 17 February 2005, finds its legal basis in what today is article 100 of the Treaty on the Functioning of the European Union laying down European Union rules for sea and air transport. It follows from article 1 and recitals 1 and 4 that the Regulation's primary objective is to ensure a high level of protection for air passengers in the European Union (see also European Commission, 2001). In this regard the Regulation's protection of passenger rights not only applies to consumers in the usual meaning of this term, but covers all purchasers of passenger air transport including companies and other professionals. Simultaneously, the Regulation shall create a level playing field amongst air carriers by ensuring that air carriers operate under harmonized conditions of competition. To this end it establishes minimum rights for the passengers (article 1(1)); rights that may not be limited or waived in any way (article 15(1)). The Regulation lays down detailed rules regarding its scope of application. Essentially it applies to all flights departing from an airport located in a member state and to all flights departing from airports outside the European Union, provided that the flight is going to an airport in the Union and that the flight is operated by a Union carrier (cf. article 3(1)).

13.2.1 When is an Airport Located in a Member State?

An airport is located in a member state if it is placed on territory of one of the 27 member states listed in the Treaty on European Union and if the European Union treaties are applicable. Arguably, this means the geographic area that has been defined in article 52 of the Treaty on European Union together with article 355 of the Treaty on the Functioning of the European Union. A return ticket – e.g. for flight transport from Germany to Manila and later return – constitutes two flights. Only the first of these departs from an airport in a member state. If the operating air carrier is not a Union carrier, only the flight departing from Germany will come within the Regulation's scope, cf. Case C-173/07, *Emirates Airlines v Schenkel*.[3]

The Regulation confers rights on passengers in three situations, namely (1) denied boarding, (2) flight cancellation, and (3) delay of a flight. It applies to ordinary circumstances as well as to extraordinary circumstances – and the legal consequences may differ depending upon whether or not a situation should be classified as extraordinary circumstances or not. In the present context it is particularly important that where a flight is cancelled passengers always have a right to care, whereas they are only entitled to compensation where the cancellation is not due to extraordinary circumstances, i.e. circumstances that could not have been avoided even if all reasonable measures had been taken (recital 14). In this regard it must be noted that the Regulation's definition as laid down in recital 14 is somewhat ambiguous. The present author takes the view that it *defines* 'extraordinary circumstances' as those circumstances 'which could not have been avoided even if all reasonable measures had been taken'. However, it may also be that the latter merely refers to a sub-group of all 'extraordinary circumstances'. Whichever of the two interpretations is the better one, the conclusion is that the limitation on passengers' rights only apply to those circumstances that 'could not have been avoided even if all reasonable measures had been taken' by the air carriers.

All the above now leads us to the question as to how the ash cloud and the ensuing flight ban should be classified under the Regulation? On the one hand there is hardly any doubt that they qualify as 'extraordinary circumstances' and not as 'ordinary circumstances' (likewise European Commission, 2010, para. 24). On the other hand the situation during the ash cloud was so extreme that to treat it merely like 'extraordinary circumstances' does not appear appropriate; the geographic scope and the duration of the flight ban was unprecedented and, almost literally, grounded the full European aviation industry for several days. Therefore, in the opinion of the present author, the situation should not merely be classified as 'extraordinary circumstances' as defined in the Regulation, but rather it should be qualified as 'exceptional circumstances' as a subgroup of 'extraordinary circumstances'.

13.3 APPLYING THE DENIED BOARDING REGULATION TO 'EXTRAORDINARY CIRCUMSTANCES'

The flight ban introduced by the authorities during the ash cloud forced the air carriers to cancel their flights (article 2(l)). According to the Denied

Boarding Regulation, cancellation of a flight obliges the air carrier to inform the passengers (article 5, implicitly), and to provide the passengers with information about possible alternative transport (article 5(2)). The burden of proving to what extent and when the passengers are informed lies with the air carrier. Moreover, the air carrier must offer the passengers reimbursement or rerouting as well as meals and refreshments and, where necessary, also accommodation (article 5(1)(a) and (b)). Under normal circumstances cancellation also gives the passengers a right to compensation (cf. article 5(1)(c)). In contrast, the Regulation, in article 5(3), also lays down that '[a]n operating air carrier shall not be obliged to pay compensation ... if it can prove that the cancellation is caused by extraordinary circumstances which could not have been avoided even if all reasonable measures had been taken'.

Since the cancellations, caused by the flight ban introduced during the ash cloud, qualify as 'extraordinary circumstances', the passengers would not be entitled to compensation under the Regulation.

13.3.1 What Constitutes 'Extraordinary Circumstances'?

According to the European Court of Justice in order to be classified as 'extraordinary circumstances' the problem giving rise to these circumstances must stem 'from events which, by their nature or origin, are not inherent in the normal exercise of the activity of the air carrier concerned and are beyond its actual control'. The Court moreover has ruled that with regard to the interpretation of article 5(3) of the Regulation the Montreal Convention is not decisive.[4]

The Regulation, however, requires also that where 'extraordinary circumstances' apply, the passengers are offered the choice between reimbursement, a return flight to the first point of departure or rerouting. It follows that in this situation it is the air carrier alone who bears the risk with regard to those conditions that entitle the passengers to reimbursement. Moreover, it is exclusively the passengers who can decide whether or not to ask for reimbursement. This means that the air carrier cannot divest itself of its obligations under the Regulation by insisting upon reimbursing the flight ticket if this is against the will of the passengers.

As just noted where a flight is cancelled, the air carrier shall offer the passengers a return flight to the first point of departure. During the ash cloud this obligation would only be possible to honour where the cancelled flight was to depart from an airport outside the no-fly zone, meaning that only in such situation could the air carrier be required to provide the passenger with a return flight. Thus, by way of illustration, if a passenger has purchased a ticket from Athens to London via Rome and the flight from Rome to London is cancelled, the passenger has a right to a return flight to Athens.

Finally, when it comes to rerouting the Denied Boarding Regulation is somewhat ambiguous regarding whether rerouting must be by air only, or whether other means of transport may also be used. On the one hand, the Regulation's wording seems to presuppose that the 'rerouting' must be by air transport as is apparent from article 5's reference to article 7 which in section 2 refers to rerouting as 'alternative flight'. Arguably, this interpretation also finds support in article 8, which provides that rerouting must be 'under comparable transport conditions'. On the other hand, the primary objective of the Regulation is to ensure a high level of passenger protection and, in general, it must be more desirable for those passengers who are subjected to a cancellation under extraordinary circumstances to be offered an alternative means of transport rather than no alternative at all (see also Bernard, Chapter 14). In this regard the situation during the volcanic ash cloud would seem to provide a convincing illustration of the need to allow rerouting by other means than air transport.

At least where a cancellation takes place under 'extraordinary circumstances' (so that the passengers are not entitled to compensation) this author finds that it will generally be in the passengers' interest that the air carriers are allowed to offer rerouting by means of transport other than air. In this respect it is worthy of note that according to the European Commission the concept of 'comparable transport conditions' is open to diverging interpretations (European Commission, 2007, section 5.3; see also European Commission, 2008, p. 11).

The Denied Boarding Regulation in article 5(1)(b) lays down that in the case of cancellation of a flight, as well as in event of rerouting, the passengers are entitled to care free of charge in accordance with the Regulation's article 9. This care must be in a reasonable relation to the waiting time (article 9(1)(a)). Whereas the provision does offer the air carrier a certain margin of discretion it is nonetheless clear that, as a minimum, an affected passenger must be entitled to receive all the principal meals that fall within the waiting time be it by the provision of a voucher or by another means. If a departure is cancelled at 10 am and the affected passenger is only rerouted to a departure at 6 pm the air carrier must, as a minimum, offer both lunch and dinner. Moreover, the voucher or the equivalent must be handed out so timely that the affected passengers have time to obtain and consume the meal before being called to the gate.

If the situation necessitates an overnight stay, the air carrier must offer the affected passenger hotel accommodation (article 9(1)(b)) as well as transport between the airport and the hotel (article 9(1)(c)). If a passenger, at his or her own cost, chooses not to sleep in the hotel provided by the air carrier – for example sleeping at home – the air carrier will normally have to pay the extra transport expenses that the affected passengers hereby incur.

Moreover, the affected passengers shall be offered free of charge two telephone calls, telex or fax messages, or emails (article 9(2)). The air carrier must offer this at its own motion and it must see to it that the affected passengers are given adequate access to make use of this right.

Lastly it should be noted that the air carriers cannot invoke *force majeure* as a defence for not offering the required care (European Commission, 2007, section 5.4).

13.4 MAKING THE DENIED BOARDING REGULATION MORE SUITABLE FOR EXCEPTIONAL SITUATIONS (EMERGENCY SITUATIONS)?

Consumer protection is the primary objective of the Denied Boarding Regulation. In essence this objective is pursued by requiring air carriers to bear (an important part of) the risks connected with overbooking, delays and cancellations.

The drafters of the Denied Boarding Regulation explicitly decided to let the Regulation cover both ordinary and extraordinary circumstances. However, the Icelandic ash cloud was not merely extraordinary; rather it brought about exceptional circumstances. In short, it produced an emergency situation.

The emergency character of the situation was not due to the fact that it was caused by an ash cloud. Indeed, air traffic problems caused by volcanic ash clouds were known before the 2010 Icelandic ash cloud spread over Europe (Brannigan, 2010). Rather, what made the situation exceptional was the fact that the authorities introduced a total flight ban applying to every single air carrier in a major part of the geographic area covered by the Regulation and for an extended period. Exceptional situations could also be caused by other factors, such as unusual weather conditions, terror or even war.[5]

Whereas the drafters of the Denied Boarding Regulation explicitly let the Regulation also cover extraordinary circumstances, there is nothing that indicates that they also specifically considered how the Regulation were to apply in emergency situations that went beyond 'normal' extraordinary circumstances. This is reflected in the Regulation's toolbox, which does not appear apt to deal with emergency situations (as a sub-group of 'extraordinary circumstances'), but merely provides tools for handling 'extraordinary circumstances' in general. From the passengers' point of view, in an emergency situation the question is not about being rerouted to another flight bound for the same destination, being offered (minimum) the same level of in-flight service and arriving at the destination at more or less the same time as originally envisaged. Rather, in an emergency situation the question is about getting to one's destination within a reasonable time and getting there under acceptable circumstances.

Following the shutdown of European airspace, under the Denied Boarding Regulation the air carriers were required to provide care to the stranded passengers in the form of food, accommodation and access to make phone calls (etc.). Certain air carriers such as Ryanair initially refused to comply with the Regulation's requirements regarding care, but later reversed this decision (BBC, 2010b). Not only did the provision of care inflict significant additional costs on the air carriers. In many locations the strong increase in demand for accommodation, caused by the many stranded passengers, also led to steeply increased prices for hotel accommodation, and in some it even proved hard to find accommodation to all the passengers.

In the opinion of the present author the extensive problems experienced during the ash cloud crisis show that there is a need to reconsider the application of the Denied Boarding Regulation in emergency situations. In this respect it is important to emphasize that the question whether there is an emergency situation should not be left to the individual air carrier, but instead should be unambiguously decided by a public authority – for example the European Commission.

At present the European Commission is undertaking a review of the Denied Boarding Regulation and has expressed its intention of taking the experience from the volcano ash cloud crisis into account in connection with this review (European Commission, 2010, para. 27). As part of this review I will suggest that the Commission takes the following four proposals into consideration:

First of all, if anything the volcano ash cloud crisis has shown that the Denied Boarding Regulation's distinction between ordinary and extraordinary circumstances fails adequately to cover those extreme situations that go beyond the 'extraordinary circumstances category'. Rather than treating these situations like 'extraordinary circumstances', as we presently do, a third category catering for this type of emergency/exceptional situations should be created.

Secondly, it could be contemplated whether in emergency situations the air carriers should be given the right to offer transport by other means than air (train, boat, car or coach); at least where the distances are not excessive. Passengers should be entitled to refuse to accept this offer of alternative – and under normal circumstances often less attractive – means of transport.

However, if a passenger insists on waiting until air transport becomes possible anew following the end of the emergency situation, then the passenger and not the air carrier should be obliged to cover his or her own costs of care during this waiting period.

Thirdly, it could be considered whether in emergency situations the air carriers and passengers should be allowed to agree to 'swap the risk'. Today the Denied Boarding Regulation provides the possibility of the air carrier reimbursing the passenger by repaying the ticket price, provided the passenger agrees to this. Such reimbursement is, however, unlikely to be attractive to a passenger who is stranded and for that reason must bear the costs of care if he accepts to have his ticket reimbursed. One could therefore envisage that, in cases of emergency, the Denied Boarding Regulation would allow the air carriers to offer a lump sum payment to passengers who agree to cover their own costs of care until the emergency situation has been brought to an end so that the air carrier may resume the flights. A somewhat similar proposal has been put forward by Nick Bernard (Chapter 14). To complete the picture it may be observed that in a report evaluating the Denied Boarding Regulation for the European Commission and prepared by the consultancy firm of Steer Davies Gleave (2010) the question of compensation in cases of *force majeure* was considered. The consultants 'suggest that the Commission should reflect on changing the Regulation so that compensation would not be payable in case of cancellations or delays due to force majeure' (p. 107). These consultants go on to propose that the Regulation should be amended so that an air carrier shall not be obliged to pay compensation, if it can prove that the cancellation is caused by circumstances (ordinary as well as extraordinary) which could not have been avoided even if all reasonable measures had been taken. In the opinion of the present author, it is misguided to consider that any event, which could not have been avoided by the airline even if all reasonable measures had been taken, qualifies as *force majeure*. However, that seems to be the basis for Steer Davies Gleave's proposal.

Fourthly, during the ash cloud incident some air carriers reportedly came close to economic collapse. If an air carrier goes bankrupt during an emergency situation this may severely affect the situation of the stranded passengers. It may therefore be considered how it is possible to ensure that the air carriers can honour their obligations *vis-à-vis* the passengers – for example through the introduction of an obligatory insurance coverage or by requiring the air carriers to set up a special fund to cover the costs of care during emergency situations. This proposal may be compared with that of Nick Bernard concerning the setting-up of a contingency fund (Chapter 14). According to Bernard's proposal the fund should cover the costs imposed by the Denied Boarding Regulation on all air carriers – and not merely those that have gone bankrupt. Moreover, the European Commission has had a report made on air passenger rights that recommends that with regard to protection in the case of insolvency further analysis must be carried out before a decision of possible further protection is taken (Milieu, 2010, p. 106).

13.5 CONCLUSION

The primary objective of the Denied Boarding Regulation is to ensure a high level of protection for air passengers in the European Union. To this end the Regulation establishes indispensable minimum rights for the passengers in three cases, namely where a flight is delayed, where passengers are denied boarding, and where a flight is cancelled. These rules may be befitting for ordinary as well the not-so-ordinary situations that passengers and air carriers are regularly faced with. However, when it comes to emergency situations like the one experienced during the Icelandic ash cloud the present author considers that the Denied Boarding Regulation provides an inadequate scheme. Four suggestions are put forward.

- First, the Regulation's two categories of 'ordinary' and 'extraordinary' circumstances are inadequate when it comes to 'extreme' or 'exceptional' situations. There is therefore a need for a third category catering for emergency situations like the ones we experienced during the ash cloud. If such category is introduced particular importance must be paid to the delimitation of this category *vis-à-vis* the existing ones.
- Secondly, in emergency situations the air carriers should be given the right – and perhaps also the duty – to offer transport by other means than plane. If in this situation a passenger refuses to accept the alternative means of transport, the air carrier should not be liable to bear the costs of care whilst the passenger is waiting for the situation to normalize. It is important that the passengers' rights are duly safeguarded in such situation. One possible way of securing this would be by requiring that the air carriers obtain prior permission from the national authorities responsible for the enforcement of the Denied Boarding Regulation before the passengers are 'forced' to use the alternative means of transport.
- Thirdly, it is suggested that the Regulation should be amended so as to enable the air carrier and the passengers to enter into an agreement whereby the latter receive lump sum payment and in return agree to cover their own costs of care whilst the emergency situation lasts. In

this respect it may be useful if some non-binding standard tariffs could be established that could form the basis for the negotiations between the two parties.

● Fourthly, it is pointed out that the passengers may end up in very unfortunate circumstances if an air carrier goes bankrupt during an emergency situation. This may be countered, for example, if an insurance system is established to protect those passengers who find themselves in such situation.

NOTES

1. In this chapter, references to 'Regulation' as well as to articles and recitals are to Regulation 261/2004 unless otherwise expressly indicated.
2. For a general examination of Regulation 261/2004, see Broberg, 2009.
3. [2008] ECR I-5237.
4. See Joined Cases C-402/07 and C-432/07, *Sturgeon and Condor* [2009] ECR I-10923, para. 72, and Case C-549/07, *Friederike Wallentin-Hermann v Alitalia* [2008] ECR I-11061, para. 34 as well as Case C-83/10, *Rodriguez y otros v Air France* (pending) and Case C-294/10, *Eglïtis and Ratnieks* (pending). For a further discussion of what constitutes extraordinary circumstances, see Broberg, 2009, pp. 736–8.
5. In this regard it may be observed that the legal consequences may differ considerably depending on the cause of the exceptional situation. For instance, there may not be insurance coverage if the situation is classified as one of war.

BIBLIOGRAPHY

BBC (2010a), 'Ash Chaos: Row Grows over Airspace Shutdown Costs' published by the BBC on 22 April 2010, available at http://news.bbc.co.uk/2/hi/uk_news/8636461.stm (accessed on 14 March 2011).

BBC (2010b), 'Volcano Ash: Europe Puts Pressure on Airlines', available at http://news.bbc.co.uk/2/hi/business/8645981.stm (accessed 14 March 2011).

Brannigan, V. (2010), 'Alice's Adventures in Volcano Land: The Use and Abuse of Expert Knowledge in Safety Regulation', *European Journal of Risk Regulation*, **1** (2), 107–14.

Broberg, M. (2009), 'Air Passengers' Rights in the European Union: The Air Carriers' Obligations vis-à-vis their passengers under Regulation 261/2004', *Journal of Business Law*, (7), 727–42.

EC Regulation 261/2004 of the European Parliament and of the Council of 11 February 2004 establishing common rules on compensation and assistance to passengers in the event of denied boarding and of cancellation or long delay of flights, and repealing EEC Regulation 295/91, OJ 2004 L46/1.

Eurocontrol (2010), *Volcanic Ash Cloud Timeline*, available at https://www.eurocontrol.int/articles/volcanic-ash-cloud-timeline-april-events (accessed 14 March 2011, no longer available).

European Commission (2001), 'Proposal for a Regulation of the European Parliament and of the Council establishing common rules on compensation and assistance to air passengers in the event of denied boarding and of cancellation or long delay of flights' COM (2001)784, final.

European Commission (2007), 'Communication from the Commission to the European Parliament and the Council pursuant to Article 17 of Regulation (EC) No 261/2004 on the operation and the results of this Regulation establishing common rules on compensation and assistance to passengers in the event of denied boarding and of cancellation or long delay of flights', COM(2007)168 final.

European Commission (2008), 'Information Document of Directorate-General for Energy and Transport – Answers to Questions on the Application of Regulation 261/2004', European Commission, 17 February 2008.

European Commission (2010), 'Information Note to the Commission – The impact of the volcanic ash cloud crisis on the air transport industry', SEC(2010)533, Brussels 27 April 2010, available at http://ec.europa.eu/commission_2010–2014/ kallas/headlines/news/2010/04/doc/information_note_volcano_crisis.pdf. (accessed 14 March 2011).

Financial Times (2010), 'Airlines Warn of Bankruptcy and Call for End to Restrictions', *Financial Times*, 19 April 2010, available at http://www. ft.com/ cms/s/0/15935c98–4b4a-11df-a7ff-00144feab49a.html (accessed 14 March 2011).

Milieu 2010, 'Final Report – Analysis and evaluation of contributions to the public consultation on air passenger rights carried out by the European Commission from 15/12/2009 to 10/03/2010', report prepared by Milieu, available at http:// ec.europa.eu/transport/passengers/consultations/doc/2010_03_01_apr_final_ report.pdf (accessed 14 March 2011).

Steer Davies Gleave (2010), 'Evaluation of Regulation 261/2004 – Final report – Main report – February 2010'. Prepared for the European Commission, available at http://ec.europa.eu/transport/passengers/studies/doc/2010_02_evaluation_of_ regulation_2612004.pdf (accessed 14 March 2011).

14. The volcanic ash crisis and EU air passenger rights

Nick Bernard

14.1 INTRODUCTION

The volcanic ash crisis gave Regulation 261/2004[1] on air passenger rights in case of denied boarding, long delays or cancellation of flights, if not its baptism of fire – the Regulation has had a good five years to bed down since it came into force – nonetheless a serious challenge to its ability to cope with unusual events giving rise to prolonged air travel disruptions. Indeed, some voices in the industry have questioned, sometimes in strong or colourful language, whether the Regulation was meant to apply to such situations as the volcanic ash crisis at all.[2] While most airlines have accepted, under the pressure from the EU Commission and national regulators, that passengers may be entitled to the 'right to care' under article 9 of the Regulation, it is clear that some have done so under protest and remain unconvinced that the Regulation should apply to events of similar magnitude.[3] While, as will be discussed below, the case for the non-applicability of the Regulation to the ash crisis situation is unconvincing, it remains true that the mechanisms established by the Regulation do give rise to difficulties in such a situation, not just from the airlines' perspective but also from that of passengers.

Whether or not the Regulation was meant to apply to the situation, it still does not entirely solve the question of who should eventually bear the cost of caring for passengers. At best, determining whether the Regulation applies enables us to decide whether passengers or the airlines should, in the first place, be nominally responsible for that cost. Beyond them, however, other actors may be called upon to contribute, in particular insurance companies and possibly EU member states in the form of state aids.

While not specifically linked to the ash crisis *per se*, the size of the event and its impact have highlighted some inherent weaknesses in the Regulation in terms of its mechanisms for enforcement. Up to a point, those weaknesses are a reflection of the general problem of diffused interests in consumer law, which the Regulation seeks to address, albeit imperfectly, by a dual-track public/private enforcement route. The specific context, however, notably its transnational nature and the existence of international instruments such as the Montreal Convention, add layers of difficulties going beyond the more generic problem of consumer law enforcement.

This chapter is divided in three main parts: in section 14.2, the question of the applicability of the Regulation to the ash crisis and to other emergency situations will be considered. Section 14.3 will address questions of allocation of costs beyond airlines and passengers. Finally, section 14.4 will be devoted to enforcement issues. Some conclusions will be drawn in section 14.5.

14.2 APPLICABILITY OF THE REGULATION TO THE VOLCANIC ASH CRISIS

Many airlines and their representative associations have been vocal in their criticism of the application of the Regulation to an event such as the volcano ash crisis, arguing that the Regulation was never meant to apply in such a situation of prolonged, general closure of airspace.[4] The criticism, however, is not always entirely devoid of ambiguity. While in some cases it is meant *de lege ferenda* – *viz.* conceding that, as a matter of law, the Regulation in fact applies but arguing that, as a matter of policy, it should not – some statements seem to suggest that there is in fact doubt as to whether the Regulation actually applies to the situation.[5]

14.2.1 Subjective/Historical Intention of the Legislator?

It is true that the wording of the Regulation does not expressly refer to an event of the magnitude of the ash crisis. But it does not expressly exclude it either. While recital 14 refers explicitly to 'meteorological conditions incompatible with the operation of the flight concerned', it would be plausible to argue that the kind of meteorological situations that the legislator had in mind were more ordinary meteorological phenomena with a more limited impact on flight operations. That said, severe disruptions due to winter bad weather lasting for several days are not unknown in Europe and it could be argued that the legislator must have had that in mind when adopting the Regulation. Moreover, the fact that recital 14 refers to situations of political instability suggests that prolonged situations were not entirely excluded from the contemplation of the legislator. Still, there is a difference between a situation of political instability in one country or one sub-region or even temporary closure of airports due to severe winter weather and the scale of the prolonged, complete shutdown of large chunks of normally very busy airspace that we faced during the volcano ash crisis. While it is true that situations of political instability or meteorological events can reach the level of an emergency situation comparable to the Eyjafjallajökull eruption, there is nothing in the text of the regulation to suggest that such an occurrence was actually contemplated by the legislator.

The *travaux preparatoires* do not throw much more light on the question in that issues of major, prolonged disruptions do not seem to have been explicitly addressed in the lengthy (six years) legislative history of the Regulation, whether by the Council, Parliament or Commission.

There is, therefore, a highly plausible argument that events such as the ash crisis were simply not in the mind of the legislator when the Regulation was adopted. This, however, does not lead us very far in terms of determining the applicability or otherwise of the Regulation to a set of events such as this one. It merely tells us that the text of the Regulation and its legislative history are silent on the matter and does not allow any compelling inference to be drawn either way.

We therefore need to turn to the overall system set up by the Regulation and consider whether this yields more conclusive answers.

14.2.2   Systemic Considerations

Systems of civil liability often follow the dual purpose of discouraging certain types of behaviour as well as indemnifying individuals who suffer a prejudice. The Regulation is no different in this respect. In addition to providing certain forms of compensation or assistance to passengers, it has an incentive structure to discourage airlines from behaving in certain ways. Thus, whereas the Regulation provides for three main rights for passengers (right to compensation in article 7, right to reimbursement or rerouting in article 8 and right to care in article 9), it also provides for some possibilities of exemption for airlines in situations of extraordinary circumstances outside the airline's control.

This possibility of exemption, however, only arises in relation to article 7, *viz.* the right to compensation. It is clear, therefore, that the right to compensation, on the one hand, and the right to reimbursement/rerouting and right to care on the other fulfil quite distinct functions within the scheme of the Regulation. Whereas the right to compensation fulfils the dual role of compensating passengers but also discouraging certain types of behaviour on the part of airlines (excessive overbooking or cancellations for commercial reasons), the same is not true of the right to care (or, for that matter, right to reimbursement/rerouting) which is purely designed to assist passengers, regardless of any act imputable to airlines. The extent to which circumstances outside the airline's control should absolve the airline of any liability with regard to the passengers' right to care was clearly a matter of discussion during the legislative process. Initially, both the European Parliament[6] and the Council[7] were in favour of excluding entitlement to right to care when the delay or cancellation was due to events amounting to '*force majeure*' or 'extraordinary circumstances'.[8] At second reading, however, Parliament had moved towards excluding any extraordinary circumstances defence to the right to care in case of delays (but not cancellations).[9] The solution eventually agreed by the Council and Parliament in the final text of the Regulation should therefore be regarded as a deliberate choice by the legislator to treat the right to compensation on the one hand and the right to reimbursement or rerouting and right to care on the other differently.

Put differently, the provisions of the Regulation relating to the right to care constitute essentially a mechanism of allocation of risk between the parties to the contract. The question, therefore, is whether there is any reason why, *de lege lata* or *ferenda*, this risk allocation to the airline side of the contract of carriage should be either excluded or limited in some ways in the case of events exceeding a certain magnitude.

De lege lata, as already noted, nothing conclusive is to be found in the Regulation itself nor does there seem to be anything of relevance in wider EU law. *De lege ferenda*, some airlines and industry bodies, such as IATA, speak of the 'unfairness' of requiring airlines to care for passengers during events such as the ash crisis without limitation in time or amounts (International Air Transport Association, 2010). However, the risk will have to be borne by someone eventually and there is nothing *a priori* inherently unfair in asking one party, the airlines, to bear the risk rather than the other party, *viz.* passengers: neither party is responsible for the realization of the risk. Simply because that risk has tended in the past to be borne by passengers rather than carriers is not a consequence of any inherent superiority of this solution from a fairness perspective but rather a reflection of the imbalance in bargaining power between the parties.[10] At the risk of stating the obvious, Regulation 261/2004 is, after all, a piece of consumer protection legislation, as repeatedly noted by the Court of Justice in support for the view that provisions in the Regulation conferring rights on passengers should be interpreted broadly and derogations interpreted narrowly.[11] If the Court was willing to find in *Sturgeon*[12] that the principle of equality required that passengers suffering long delays should be treated in the same way as passengers whose flight had been cancelled, it would seem strange that passengers suffering from longer delays due to prolonged closure of the air space could be treated less well than passengers suffering from shorter delays due to some other reason and be denied in the former case of a right to care to which they would be entitled in the latter. Yet both the

maritime and inland waterways passenger rights regulation[13] and the bus
and coach passenger rights regulation[14] limit the number of nights, as well
as the amount per night, for which the transport operator may have to
provide accommodation for passengers in case of cancelled or delayed
transportation.[15] However, as noted by several member states in Council
negotiations during the adoption of the maritime passenger rights Regulation,[16] the presence of a large number of small and medium size undertakings in the fields of sea and inland waterways passenger transport makes
the full allocation of the risk on the transport operator more difficult.[17] The
same is true of road passenger transport. There may therefore still be a case
for a different approach in the field of air transport.

In terms of logistics and efficiency, there is also something to be said in
favour of airlines being responsible for the right of care. Airlines will
generally have better knowledge of, and access to, local resources as well as
bargaining power with respect to local hospitality service providers. Overall, therefore, it would seem that allocating the risk to the airlines rather
than passengers through a right to care obligation is likely to lead to a lower
aggregate cost for dealing with the passenger care dimension of flight
disruptions.

That said, the experience of the ash crisis would suggest that events of
that magnitude clearly exceed the logistical capacities of airlines: in effect,
the duty to care often turned into a duty to compensate: airlines were
unable to organize reaccommodation and other aspects of the duty of care
obligation for a very large number of passengers and passengers had, in the
main, to organize themselves and turn to airlines at a later stage for
reimbursement. A shortcoming of the Regulation in this respect is that the
role it reserves to passengers is a rather passive one. The responsibility of
finding suitable rerouting options and accommodation is left entirely to the
airlines with the passenger having no say other than perhaps objecting to
options which are offered when these fall below the standards specified in
the Regulation (for instance objecting to rerouting options which are not
under 'comparable transport conditions' under article 8). It is true that the
passenger always has the option of seeking reimbursement of their ticket
and make their own arrangements for rerouting, albeit at their own costs.
However, in the case of a very large proportion of passengers who are on
advanced purchase discounted fares, reimbursement of the fare will typically represent a small fraction of their rerouting costs. And since the
passenger will cease to be entitled to any assistance once reimbursement is
requested, there is a clear incentive for passengers to do nothing and wait
until the airline provides a solution. Proactive passengers who find a
reasonable solution to their rerouting problems, such as finding a rail or
multimodal alternative, may end up penalized for doing so.

This, however, does not in itself point towards a limitation of airlines' liability in case of especially prolonged and severe disruptions. Admittedly, a temporal limitation of the right to care, as in the case of maritime and road transport, would create an incentive for passengers to be more proactive in attempting to resolve the crisis situation in which they find themselves. However, it would do so at the cost of shifting the bulk of the cost of either repatriation or care to the passengers. Merely shifting the burden from one party to another does not address the issue of finding an effective and fair way to deal with passenger care in situations of severe and prolonged disruptions. It may, however, point to consideration of alternative mechanisms, such as, in particular, a compensation-based mechanism rather than a duty of care-based mechanism.

14.2.3   A Right to Compensation as an Alternative to the Obligations of Care and Rerouting?

A right to fixed compensation could present a number of advantages compared to the current system in the case of prolonged disruptions. The main strength of this approach is to make the passenger an active player in finding a solution to the problem rather than being the passive recipient of airline assistance. This may enable more options to be considered, notably with respect to other modes of transport including combinations of several modes of transport: airlines tend not to offer options other than air transport, which is clearly problematic in situations of major disruptions to air traffic. It would also have the advantage of creating an incentive to keep rerouting and accommodation costs relatively low: with a fixed budget, passengers are free to choose the most economical solution or, if they prefer, supplement that budget out of their own pocket for other, more expensive solutions. For the airlines, it would make it easier to estimate their potential liabilities as well as make the system simpler to administer.

A major difficulty with such a system, however, would be to determine both the trigger and the level of compensation. As to the level of compensation, it would have to be sufficiently high to make a significant help towards the likely average cost of repatriation and it may be that such a cost may prove uneconomic for the airlines. As to the trigger, it is clear that such a system only makes sense for prolonged disruption and would have to be excluded for more ordinary flight disruptions of a shorter duration. However, even if a trigger threshold is defined, it may prove difficult to estimate from the start how long the disruption will last, as indeed was the case in the ash crisis. If so, such a system, premised on a relatively large one-off payment instead of gradual accrual of expenses under the right to care would be problematic.

14.3 SOCIALIZING THE COST OF DEALING WITH SEVERE FLIGHT DISRUPTIONS: INSURANCE MECHANISMS AND STATE AIDS

Even if the cost of care is allocated to the airlines through a duty of care obligation or left on passengers themselves, it does not follow that either will ultimately bear that entire cost.

In the first place, insurance mechanisms may have a role to play. Travel insurance is relatively widespread in Europe and this might be an argument for placing the onus on passengers rather than airlines. However, experience during the ash crisis suggests that many travel insurance policies exclude cover for exceptional events such as the ash crisis and, even where they do not, the level of cover may be wholly inadequate to cope with prolonged disruptions. While the events raised – at least in the short term – the level of awareness in the general public regarding variations in cover between travel insurance companies, the highly competitive and heavily price-driven nature of the travel insurance market in some member states means that it is to be expected that a substantial number of passengers would remain uninsured for future occurrences of comparable events.

The very existence of an obligation of care to passengers under a strict liability regime as in Regulation 261/2004 could itself be described as a mechanism of compulsory insurance of all passengers with the airline acting as *de facto* insurer.[18] Beyond this, the airlines themselves have tended to self-insure with regard to their passenger care obligations. There does not seem to be any overwhelming reason why airlines could not obtain insurance themselves for their liabilities under Regulation 261/2004. In the aftermath of dramatic events, insurance premiums can spike and the risk may even become temporarily uninsurable, as was the case immediately after the 9/11 events in relation to cover for risks of war and terrorism (EU Commission, 2001, 5–6, 2002). However, there is *a priori* no reason to assume that the commercial insurance market should not be able to offer cover at reasonable rates in the medium-term.[19]

An alternative approach could consist of setting up a contingency fund similar to the arrangements to deal with tour operator insolvency in the context of the Package Travel Directive.[20] That said, if the commercial insurance market is capable of offering adequate products, the case for such a fund appears rather weak. In addition, as a stand-alone fund, administration costs may be disproportionate to the problem being addressed. If a fund was contemplated for other purposes such as dealing with scheduled airline insolvency, there might be a case for extending the coverage of the fund to include other catastrophic events. The case for such a fund, however, is itself not straightforward.[21]

Finally, the question arises of the potential role of state aids for such events. Under article 107(2)(b) TFEU, aid to make good the damage caused by natural disasters or exceptional occurrences constitutes aid that is compatible with the internal market. This article[22] was used in the aftermath of 9/11 to authorize state aids to airlines. There is little doubt that the volcanic ash crisis qualifies as a natural disaster or exceptional occurrence within the meaning of article 107(2)(b). Commissioner Kallas said as much in his information note of 27 April 2010 on the impact of the volcanic ash crisis on the air transport industry (Kallas, 2010). As in the case of post-9/11 state aid, however, the Commission was insistent on the need for the aid to be strictly circumscribed so as to limit potential market distortions (Kallas, 2010, 9). In the context of 9/11, this was interpreted as meaning that aid could be granted for the direct consequences of the closure of US airspace between 11 and 14 September 2001 and for the extra costs of insurance resulting from withdrawal of cover by commercial insurers (EU Commission, 2001, 7–9) but not for other costs borne by airlines after the reopening of US airspace, even if those costs were related to measures taken as a result of the events of 9/11, such as increased security measures mandated by US authorities.[23] The latter were regarded by the Commission as too indirect and not fundamentally different from similar constraints for air service to countries posing a particular political risk, which are not normally regarded as being sufficiently exceptional to justify the application of article 107(2)(b).[24] Transposing this to the volcanic ash crisis, it is probable that aid to compensate for losses due to the non-operation of services during the period of closure of airspace and aid for any special measures taken to repatriate stranded passengers and for complying with Regulation 261/2004 obligations during the same period would be regarded as compatible with the internal market. It is less clear that aid related to costs incurred in clearing the backlog of stranded passengers after the airspace reopened would necessarily have been covered although it could probably be regarded as still directly related to the crisis and therefore allowable. As it happened, member states and the Council were rather more lukewarm about state aids in this situation. In its Volcano Crisis Report of 30 June 2010, the Commission stated that, as it had not received any volcanic ash crisis-related state aid notification, it had abstained from issuing the communication clarifying the extent of allowable aid envisaged in the information note of 27 April 2010 (EU Commission, 2010, para. 41).

14.4 ENFORCING REGULATION 261/2004

Regulation 261/2004 envisages two modes of enforcement: private enforcement by passengers themselves seeking vindication of their rights before courts and public enforcement by public authorities, the national enforcement bodies ('NEBs') referred to in article 16 of the Regulation. It also envisages a hybrid route in the form of passenger complaints to NEBs. All three routes present potential problems. While these problems are fairly standard issues of enforcement of consumer law in general, they present themselves with particular characteristics in the context of Regulation 261/2004.

14.4.1 Public Enforcement by National Enforcement Bodies

Under article 16 of the Regulation, each member state must designate a body responsible for ensuring compliance of air carriers with their obligations under the Regulation. Most member states have designated the body responsible for regulating civil aviation as the NEB under article 16, although a few have allocated this task to statutory consumer protection bodies. After some initial teething problems and the threat of enforcement proceedings by the Commission, these bodies have generally been given powers to sanction non-complying carriers.

An advantage of designating a civil aviation authority or similar body as an NEB is that such a body has better technical expertise in the field (notably when it comes to evaluating whether the carrier can rely on the 'extraordinary circumstances' clause in article 5(3) of the Regulation). On the other hand, those bodies are also more susceptible to regulatory capture by the industry. It should be borne in mind, in that respect, that NEBs are normally responsible for compliance with the Regulation for flights departing from their territory or, in the case of flights originating outside the EU, for flights to an airport situated within their territory. A consequence of this is that, where an NEB adopts a strict policy with regard to enforcement, the carriers that will be most affected by this are the national carriers of the country of the NEB.

In addition, some member states have made no secret of their lack of enthusiasm towards robust enforcement when adopting implementing legislation for the Regulation. In the UK, for instance, the government explicitly stated in its response to its second consultation on the proposed UK implementation of the Regulation that it favoured a 'light touch' approach to enforcement (Department of Transport, 2005a) and the Regulatory Impact Assessment annexed to the explanatory memorandum to the

UK regulations implementing Regulation 261/2004 (Department for Transport, 2005b) is quite clear that enforcement measures should only be envisaged in cases of 'flagrant' or 'systematic' failure to comply by the airline concerned. Moreover, the manner in which the Regulation has been implemented, in particular the existence of a 'due diligence' defence available to carriers, makes enforcement difficult in practice.

A 2010 Report prepared for the Commission on the evaluation of Regulation 261/2004 (Steer Davies Gleave, 2010) highlights stark variations on enforcement practices between member states. Up until the end of 2008, despite the UK being one of the larger member states and the Air Transport Users Council (AUC)[25] handling a rather large number of passenger complaints, the UK CAA had not imposed a single sanction on a carrier whereas, at the other end of the spectrum, the Italian NEB had issued 452 sanctions.[26]

In the context of the ash crisis itself, NEBs reacted with varying strength and results in the face of non-compliance by airlines. In Ireland, for instance, the Irish Commission for Aviation Regulation reacted quickly to Ryanair's announcement that the airline would not reimburse passenger expenses linked to the volcanic ash crisis, reminding the airline of its obligations under the Regulation (Commission for Aviation Regulation, 2010). A reversal of Ryanair's declared policy on this issue followed two days later (Ryanair, 2010). Some NEBs, on the other hand, were less vocal and/or less effective at obtaining a clear statement from airlines primarily under their jurisdiction of their intention to fully comply with their regulatory obligations.[27]

14.4.2   Private Enforcement by Passengers

Many NEBs have limited resources to devote to passenger rights and many regard private enforcement by passengers before courts as the main way to obtain redress when a carrier fails to comply with its obligations.

In most member states, some form of small claims court, with low-cost, simplified procedure, is available for consumers to bring low value disputes, such as those typically arising out of Regulation 261/2004.

Litigation in consumer rights cases works best when legal issues are straightforward and entitlements are clear. In this respect, a number of issues can arise under Regulation 261/2004 where the extent of the obligations imposed on air carriers and the corresponding passenger rights are not altogether clear. In particular, in ash crisis-type situations, the scope of the Article rerouting obligation can give rise to difficulties. For instance, when a passenger identifies a rerouting option regarded by the passenger as suitable but rejected by the airline, it is not clear whether such refusal can ever be regarded as a breach of article 8 and, if so, in what circumstances. It is certainly arguable that rerouting by alternative modes of transportation (such as rail) or a multi-modal transport solution may, in some cases, be regarded as 're-routing, under comparable transport conditions, to their final destination at the earliest opportunity' within the meaning of article 8(1)(b) of the Regulation. While, admittedly, a different mode of transport might arguably be regarded as not constituting *comparable* transport conditions, the condition of comparability would seem to be imposed primarily to protect the passenger and should therefore not be regarded as a reason to reject that possibility when it is actually sought by the passenger.[28] Yet airlines, as noted above, rarely consider alternative modes of transportation when rerouting passengers. Passengers may therefore apply for a refund under aticle 8(1)(a) rather than insisting on rerouting whereas they might conceivably have been better off had the airline covered the cost of the alternative transport.

A particular problem has arisen before UK small claims courts on the relationship between the rights granted by the Regulation and the Montreal Convention. Several small claims courts have taken the view that the Regulation does not give rise to a cause of action by private parties, at any rate under articles 8 and 9, and that any claims must be brought under the Montreal Convention. The argument seems to be a variation of the argument put forward (and rejected by the Court) in Case C-344/04, *R v Department of Transport, ex parte IATA and ELFAA*.[29] In that case, the applicants had argued that article 6 of Regulation 261/2004 was incompatible with the Montreal Convention, to the extent that the latter limited the liability of carriers in cases of delays or even excluded it where the carrier could show that it had taken all the measures that could reasonably be taken to avoid the damage. By contrast, the right to care under the Regulation is unlimited and, in so far as article 29 of the Montreal Convention reserves exclusivity to itself and rules out any other action for damages, however founded, no action should be allowed under Regulation 261/2004 that conflicts with the Montreal Convention. The Court, however, drew a distinction between individual redress, based on the particular circumstances of the passenger seeking damages and the general duty of immediate care under article 9 of the Regulation (or for that matter, article 8).[30] According to the Court, therefore, the Montreal Convention did not prevent the Community legislator from adopting measures providing for a right to care on a standardized basis, irrespective of the individual circumstances of the passenger.

Whatever view one takes of the judgment – and some aviation lawyers were clearly unconvinced by the reasoning of the Court [31] – the fact remains that the case still represents current law and it would seem to follow from this that the rights that passengers derive from the Regulation must be regarded as rights that are distinct and unrelated to the Montreal Convention. If that is so, then it is difficult to regard judgments of UK small claims courts denying the existence of a private cause of action under Regulation 261/2004 as anything other than a denial of remedy for breach of an EU law right, which would be a clear breach of the well-established case-law of the Court of Justice on remedies for breach of EU Law: the Court of Justice has made clear on countless occasions that, while enforcement of EU law rights is, as a rule, left to national legal orders, national rules must not be such as to make enforcement of EU law rights virtually impossible. To the extent that article 9 (and 8) of Regulation 261/2004 are clearly meant to confer rights on individuals, national courts are duty-bound to find in its national legal order mechanisms to vindicate those rights and set aside any national rule that would in effect render the exercise of those rights impossible in practice.[32]

The significance of these couple of examples for our present purposes lies not so much in determining which is the 'right' legal answer to the problem posed. What matters here is that these show that enforcement of the Regulation is not just a matter of 'facts' but can raise complex legal issues. Small claims courts are not especially well-suited for such disputes. Claimants, who typically represent themselves before these courts without benefiting from formal legal advice, are ill-equipped to engage in complex legal arguments with airlines who will normally have the benefit of legal advice and representation by law firms specializing in aviation law.

14.4.3 Passenger Complaints and National Enforcement Bodies

In addition to the 'purely public' and the 'purely private' enforcement mechanisms, article 16(2) of Regulation 261/2004 also seems to contemplate a hybrid route, by which individuals can bring a complaint to an NEB. That route, however, also presents some difficulties.

The NEB responsible under article 16(2) is in principle the same as for the purely public enforcement route on article 16(1), *viz.* that of the member states from which the flight departed or, in case of flights originating in third countries, that of the country of destination of the flight. A difficulty for passengers, however, is that this NEB may not necessarily by the one from their country of residence. While the wording of article 16(2) is open enough to allow an individual to submit a complaint to a NEB other than the one designated in article 16(1), an agreement between NEBs concluded under the auspices of the Commission confirms that the competent NEB is that on whose territory the incident happened, which, in practice, means the one from whose territory the flight departs.

While this is understandable from the perspective of actual capacity to investigate, it remains the case that it is not the most consumer-friendly arrangement. The NEB–NEB agreement envisages that a passenger may address a complaint to another NEB, in particular for linguistic reasons, such as that of the country of residence of the passenger. However the NEB concerned is expected to act primarily as a letterbox and to transmit the file to the competent NEB (albeit with a summary in English). In so far as most NEBs only accept complaints and reply to them in their own national language or in English, this is clearly a major barrier for passengers. In many right to care issues, and especially those that arose in the context of the volcanic ash crisis, there is a high likelihood, at least for intra-European flights and save for domestic flights, that the responsible NEB will not be that of the country of residence of the passenger, even where the passenger has purchased a ticket in his/her country of residence on a home state carrier.

The NEB–NEB agreement does allow an NEB that would not normally be competent to seize themselves of the matter. *Prima facie*, this might seem a sensible solution in some cases, notably when the carrier concerned is based in the same member state as the NEB. However, the NEB is then expected to take full responsibility including actual enforcement. Given that most NEBs have limited resources and given the greater difficulty of collecting evidence in relation to facts taking place in another member state, the likelihood of them voluntarily taking over responsibility of cases normally falling under the responsibility of another NEB is rather low.

Arguably, while the idea of leaving investigative competence primarily in the hands of the NEB on whose territory the incident happened is sound, it would make sense for the NEB of the country of residence of the passenger to play a more active role as intermediary between the handling NEB and the consumer than is currently contemplated in the NEB–NEB agreement. While the Consumer Protection Cooperation Network set up by the Regulation on consumer protection cooperation[33] can be used in the context of Regulation 261/2004, very little use of that network seems to be made by NEBs.[34]

14.5 CONCLUSION

As a matter of current law, it seems difficult to sustain that the system of rights and remedies established by Regulation 261/2004 should not be applicable to disruptions of the kind encountered during the volcanic ash crisis. As a matter of future policy, while the regulations on the rights of maritime and road transport passengers[35] create a precedent for limiting in time the right to care obligations of transport operators, the different structure of the passenger air transport sector, or for that matter the passenger rail transport sector,[36] consisting primarily of large operators rather than small- and medium-size undertakings may call for a different approach based on the *status quo*. While there is certainly a case that could be made for specific measures, notably in terms of state aid, to be taken to assist airlines when faced with especially severe and unusual events, there does not seem to be much appetite for this at present.

If, therefore, the regime of Regulation 261/2004 is probably here to stay, it does not follow from this, however, that it is perfect and requires no alteration at all. More than anything else, Regulation 261/2004 would benefit from much greater clarity in terms of the extent of air carriers' obligations and corresponding passenger rights as well as greater attention to the mechanisms of enforcement, and in particular the role played by national enforcement bodies. Separating much more clearly the task of actual enforcement through criminal and/or administrative sanctions on the one hand and that of handling of passengers' complaints on the other would make for a more user-friendly system. It would also be helpful for more attention to be paid as to what NEBs actually do with respect to each of those two tasks. The Commission consultation carried out earlier this year raised the question of more systematic and regular reporting by the NEBs on their activities and there seems to be a reasonably broad consensus among stakeholders that this would be desirable.[37] This could be a good starting point for a more systematic consideration of the role of NEBs. Such improvements to the passenger rights regime, however, are not directly linked to the emergency nature of events such as the volcanic ash crisis but are of a more general nature. If there is one problematic aspect of Regulation 261/2004 that is raised with particular acuity in a crisis situation, it would be the failure of Regulation 261/2004 to ensure that all stakeholders, and in particular passengers, are enlisted to take an active role in the resolution of the crisis rather than passively waiting for solutions to be provided by someone else. Finding an effective way to do this without either generating excessive burdens on airlines or significantly curtailing passenger rights is not, however, a straightforward matter.

NOTES

[1.] European Parliament and Council Regulation 261/2004/EC of 11 February 2004 establishing common rules on compensation and assistance to passengers in the event of denied boarding and of cancellation or long delay of flights, and repealing EEC Regulation 295/9, [2004] OJ L46/1.

2. The Director General of the European Regional Airlines Association, for instance, has thus argued that 'anybody who believes seriously that Regulation 261/2004 (passenger compensation and assistance) is appropriate for application during the 'volcanic ash' crisis, has about as much credibility as the proponents of the flat earth society.' (Ambrose, 2011)

3. Among others, see Ryanair (2010).

4. Among others, see International Air Transport Association (2010) complaining of 'Unfair Passenger Care Regulations' which were 'never meant for such extra-ordinary situations'; Association of European Airlines (2010a) stating that the rules on air passenger rights were 'designed for an event horizon encompassing isolated incidents, involving individual airlines, not a prolonged disruption of all services'; KLM (2010) arguing that the regulations 'were intended for individual flight delays and cancellations, and not for circumstances in which the entire airspace was closed for a lengthy period due to a natural disaster' and that 'it would be unreasonable to expect the airline to carry all of the costs.'

5. For instance, the Association of European Airlines repeatedly called for the Commission and Council to provide 'guidance' and 'clarify' the 'ambiguities' in the Regulation as to whether and how it should apply in exceptional circumstances for which it was not drafted (see Association of European Airlines (2010b) and (2010c)).

6. See articles 10(1) and 11(1) of the proposal, as amended by Parliament at first reading: European Parliament, Legislative resolution on the proposal for a European Parliament and Council regulation establishing common rules on compensation and assistance to air passengers in the event of denied boarding and of cancellation or long delay of flights, P5_TA(2002)0514.

7. See articles 5(1)(b) and 6(1) of Common Position (EC) No 27/2003 adopted by the Council on 18 March 2003, [2003] OJ C125E/63.

8. Parliament preferred the phrase of '*force majeure*' whereas the Council preferred that of 'extraordinary circumstances'.

9. See articles 5(1)(b) and 6 of the common position, as amended by Parliament at second reading: European Parliament, Legislative resolution on the Council common position for adopting a European Parliament and Council regulation establishing common rules on compensation and assistance to passengers in the event of denied boarding and of cancellation or long delay of flights, and repealing Regulation (EEC) No 295/91, P5_TA(2003)0329.

10. Regulation 1177/2010 of the European Parliament and Council of 24 November 2010 concerning the rights of passengers when travelling by sea and inland waterway and amending EC Regulation 2006/2004, [2010] OJ L334/1, which establishes a comparable passenger rights regime for maritime passenger transport, expressly refers in its preamble to the passenger being the weaker party to the transport contract as justification for the protection of passenger rights.

11. See Case C-549/07, *Wallentin-Hermann* [2008] ECR I-11061, at para. 17 or joined Cases C-402/07 and C-432/07, *Sturgeon* [2009] ECR I-10923.

12. Joined cases C-402/07 and C-432/07, n. 126.

13. Regulation 1177/2010, n. 125.

14. Regulation 181/2011 of the European Parliament and of the Council of 16 February 2011 concerning the rights of passengers in bus and coach transport and amending EC Regulation 2006/2004, [2011] OJ L55/1

15. The limits are three nights for maritime transport and two nights for road transport, with a ceiling of €80 per night per passenger in both cases: see article 17 of Regulation 1177/2010 for maritime transport and article 21 of the European Parliament and Council joint text (2008/0237 (COD) C7–0015/2011).

16. Council of the European Union, Political Agreement on a proposal for a Regulation of the European Parliament and of the Council concerning the rights of passengers when travelling by sea and inland waterway and amending EC Regulation 2006/2004 on

cooperation between national authorities responsible for the enforcement of consumer protection laws, 5 October 2009, Council Document 13874/09, p. 4.

17. It should also be noted that, in relation to maritime transport, the limitation to three nights only applies to accommodation ashore. On board accommodation, where applicable, is not limited in time: see article 17 of Regulation 1177/2010.

18. This remains true whether the airline charges the notional insurance premium to passengers (*viz.* passes on the cost of care through higher fares) or does not due to an inability to raise fares as a result of competitive pressure.

19. On the return to more reasonable premiums for war and terrorism cover after 9/11, see EU Commission (2008a, 6–7).

20. Council Directive 90/314/EEC of 13 June 1990 on package travel, package holidays and package tours, [1990] OJ L158/59.

21. See Booz & Co (2009, 109–12). The Report published by the consultant contracted by the Commission to analyze the results would seem to suggest that while, predictably, consumers and their organizations tended to be more in favour of such a fund than industry respondents, even among the former group only 50 per cent seemed to be in favour of compulsory protection: see Milieu Ltd (2010).

22. Article 87(2)(b) of the EC Treaty at the time.

23. See Commission Decision 2003/196/EC of 11 December 2002 concerning assistance to French airlines, [2003] OJ L77/61.

24. Ibid, recital 37.

25. In the UK, the function of actually enforcing the Regulation (by means of imposition of criminal sanctions) is entrusted to the Civil Aviation Authority whereas the function of handling passenger complaints is left to a separate body: the Air Transport Users Council ('AUC').

26. It should be noted, however, that the imposition of a large number of sanctions does not, in itself, mean that those sanctions are effective. Low level of sanctions and poor collection procedures can severely affect the deterrent effect of sanctions. The latter problem seems to be particularly acute in Italy.

27. See, for instance, the ambiguity of KLM's press release of 20 August 2010 (KLM, 2010) regarding its willingness to bear the costs related to its duty of care obligations under Regulation 261/2004 in the context of the volcanic ash crisis.

28. In an informal information document, the Commission (DG Tren) also seemed to have shared the view that re-routing could be by alternative transport modes: see answer to question #22 in EU Commission (2008b).

29. [2006] ECR I-403.

30. See paras 44–48 of the judgment.

31. See Balfour (2007), who acted for IATA in the case.

32. See, e.g., Case C-453/99, *Courage v Crehan* [2001] ECR I-6297. Among the many cases reaffirming that principle in just about any area of EU law, it is perhaps especially worth mentioning case C-253/00, *Muñoz* [2002] ECR I-7289, where an almost identical argument that a Regulation only gave rise to a private cause of action was firmly rejected by the Court based on the principle of effectiveness of EU law.

33. Regulation 2006/2004/EC of 27 October 2004 on cooperation between national authorities responsible for the enforcement of consumer protection laws, [2004] OJ L264/1

34. In 2007 and 2008, there were a grand total of 12 requests for mutual assistance under Regulation 2006/2004 in relation to the enforcement of Regulation 261/2004: see EU Commission (2009: Annex I).

35. Regulations 1177/2010 and 181/2011, nn. 125 and 129.

36. See Regulation 1371/2007 of the European Parliament and of the Council of 23 October 2007 on rail passengers' rights and obligations, [2007] OJ L315/14 which, like Regulation 261/2004, does not limit in time the duty of care of rail operators towards stranded passengers.

37. See Milieu's analysis of the responses to the consultation, n. 136, at pp 46–9.

BIBLIOGRAPHY

Ambrose, M. (2010), 'The Earth is Not Flat but Europe Thinks It Is', *Regional international*, June 2010, p. 5 available at http://www.eraa.org/publications/regional-international (accessed 18 February 2011).

Association of European Airlines (2010a), 'Airspace Closures – The Human Dimension. "We Will Fight for our Affected Passengers" says AEA', Press Release of 22 April 2010, available at http://files.aea.be/News/PR/Pr10–018.pdf (accessed 18 February 2011).

Association of European Airlines (2010b), 'EU Transport Ministers did not Fulfil Airline Expectation – AEA: "Opportunity Missed"', Press release of 25 June 2010, available at http://files.aea.be/News/PR/Pr10–028.pdf (accessed 18 February 2011).

Association of European Airlines (2010c), 'AEA annoyed that the EU Commission is targeting individual airlines over Ash Cloud Compensation Delays', Press release of 17 August 2010 available at http://files.aea.be/News/PR/Pr10–031.pdf (accessed 18 February 2011).

Balfour, J. (2007), 'Further Comment on Case C-344/04, The Queen ex parte International Air Transport Association, European Low Fares Airline Association v. Department for Transport, Judgment of the Court (Grand Chamber) of 10 January 2006', *Common Market Law Review*, **44**, 555.

Booz & Co (2009), 'Study for the EU Commission (DG TREN) on Consumer Protection against Aviation Bankruptcy', available at: http://ec.europa.eu/transport/air/studies/doc/internal_market/2009_01_bankruptcy_study.pdf (accessed 18 February 2011).

Commission for Aviation Regulation (2010), 'CAR Response to Ryanair Announcement that Passenger Expenses will not be Reimbursed', news release of 20 April 2010, available at http://www.aviationreg.ie/CAR_response_to_Ryanair_announcement_that_passenger_expenses_will_not_be_reimbursed/Default.467. html (accessed 18 February 2011).

Department of Transport (2005a), 'Second Consultation on Denied Boarding Compensation Regulation (EC) No. 261/2004 – Summary of responses', available at http://webarchive.nationalarchives.gov.uk/+/http://www.dft.gov.uk/consultations/archive/2005/dbcrsecc/deniedboardingcompensationre1295 (accessed 18 February 2011).

Department for Transport (2005b), Explanatory Memorandum to the Civil Aviation (Denied Boarding, Compensation and Assistance) Regulations 2005, available at http://tna.europarchive.org/20081027082750/http://www.opsi.gov.uk/si/em2005/uksiem_20050975_en.pdf (accessed 18 February 2011).

EU Commission (2001), 'Communication from the Commission on the Repercussions of the Terrorist Attacks in the United States on the Air Transport Industry', COM (2001) 574.

EU Commission (2002), 'Communication from the Commission on Insurance in the Air Transport sector following the terrorist attacks of 11 September 2001 in the United States', COM (2002) 320.

EU Commission (2008a), 'Communication from the Commission on Insurance Requirements for Aircraft Operators in the EU – A Report on the Operation of Regulation 785/2004', COM (2008) 216.

EU Commission (2008b), 'Information Document of Directorate-General for Energy and Transport: Questions and Answers to Questions on the application of Regulation 261/2004' of 17 February 2008, available at http://ec.europa.eu/transport/air_portal/passenger_rights/doc/2008/q_and_a_en.pdf (accessed 18 February 2011).

EU Commission (2009), '2007–2008 Report from the Commission to the European Parliament and Council on the application of Regulation (EC) No 2006/2004', COM (2009) 336.

EU Commission (2010),'Report on the Actions Undertaken in the Context of the Impact of the Volcanic Ash Cloud Crisis on the Air Transport Industry', 30 June 2010, available at http://ec.europa.eu/transport/doc/ash-cloud-crisis/2010_06_30_volcano-crisis-report.pdf (accessed 18 February 2011).

International Air Transport Association (2010), 'Volcano Crisis Cost Airlines $1.7 Billion in Revenue – IATA Urges Measures to Mitigate Impact', Press release of 21 April 2010, available at http://www.iata.org/pressroom/pr/Pages/2010-04-21-01.aspx (accessed 18 February 2011).

Kallas, S. (2010), 'Information Note to the Commission: The Impact of the Volcanic Ash Cloud Crisis on the Air Transport Industry', SEC(2010)533.

KLM (2010), 'European Commission Denies Statements about KLM', Press release of 20 August 2010 available at http://www.klm.com/corporate/en/newsroom/press-releases/archive-2010/European-Commission-denies-statements-about-KLM.html (accessed 18 February 2011).

Milieu Ltd (2010), 'Final Report on Analysis and Evaluation of Contributions to the Public Consultation on Air Passenger Rights Carried Out by the European Commission from 15/12/2009 to 10/03/2010', available at http://ec.europa.eu/transport/passengers/consultations/doc/2010_03_01_apr_final_report.pdf (accessed 18 February 2011).

Ryanair (2010), 'Ryanair will Comply with Unfair EU261 Regulations', News release of 22 April 2010, available at http://www.ryanair.com/en/news/ryanair-will-comply-with-unfair-eu261-regulations (accessed 18 February 2011).

Steer Davies Gleave (2010), 'Report of 3 February 2010 on Evaluation of Regulation 261/2004 prepared for the Commission (DG Tren)', available at http://ec.europa.eu/transport/passengers/studies/doc/2010_02_evaluation_of_regulation_2612004.pdf (accessed 18 February 2011).

PART 6

New ideas for emergency risk regulation

15. The fallout from the fallout: hazards, risk and organizational learning

Christopher Lawless

15.1 INTRODUCTION: UNDERSTANDING RISK IN A COMPLEX WORLD

In a world of choices, risk is an inevitable and unavoidable aspect of everyday life. Yet while we as individuals may experience the outcomes of risk, the manner in which risks arise, and the practices and procedures through which risk is comprehended and understood, display a distinctly socialized character. Sociologists have for some time emphasized the instrumental organizing role risk plays in modern societies. The work of Beck (1992) has proved particularly influential in demonstrating how awareness of the increasingly hazardous, but also unpredictable, nature of technological advancement is serving to define the social condition, at least in the western world. Beck's conception of the 'Risk Society' has since been joined by numerous other sociological analyses that have explored the way risk is addressed in various settings.

The relationship between risk and organizations has been found to be significantly complex. Risk may not be 'clearly identifiable and manageable, but emerges and is constructed from complex but fractured processes of organizational attention involving information systems, incentive structures and narratives of explanation which are the source of further uncertainties' (Scheytt et al., 2006, p.1333). Related studies have described how 'risks' are rendered as 'decidable' by societies (*ibid.*); 'how one *views* risk determines how one *assesses* it' (Corvellec, 2010, p.145, emphasis added).

Hutter and Power (2005) argue that risk is an inherently *organized* phenomenon. Organizations themselves may become 'producers and managers of risk' (Hutter and Power, 2005), and a significant canon of literature now exists that demonstrates how risk events are themselves the product of distinctly organizational shortcomings. For example, Vaughn (1996), in a landmark study of the 1986 Space Shuttle disaster, describes how political pressures, coupled with deficiencies in communication structures, served to construct epistemic barriers that led to failures to address fatal flaws in the design of O-ring seals in the booster rockets of the shuttle. In a notable theoretical intervention, Perrow (1999) has put forward the 'normal accident' theory, which posits that catastrophic failures are inevitable in complex, tightly coupled systems, albeit with consequences that are impossible to predict. On the other hand, a number of theorists have drawn attention to so-called 'high reliability organizations' (HROs), which successfully operate in situations where risk, and the potential impact of that risk, is extremely high. HROs consciously identify certain events that must simply never happen. Organizational theorists have argued that prevention does not occur through technological interventions alone, but through 'organizational strategy and management' (Boin and Shulman, 2008, p. 1051). Studies of HROs have sought to understand how they are able to avoid the kinds of disastrous consequences anticipated by normal accident theory.

Commentators on risk have also studied the evolution of statutory procedures for the management of such risks. Studies of 'regulatory regimes' (Hood, 2001) have demonstrated the increasingly complex relationship between risk and regulation. For example, Rothstein et al. (2006) argue that in attempting to address societal risks, regulators themselves inevitably risk losing their authority through being pressured toward greater coherence, transparency and accountability. In confronting societal risks, regulators face 'institutional risks'; attempts to manage the latter impact upon the way in which the former are constructed and perceived. Hence consideration of regulatory strategy exposes a second order dilemma, namely how the practice risk management itself presents considerable risks.

The significant recent growth in risk scholarship raises questions over whether modern societies are inherently more risky, or whether risk has merely provided new way of perceiving, and framing the world around us (Hutter, 2010, p. 5). While this philosophically complex question deserves more concerted scrutiny, it is certainly the case that technologically advancing, interconnected societies place ever higher demands on resources and power. It is recognized that these societies require a complex array of critical infrastructures (CIs) to continue to function. Broadly speaking, CIs as a category encompass *inter alia* energy utility networks, telecommunications systems, finance flows and transport links (Hutter, 2010, p.8). It has also been recognized, however, that CIs exhibit a particularly vulnerable character, and that any breakdown may incur extremely high social and financial costs (Perrow, 2007). A growing amount of risk literature has sought to assess these kinds of threats (Boin and McConnell, 2007).

It has been shown how risks to CI may display a distinctly transboundary character, which national regimes of risk regulation struggle to cope with (Boin, 2010). The disruptions caused during the April 2010 volcanic ash crisis represented a clear example of this dimension of infrastructural vulnerability. As well as starkly exposing the shortcomings of existing regulatory frameworks, this crisis revealed the complex set of interdependencies which revolve around the necessity to maintain fully functioning air transport, and the consequent high levels of systemic risk. More significantly still, it exposed the epistemic deficiencies across all parts of the aviation sector with regard to volcanic ash. Over the course of just a few days, however, the risk of volcanic ash became quickly redefined. While the solution to the crisis may perhaps not have reflected the conventional norms of scientific propriety, it encapsulated some of the aspects that have led sociologists of science to distinguish regulatory science as a problematic site where politics and science meet. They have shown how it is considerably removed from the image of science as a universalizing, politically disinterested mode of inquiry. In what follows I introduce some of the key works that have explored the complex character of this form of technical decision-making.

15.2   REGULATORY SCIENCE – A MUTUAL PROBLEM FOR SCIENCE AND SOCIETY

The relationship between risk regulation and science constituted the focus of a landmark paper by Weinberg (1985). Influenced by the then nascent Sociology of Scientific Knowledge (SSK) programme, Weinberg argued for the need to define 'regulatory science' as possessing 'less demanding' norms than 'ordinary science' (Weinberg, 1985, p. 68). This was in response to what he saw as the intractable demands placed on scientific inquiry from policymakers to ensure certainty:

> Regulators, instead of asking science for answers to unanswerable questions, ought to be content with less far-reaching answers; where uncertainty bands can be established, they should regulate on the basis of that uncertainty; where uncertainty bands are so wide as to be meaningless, they need to recast questions so that regulation does not depend on answers to the unanswerable. (Weinberg, 1985)

The problem of regulatory science has subsequently gained attention from numerous commentators drawn from the fields of law, politics, and sociology. The work of Jasanoff (1987, 1990, 1993) has been particularly influential. Jasanoff has illuminated the contested nature of scientific knowledge used in the context of regulatory decision-making (Jasanoff, 1987). She demonstrates the decidedly contingent nature of such knowledge, showing how complications arise when regulatory controversies extend beyond scientific technicalities to encroach on political issues. In these cases the boundary dividing scientific and policy concerns can be highly ambiguous and fluid. Here, terms such as 'science policy', 'risk assessment', 'risk management', 'peer review' etc. can be used as rhetorical devices in the course of shaping particular views about the role of science in policymaking:

> The fluidity of these concepts arises from fundamental social disagreements about the extent to which science and scientists should control decision-making at the frontiers of knowledge. Since these boundary-defining terms affect the allocation of power, their meaning *cannot be established independently of the political process*. (Jasanoff, 1987, p. 226, emphasis added)

Many studies have supported the view of the problematic character of regulatory science, aligning with Weinberg and Jasanoff in pointing to the presence of intractable ontological barriers that preclude absolute scientific understanding of a specific risk, even though decision-makers may demand absolute knowledge. In their study, Irwin et al. (1997) highlight a number of aspects of the 'heterogeneous and hybrid' character of regulatory science. Firstly, they show how the practice of regulatory science is located *across* a variety of institutional locations, which may include academic, industrial and government sites. Second, it involves a wide range of activities, reflecting a complex mix of 'speciality and disciplinary orientations' (Irwin et al., 1997, p. 22), and which reflects varying levels of scientific uncertainty, 'from complex and innovative work on mechanisms through to routine testing' (*ibid.*). It encompasses a heterogeneous combination of 'intellectual and practical activities' that 'span the technical and the bureaucratic' (*ibid.*), and, that represents the nexus of scientific, political and economic factors. Finally, it is both regulatory and innovative in character. Although this kind of scientific activity may seek to understand an existing risk, it may itself create altogether new ways of perceiving the world through forging new coherence amongst previously fractured ontologies.

Regulatory science therefore possesses a markedly different epistemic character than the kind of endeavours of discovery traditionally associated with 'pure' scientific research, as practised within the disciplinary confines of academic departments. Either by accident or design, regulatory science forces down these disciplinary barriers. Hence risk regulation possesses an inherently multivalent character. The products of such regulatory practices hold consequences for how 'scientific' activity is understood, and how policymaking proceeds in a particular problem areas.

While risk regulation poses significant challenges at national level, hazards that transcend sovereign boundaries present further complications. Different nations have been shown to possess significantly varying cultures of scientifically informed regulation. Another landmark study by Jasanoff (1993) found that UK regulators were more likely to favour a decision-making style based on empirical observations, in contrast to their US counterparts, who preferred greater use of theoretical models. Such observations have become increasingly relevant as scholars have begun to turn ever greater attention to transboundary risks (see for example Linnerooth-Bayer et al., 2001). It is only more recently that attention has been focused on regulatory responses to hitherto unforeseen events. Incidents such as the recent global financial crisis have transcended pre-existing academic understandings, as much as they have impacted upon practitioners and civil society. Studies have, *inter alia*, emphasized the wider cultural contexts that surround decision-making under uncertainty, and which influence orientations to both the 'known' and the 'unknown' (Wynne and Dressel, 2001; Hutter, 2010).

Social studies of scientific knowledge production have therefore played a significant role in highlighting the manner in which scientific controversies are resolved. Many of these kinds of commentaries focus on the highly emergent nature of knowledge production, pointing to the distinctly social practices required to ensure the closure of technical disputes. The need to manage uncertainty constitutes a key theme in a number of these studies. Often, this uncertainty is the inevitable side-effect of a lack of ontologically reconcilable solutions. As this section has demonstrated, political imperatives may place demands that scientific practice struggles to meet. A brief focus on some of the scientific issues in relation to volcanic ash is sufficient to indicate how the construction of regulatory expertise presents clear difficulties.

15.3 THE VOLCANIC ASH RISK: INCIDENTS AND UNCERTAINTIES

Scientific understanding of the effects of ash is greatly complicated by numerous sources of uncertainty. Firstly, the composition of volcanic ash varies significantly. Not only is there considerable geographic variance across volcanic sites, but the precise composition of ash clouds may also vary between individual eruptions occurring from the same volcano. Second, measuring concentrations of ash in the atmosphere presents considerable challenges. The density of ash may vary enormously within a plume, meaning that sample measurements may fail to capture the variance in distribution. Local pockets of high ash concentrations may fail to be detected. The potential adverse effects on jet engines also presents obvious problems in trying to provide samples via airbourne methods.

Third, controversy exists within the relevant scientific communities over the reliability of theoretical models used to estimate ash cloud parameters. Although the UK Met Office claims its own models are relatively reliable, other national weather agencies, who use the same model, interpret the data in markedly different ways, adding further uncertainty (Flight International, 2010). Fourth, relatively little is known about the precise effects of ash on jet engines, in terms of the concentrations in which engines can safely operate. Manufacturers have historically been reluctant to disseminate the results of related experiments for fear of litigation. As Downer (2007) has previously pointed out in his study of engine testing, there are intractable difficulties in attempting to guarantee that experimental conditions match actual flight conditions. Inevitably, manufacturers are highly wary of making decisive claims about test data for fear of legal reprisals in the event of an accident.

In the absence of ontological certainty, the way in which scientific knowledge is represented plays an important role. In many cases, these studies have demonstrated how projections of authority and credibility rely strongly on the practices involved in portraying knowledge. One especially prominent perspective, Actor-Network Theory (ANT), emphasizes the way in which representative practices actively construct linkages between actors and artefacts. The resulting 'actor-networks' exist as complexes through which information flows. The success of actor-networks in projecting credibility is regarded as a function of their ability to 'recruit' elements. Writers such as Bruno Latour, Michel Callon and John Law have built upon the original tenets of ANT to develop a series of concepts that seek to account how actor-networks gain power (Callon, 1986; Latour, 1987, 1999; Law, 1991). For example, actors seeking to create networks need to position themselves as 'obligatory passage points' in order to control the way in which information is shaped and transferred. Differing interests also need to be reconciled, which may also influence the way in which networks are shaped.

One of the key aspects of ANT is the way in which it is able to account for how scientific and social orderings emerge simultaneously. It represents one notable way in which researchers have sought to understand how actors dynamically make sense of highly fluid situations of high epistemological and ontological flux. The notion of the simultaneous 'co-production' of scientific knowledge and organizational arrangements has been developed through these kinds of studies. In what remains I adopt a similar perspective to illuminate aspects of the volcanic ash crisis.

15.4 A UNIFIED SKY?

Sociologists and anthropologists have utilized the term 'liminal space' (Derksen, 2000; Turner, 1976) to describe certain transitional phases, where the values and norms associated with one set of social arrangements are being left behind, but where a competing set of values and norms have yet to be fully established. Liminal spaces may be sites of considerable uncertainty and flux, which represent thresholds between historical attitudes.

European airspace appears to be entering a similar state of transition. The long-standing norm of sovereign control of airspace, codified by the 1944 Chicago Convention, is being challenged by a new paradigm of airspace management. The 'Single European Sky' (SES) initiative seeks to replace state-by-state control of national airspace with 'a single operating airspace where common procedures for design, planning and management ensure the efficient and safe performance of air traffic management' (European Commission, 2001). Central to the SES concept is the redesign of European airspace to reflect air traffic flows instead of national borders (Alemanno, 2010, p. 104). SES seeks to transcend national boundaries, replacing state-by-state airspace oversight with a route-by-route strategy, intended to better reflect 'operational and technical realities' (Schubert, 2003, p. 33).

Although SES was approved in principle in 2004, the response by European nations to the 2010 Eyjafjallajökull eruption exposed an enduring degree of fragmentation of airspace control, and reignited the debate over the future of the European sky. The experience of the ash crisis has therefore drawn greater attention to the liminal status of the latter. Yet it is not only airspace that is being reconstructed, as the uncertain status of European sky creates a space in which the nature of risk itself is able to be contingently redefined. In what follows I describe how the UK CAA's response to the ash cloud, and the subsequent response of European authorities, not only parallels the contingent aspects of regulatory science, but also shows how perceptions of risk (particular in terms of its geographical dimensions), are mutually shaped.

15.5 CONSTRUCTING EMERGENCY REGULATORY SCIENCE

In the absence of the ability to gain universal information about volcanic ash, but nonetheless experiencing pressure from airline executives and politicians, the UK's regulator, the Civil Aviation Authority (CAA), came up with a solution that represented a shift from the so-called 'zero-tolerance' policy. At the peak of the crisis, between 15–19 April, it convened a round of emergency teleconferences, consisting, *inter alia*, of members of the UK Met Office, aircraft and engine manufacturers, airline operators, and scientific agencies engaged in research on the behaviour of volcanic ash (CAA, 2010). Discussions sought to identify ways of restoring air flights. Efforts focused on attempting to determine ash concentrations under which aircraft could safely fly. The Met Office's own ash dispersal models indicated that there were two areas in the UK where ash concentrations were around 200 micrograms per cubic metre, while the rest of the country was covered by concentrations of greater than 2,000 micrograms per cubic metre. Meanwhile, incident reports of past encounters with volcanic ash were consulted, which enabled rough estimates to be made about the predicted tolerance levels of jet engines. Following a series of test flights, and subsequent post-flight inspections, these various strands of data were drawn together to inform a new series of guidelines. Areas where ash concentrations exceeded 2,000 micrograms per cubic metre were maintained as strict no-fly zones (CAA, 2010, p. 2). However, areas where ash concentrations were between 200–2,000 micrograms per cubic metre became defined as 'enhanced procedures' zones. Aircrafts were permitted to fly in these zones, 'subject to additional inspections if evidence of ash contamination was found' (CAA, 2010, p. 2). Any areas of airspace containing ash concentrations of less than 200 micrograms per cubic metre was announced as safe to fly.[1]

These new guidelines did not come about as a result of a pan-European decision-making process. Instead, they were largely driven by the initiative of a national regulator, working together with a variety of experts and stakeholders. Nor did they come about through a systematic and gradual accumulation of scientific knowledge (Brannigan, 2010). On the contrary, they were a result of an *ad hoc* process of consultation between experts, reliant on a certain degree of ingenuity in terms of how they combined limited quantities of data. As Andrew Haines, Chief Executive of the CAA, put it, 'we achieved what often takes years in 96 hours' (The Guardian, 2010).

Further airspace closures occurred in the UK and Ireland on the 4th and 17–18 May. In response to ongoing disruptions, the CAA announced a revised series of guidelines that doubled the tolerable limit of ash concentration for aircraft, leading to a new maximum permitted flying concentration of 4,000 micrograms per cubic metre (Learmount, 2010; Roberts, 2010). A so-called 'time-limited zone' of between 2,000–4,000 micrograms per cubic metre was also introduced, which allowed aircraft to fly for a certain amount of time as agreed by airlines and engine manufacturers. What was significant about these later moves was that they came about unilaterally, largely as the result of impatience with the perceived sluggishness of the European Union (EU) to respond to a fast-moving situation. The CAA claimed it 'could not wait' for the EU to decide on whether to accept its actions (Learmount, 2010, p. 10). The CAA also criticized European counterparts for taking a passive and uncoordinated approach to the problem (*ibid.*), but justified its unilateralism by arguing that as the UK and Ireland were closer to Eyjafjallajökull, and hence worse affected than the mainland, they were more 'highly motivated to find solutions' (*ibid.*).

The UK and Ireland originally stood alone in seeking a solution in the form of a graded series of regulated flying zones. In using geographical location to justify such a decision, and ignoring wider concerns about continental co-ordination, volcanic ash was portrayed as a localized risk.

Since then however, there are signs that the European Commission is now endorsing the need to develop more precise regulatory guidelines concerning volcanic ash. At a conference organized by the European Commission, which took place in Reykjavik in September 2010, it was agreed to endorse a 'no-fly' guideline of areas predicted to be in excess of 4,000 micrograms per cubic metre, or where the actual ash density exceeded 2,000 micrograms per cubic metre (Palsson, 2010, pp. 2–3). The quoting of such figures represents a commitment to newly agreed 'guiding principles' (*ibid.*) of regulatory science, which may lead to even more precise understandings of the effect of ash on aircraft. Significantly the use of such methodology is being incorporated into a framework that marks an 'evolution' (*ibid.*) from a state-to-state policy, to greater emphasis on route-by-route decision-making. It posits a shift from national authorities making decisions, to airlines themselves taking 'more responsibility for such decision making based on a suitable "approved risk management system"' (*ibid.*).

15.6 CONCLUSION

In this chapter I have reviewed literature that has emerged from organizational studies of risk and regulation, as well other studies that have focused on the social shaping of science and technology. I have done so in order to indicate the possibilities available to those seeking an enhanced understanding of how the plurality of actors and interests, which are accommodated in aviation regulation, combined to shape a particular risk response. I have therefore drawn upon such literature in order to make the point that a holistic, integrated and sociologically oriented perspective is needed to understand risk regulation, and to effectively supplement those interventions that take a consciously technical or economic approach.

Previous sociological explorations of the relationship between risk and organizations have questioned the status of risk as a 'culturally independent given' (Hutter and Power, 2005, p. 8). Instead, studies of 'organizational encounters with risk' have demonstrated how such events are important redefining moments for organizations themselves. Encounters that 'escape existing mechanisms of predictability' (*ibid.*, p. 18), may alter the way in which actors view the world. Building on such arguments, this chapter has sought to challenge the notion of a 'simplistic duality of organization and environment' (*ibid.*).

Responses to risk may involve social reorderings through which shared perceptions of reality become reconfigured. The 2010 volcanic ash crisis provides a useful case study in charting how localized risks become transformed into transboundary risks through organizational dynamics. The crisis exposed the hazards of a fragmented and uncoordinated nation-by-nation response, and has reinvigorated calls for greater unification of airspace, which might eventually lead to the kind of route-by-route approach promulgated by SES. Ironically however in this case, renewed attempts at developing common regulatory procedures have their roots in an initially localized risk response. The regulatory decisions of the CAA were an *ad hoc* response to the pressures of the crisis, and justified by local geography, yet they are now informing strategy at the pan-European level. It should also be noted however that the CAA was placed under considerable pressure from airlines (Interview, CAA representative, 2010). An interest in delegating responsibility to a supranational body in the light of such pressures may also have helped to drive the delocalization of the volcanic ash problem. Hence whilst exercising sovereignty in regulatory decision-making on the one hand, incentives may still exist for national regulators to help reconstruct a risk as a transboundary phenomenon, even if that endangers some eventual loss of sovereign control. Making sense of this tension remains an area for further inquiry.

The response to the ash crisis nonetheless raises the question of whether a common European decision-making structure would possess the necessary organizational flexibility to allow for such improvization in the light of unanticipated events. The system of functional airspace blocks proposed under the SES framework may potentially allow more flexibility for airspace management than the current statist system (article 8, EC Regulation 549/2004, European Parliament 2004; Eurocontrol, 2008). What remains to be seen, however, is how such reforms may be linked to incentives for airlines. Incorporating effective risk regulation measures into a more integrated airspace will naturally require the full cooperation of airlines, many of whom were extremely vocal in their criticisms of official handling of the volcanic ash crisis (Alemanno, 2010; Brannigan, 2010). How the diverse and fractious airline market would cooperate with SES is an area that invites further investigation.

This chapter has highlighted the intractable dimensions of uncertainty in scientifically evaluating, and therefore anticipating, the problem of volcanic ash. At the same time, European airspace currently occupies a contested liminal status whose future is uncertain. It is this liminality that plays an important role in mutually *constructing* understandings of the ash risk and of European airspace management. The future of European sky will progress in tandem with the further development of regulatory-scientific approaches to the hazard of volcanic ash. It should be borne in mind that this particular process of co-production is likely to continue to be a space encompassing multiple dimensions of contestation. Understanding the strategies through which the key players attempt to control this process is a fruitful source of inquiry for social scientists interested in the relationship between science and politics.

NOTE

1. Eurocontrol, the body responsible for overseeing airspace management of most of Europe, initially insisted on the creation of a 60-nautical-mile buffer zone around the 'no-fly' zone to allow for possible errors in ash drift calculations. The buffer zone requirement was subsequently removed on 10 May 2010 (CAA, 2010).

BIBLIOGRAPHY

Alemanno, A. (2010), 'The European Regulatory Response to the Volcanic Ash Crisis: Between Fragmentation and Integration', *European Journal of Risk Regulation*, **1** (2), 101–6.

Beck, U. (1992), *Risk Society: Toward A New Modernity*, London: Sage Publications.

Boin, A. (2010), 'Preparing for Future Crises: Lessons from Research', in B.M. Hutter (ed.), *Anticipating Risks and Organizing Risk Regulation*, Cambridge: Cambridge University Press, 231–48.

Boin, A. and A. McConnell (2007), 'Preparing for Critical Infrastructure Breakdowns: The Limits of Crisis Management and the Need for Resilience', *Journal of Contingencies and Crisis Management*, **15** (1), 50–59.

Boin, A. and P. Schulman (2008), 'Assessing NASA's Safety Culture: The Limits and Possibilities of High-Reliability Theory', *Public Administration Review*, Nov/Dec, 1050–62.

Braithwaite, J. (2003), 'Meta Risk Management and Responsive Regulation for Tax System Integrity', *Law & Policy*, **25** (1), 1–16.

Brannigan, V. (2010), 'Alice's Adventures in Volcano Land: The Use and Abuse of Expert Knowledge in Safety Regulation', *European Journal of Risk Regulation*, **1** (2), 107–14.

Callon, M. (1986), 'Some Elements of a Sociology of Transition: Domestication of the Scallops and the Fisherman of St Brieuc Bay', in J. Law (ed.), *Power, Action and Belief: A New Sociology of Knowledge*, London: Routledge and Kegan Paul, 196–223.

Civil Aviation Authority (2010), 'In Focus – Volcanic Ash: A Briefing from the Civil Aviation Authority', 14 May 2010, available at https://www.caa.co.uk/docs/2011/VolcanicAshBriefing.pdf (accessed 1 March 2011).

Corvellec, H. (2010), 'Organizational Risk as it Derives from what Managers Value: A Practice-Based Approach to Risk Assessment', *Journal of Contingencies and Crisis Management*, **18** (3), 145–54.

Derksen, L. (2000), 'Towards a Sociology of Measurement: The Meaning of Measurement Error in the Case of DNA Profiling', *Social Studies of Science* **30** (6), 803–45.

Downer, J. (2007), 'When The Chick Hits The Fan: Representativeness and Reproduceability in Technological Tests', *Social Studies of Science*, **37** (1), 7–26.

Eurocontrol (2008), *Evaluation of Functional Airspace Block (FAB) Initiatives and their Contribution to Performance Improvement*, Executive Final Report of the Performance Review Commission, Eurocontrol October 2008, available at http://ec.europa.eu/transport/air/studies/doc/traffic_management/evaluation_of_fabs_final_report_execsum.pdf (accessed 1 March 2011).

European Commission (2001), *Proposal for a Regulation on the organization and use of the airspace in a Single European Sky*.

European Parliament and of the Council (2004) EC Regulation 549/2004 of 10 March 2004 Laying Down the Framework for the Creation of the Single European Sky.

Flight International (2010), 'Through the Ash', 18–24 May 2010.

Guardian (2010), 'How the Battle for the Skies Ended in Victory for the Airlines', 22 April 2010.

Hood, C., H. Rothstein and R. Baldwin (2001), *The Government of Risk: Understanding Risk Regulation Regimes*, Oxford: Oxford University Press.

Hutter, B.M. (2010), 'Anticipating Risk and Organizing Risk Regulation: Current Dilemmas', in B.M. Hutter (ed.), *Anticipating Risks and Organizing Risk Regulation*, Cambridge: Cambridge University Press, 3–22.

Hutter, B.M. and M. Power (2005), 'Organizational Encounters with Risk: An Introduction' in B.M. Hutter and M. Power (eds), *Organizational Encounters with Risk*, Oxford: Oxford University Press, 1–32.

Irwin, A., H. Rothstein, S. Yearley and E. McCarthy (1997), 'Regulatory Science – Toward A Sociological Framework', *Futures*, **29** (1), 17–31.

Jasanoff, S. (1987), 'Contested Boundaries in Policy-Relevant Science', Social Studies of Science, **17**,195–230.

Jasanoff, S. (1990), *The Fifth Branch: Science Advisers as Policy Makers*, Cambridge, MA: Harvard University Press.

Jasanoff, S. (1993), 'Bridging the Two Cultures of Risk Analysis', *Risk Analysis* **13** (2), 123–9.

Jasanoff, S. (2004), *States of Knowledge: The Co-production of Social and Scientific Order*, London: Routledge.

Latour, B. (1987), *Science in Action: How to Follow Scientists and Engineers Through Society*, Cambridge, MA: Harvard University Press.
Latour, B. (1999), *Pandora's Hope: Essays on the Reality of Science Studies*, Cambridge, MA: Harvard University Press.
Law, J. (1991), *A Sociology of Monsters: Power, Technology and Domination* London: Routledge.
Learmount, D. (2010), 'Europe Drags its Feet on Ash Policy', *Flight International*, 25–31 May 2010, p. 10.
Linnerooth-Bayer, J., R. Lofstedt and G. Sjostedt (2001), *Transboundary Risk Management*, London: Earthscan.
Palsson, T. (2010), *Atlantic Conference on Eyjafjallajökull and Aviation: Conference Summary and Conclusions*, Rejkjavik, 15–16 September 2010.
Perrow, C. (1999), *Normal Accidents: Living With High-Risk Technologies*, Princeton: Princeton University Press.
Perrow, C. (2007), *The Next Catastrophe: Reducing Our Vulnerabilities to Natural, Industrial and Terrorist Disasters*, Princeton, NJ: Princeton University Press.
Roberts, P. (2010), 'Changes to the Operating Procedures in the Vicinity of High Ash Concentration Areas', Open letter published 17 May 2010, available at http://www.caa.co.uk/default.aspx?catid=2011&pagetype=90&pageid=12018 (accessed 1 March 2011).
Rothstein, H., M. Huber and G. Gaskell (2006), 'A Theory of Risk Colonization: The Spiralling Regulatory Logics of Societal and Institutional Risk', *Economy and Society*, **35** (1), 91–112.
Schubert, F. (2003), 'The Single European Sky: Controversial Aspects of Cross-Border Service Provision', *Air & Space Law*, **28** (1), 32–49.
Schyett, T., K. Soin, K. Sahlin-Andersson and M. Power (2006), 'Special Research Symposium: Organizations and the Management of Risk. Introduction: Organizations, Risk and Regulation', *Journal of Management Studies*, **43** (6), 1331–7.
Turner, V. (1976), *The Forest People of Symbols*, Ithaca: Cornell University Press.
Vaughn, D. (1996), *The Challenger Launch Decision: Risky Technology, Culture and Deviance at NASA*, Chicago: Chicago University Press.
Weinberg, A.M. (1985), 'Science and its Limits: The Regulator's Dilemma', *Issues in Science and Technology*, **2** (1), 59–72.
Wynne, B. and K. Dressel (2001),'Cultures of Uncertainty – Transboundary Risks and BSE in Europe', in J. Linnerooth-Bayer, R. Lofstedt and G. Sjostedt (eds), *Transboundary Risk Management*, London: Earthscan, 121–54.

16. Rising from the ashes: a governance perspective on emerging systemic risks

Giuliano G. Castellano

16.1 INTRODUCTION

Unpredictable events – like an infrastructure failure such as a blackout (e.g. the 1999 southern Brazil blackout or the northeast blackout of 2003 that occurred in the US and Canada), a large-scale financial crisis with deep consequences on the real economy (e.g. the Icelandic and the Greek crises), a non-conventional terrorist attack (committed with chemical, biological, radiological, nuclear weapons), the risk related to the exploitation of new technologies (typically nanotechnologies), or a geophysical event (as the 2010 volcanic ash crisis or the 2011 Japan earthquake) – may suddenly cause large-scale losses. The knock-on effect of these events grows beyond the direct social and economic impact on a specific geographic area, affecting simultaneously different regions and imposing immediate regulatory answers.

The chapter addresses those risks here defined as 'emerging', since they lack previous records but are expected to increase in frequency and impact. The main feature of this 'line of risk' – to use the insurers' terminology – is the lack of sufficient knowledge. By showing that this feature also characterizes the 2010 volcanic ash crisis – which may be considered an unexpected infrastructure failure – this chapter attempts to identify the core policy issues to be addressed through a risk-based governance model that stimulates preventive strategies and minimizes losses. Such an approach requires both public actions and private sector's interventions (typically the insurance and reinsurance industries) to absorb large-scale losses. The *ex ante* perspective here presented is opposed to the *ex post,* centralized 'zero-risk approach' adopted to manage the 2010 volcanic ash crisis. Such an approach, even if it is meant to protect travellers' lives, might be considered an over-reaction that ultimately increases the severity of the occurrence.

Section 16.2 presents the 2010 volcanic ash crisis as an emerging systemic risk. The main features of this line of risk are in fact characterizing the 2010 volcanic ash crisis. In section 16.3 a governance perspective is taken and a trade-off, between precaution and over-prevention, is introduced to understand whether the zero-risk approach adopted by EU regulators belongs, indeed, to the realm of over-reaction. A different risk allocation could be the first step to draw a more reliable and holistic strategy to minimize the impact of emerging systemic risks. Under this light, *disciplinary* and *risk-based governance* models are taken into account, being two alternative devices to cope with these unexpected occurrences. It appears that, in order to avoid over-reacting measures and to apply a risk-governance approach, a shift in the policy goals is necessary. Precisely, the governance action should be designed *ex ante* to tackle directly ignorance by increasing the level of information. Against this backdrop section 16.4 illustrates how changing policy objectives might lead to the establishment of a correct set of incentives that – with different insurance and reinsurance techniques – helps to reduce the impact of unexpected events ensuring a recovery of large-scale losses.

16.2   THE 2010 VOLCANIC ASH CRISIS AS AN EMERGING SYSTEMIC RISK

New forms of large-scale disasters, usually defined as *emerging systemic* (or *catastrophic*) *risks*, have gained more attention at international level, as the frequency of these occurrences increased and policy actions are required to prevent and minimize losses (OECD, 2003). Typically this category of risks is related to the implementation of new technologies, the collapse of critical infrastructures, the unpredictable effects of climate changes or global geophysical events. At first glance, it might appear that these occurrences overlap with the traditional nature- or man-made catastrophic events categories, which are as well characterized by a low-probability/high-impact ratio. In fact a blurred line separates emerging systemic risks from catastrophic events. Both categories are considered 'catastrophic', since they rarely occur and generate high economic losses. Nevertheless, emerging systemic risks are more complex as they are characterized by a more substantial lack of information. From a regulatory perspective, this category of occurrences requires a prompt and immediate regulatory action, to minimize the socio-economic impact. In this sense the insurance sector defines this line of risk as 'an issue that is perceived to be potentially significant but which may not be fully understood'.[1] Thus, it is possible to note that emerging catastrophic risks are characterized by a higher level of unpredictability.

16.2.1 Emerging Systemic Risks and Catastrophes

To understand better what differentiates an emerging systemic risk from an event with a low-probability/high-impact ratio, let us consider first earthquakes and risk related to nuclear plants. Even if we are not able to predict the precise moment in which an earthquake will occur nor its magnitude, we know that certain geographical areas are more prone to such occurrences. In this sense, a sufficient number of data can be collected to identify the riskier areas and different policy actions can be shaped accordingly to enact preventive measures. Similarly, risks related with nuclear plants, even if they can be hardly fully estimated, allow for an approximate calculation of the potential costs in case of malfunctioning. Differently, when emerging risks are concerned, the general unpredictability over an uncontrolled event increases at the point that it can be considered 'ignorance', meaning a significant lack of previous records. In other words, in these circumstances, even if it is recognized that there is a likely probability that a large-scale loss will occur, there are no sufficient previous records to estimate the impact of these events. When it comes to infrastructure, like a highway or railway, *a priori* it is only possible to imagine some of the risks affecting the infrastructure system. Other risks, such as an abrupt change in meteorological conditions affecting the workability of the infrastructure, are hardly imaginable, as there is not sufficient previous record and the knock-on effects are unpredictable. Fires following earthquakes, for instance, are a clear example of how a single event can have consequences that are far beyond the initial damages – as happened in San Francisco (US) in 1906; in Kobe (Japan) in 1995 and, most recently, on 11 March 2011, again in Japan where a tsunami (generated by an earthquake in the Tohoku region) damaged the Fukushima Dai-ichi nuclear power plant, transforming a geophysical disaster into a nuclear accident with widespread health and environmental effects.[2] . Infrastructures are generally protected from first-order hazards, to make them resistant to what are considered the most common risks. Thus, water, electricity, airports, and communications are protected from extreme weather conditions or sabotage and terrorist attacks (let us consider the measures taken to increase the security level at airports after 9/11).[3] However, since the interdependence and the complexity of such systems are constantly rising, hazard mitigation should also be concerned with secondary and tertiary failure effects (H. Skipper and W. Kwon, 2007, p. 134). Therefore – leaving completely unpredictable events aside – insurers, infrastructure managers, and policymakers acknowledge that there is an expanding number of 'new risks' that are likely to increase in their frequency and to impact negatively on infrastructure's workability. Precisely, these emerging systemic risks are characterized by: high losses, increasing occurrence, and ignorance.

The identification of such characteristics is the starting point to define a clear policy action aiming at: (1) minimizing the frequency of these events and/or their impact; (2) managing the event; and (3) establishing a compensatory mechanism to ensure victims' pecuniary relief.[4] The resources necessary to accomplish these results are massive and they mainly come from public funds. These tend to be insufficient not only for poorest countries but also for industrialized countries, such as EU member states. A general coordination involving different jurisdictions as well as the private sector, notably the insurance industry, should be designed to achieve the policy objectives just introduced. Even more, by ensuring a public–private mechanism of victims' compensation, as will be illustrated below, preventive measures are incentivized and total losses are eventually reduced.

16.2.2   The 2010 Volcanic Ash Crisis

To understand whether this general framework is applicable to the 2010 volcanic ash crisis the first question asked is this: is the 2010 volcanic ash crisis an emerging systemic risk? In other words, is the level of ignorance the main feature characterizing such an event? As will be shown in the following section, this answer is crucial to design a consistent governance approach to both minimize and prevent the impact of these occurrences. A first blunt answer can be given by considering that the geophysical event, i.e. the eruption of the volcano Eyjafjallajökull *per se*, occurred in a geographic area known to be subject to these occurrences.[5] Nevertheless, even though the airspace of different volcanic regions in the world have been closed in the past, the consequences of the 2010 eruption are quite unique (Alemanno, 2010, p. 1). The uniqueness of such an event is due to the expansion of the airline industry and infrastructure. The constantly increasing air traffic leads to an evolving infrastructure and a higher number of people and industries are relying on it. The growing interconnection between people, markets and economies, together with the new opportunities offered by technological development, generate a totally new scenario from the one that would have been recorded only ten years ago. As a consequence, known events assume the traits of ignorance as they nowadays have new unpredictable consequences. Pandemic diseases, for instance, in the past century used to be more localized, while, nowadays, due to the frequency of overseas travel, they are global threats. Similarly, the impact of the cloud of ash generated by the eruption of Eyjafjallajökull, even if of low intensity, affected directly crucial nodes of the airline network and caused an infrastructure failure with consequences suffered at a global level. In this sense, the difficulties of assessing the costs, even afterwards, are symptoms of the complexity of the situation. Even if *a priori* it can be predicted that a volcanic eruption in Europe might impact the airlines' infrastructure, the volatility of the consequences of a volcanic eruption within the European sky is still high. As a consequence it appears that the risk to be targeted is not the one related to the geophysical event, but the risk of the collapse of a critical infrastructure.

The difficulties of collecting sufficient data to estimate the economic impact of this systemic failure is due to a number of factors, concerning both the event *per se* and the measures subsequently adopted by policy-makers (Alemanno, Chapter 1). In this sense, a first difficulty in assessing the economic impact is represented by the unpredictability of the natural event, which was emphasized by weather conditions. Secondly, the action taken by EU regulatory bodies, by opting for a zero-risk approach (impos-ing a flight ban), impacted not only the airlines' business activity but also different industries (e.g. the tourism industry) (Ragona, Chapter 3). Moreover, the adaptive behaviour of people that went for alternative means of transportation moved financial resources from one market to other alternative markets. Finally, the rise in risk perception of travellers and policymakers also added further complexity to the event. Even if, after the first flight ban, normality was soon re-established, potential passengers were likely to decide to modify or cancel their flights fearing a new ban. People are known to not only react to actual risk but also in response to fears that affect risk perception and induce them to take countermeasures, like investing in alternative markets (Becker and Rubinstein, 2004, pp. 45–6). As a result, if airlines, oil industry, and tourism had to face immediate costs, it has to be considered that trains, notably Eurostar, car rental companies, and the ferries industry benefitted from the situation.[6] Moreo-ver, the flight ban also lead to airlines saving the cost of fuel.[7] An attempt to calculate the costs, including all the main variables, has been made, estimat-ing a loss of about €3.35 billion over one month, for nine selected European flag carriers (Mazzocchi, Hansstein, Ragona, 2010, p. 99).

The lack of sufficient information also characterizes the crisis-management phase. Although it is undisputed that that a volcano's ashes may provoke serious damages to an aircraft's turbines, the critical level of ash concentration in the air still belongs to the realm of the unknown. In this sense the International Civil Aviation Organization (ICAO), in the manual on volcanic ash, states at paragraph 3.4.8: '... at present there are no agreed values of ash concentration which constitute a hazard to jet aircraft engines'.[8] Following that limited knowledge of the phenomenon a flight ban was considered the most reliable policy to be followed, under the condition of emergency in which EU policymakers had to operate. Precisely, the flight ban was relying on scientific advice provided by the Volcanic Ash Advisory Centre (VAAC), coordinated by the European Organization for the Safety of Air Navigation (Eurocontrol) and was implemented by EU member states (see also Johnson and Jeunemaitre, Chapter 4). Airline companies claimed that the European authorities were over-reacting, since the level of risk could have been differentiated by eliciting different areas of risk, in accordance with the level of ash contamination of the air. For the purpose of this work, however, it is worth noting that the model used by the VAAC was the Numerical Atmospheric-dispersion Modelling Environment (NAME), as originally developed to track radioactive fallout from the Chernobyl nuclear disaster in 1986 (Alemanno, 2010, p. 102). NAME evolved into an all-purpose dispersion model used to predict the transport, transformation, and deposition of different materials in the atmosphere. Nevertheless several flight tests have questioned the validity of the model in such a circumstance. The regulatory response – built upon a limited knowledge – revealed a lack of coordination in establishing a single European sky.

In light of the above it is possible to conclude that, even though the problem has already been faced in the past (as the mere existence of ICAO's Manual on Volcanic Ashes proves), there is a high level of ignorance characterizing the impact of ashes on the airline infrastructure. For this reason, to answer the question raised at the beginning of this section, one may conclude that, being an unexpected infrastructure failure, the risk here examined is an emerging systemic risk. This represents a key point in shaping a consistent regulatory response.

16.3   A GOVERNANCE PERSPECTIVE TO TARGET NEW POLICY GOALS

From a governance perspective, it appears that there are two, interrelated, fundamental issues to be addressed in such a circumstance: the lack of information and the risk of over-reaction. The lack of adequate sources of information (together with the lack of information sharing) characterizes the 2010 volcanic ash crisis. The effort to adapt a model designed for other extreme circumstances is, indeed, a symptom of a lack of previous (more specific) record. Such an ignorance condition influenced the emergency regulatory action and EU policymakers opted for a zero-risk approach. The zero-risk option, however, in the light of empirical tests, was revealed to increase the severity of the total socio-economic losses.[9] Even if it revealed a life-saving option, this approach is not a viable solution to be replicated, since having a zero-risk tolerance magnified the scope and the intensity of the problem. In this sense the problem should be analyzed not only under the light of the emergency regulation, but under a broader governance perspective that can be enacted before the systemic failure to reduce the level of ignorance. By reducing the level of ignorance a larger spectrum of policy options becomes available to regulators that can better fine-tune their emergency regulation.

A governance perspective, in fact, allows all the possible actors, private or public, that can play a crucial role in furthering the technical knowledge of these phenomena, to be considered. In other words, a correct set of incentives – designed to minimize the impact of emerging systemic risks and to ensure a compensatory mechanism to recover the subsequent costs – has to be established *ex ante*. Before considering the possible governance actions, the boundaries of public intervention are presented to identify when an excessive precaution can lead to a more costly over-reaction.

16.3.1   Between Precaution and Over-reaction

In general terms, when it comes to new risks, regulators should follow the *precautionary principle,* which holds that a preventive measure should be taken every time there is a danger – even if not completely estimated – of harms to people or to the environment. In other words the lack of sufficient scientific knowledge should not block the enactment of preventive measures when the threat of a potential damage is sufficiently real. However, when it comes to preventing harm, especially from unknown (potentially disastrous) events, one may observe that – as illustrated by previous regulatory experiences with asbestos, thalidomide, and Mad Cow disease – an excessive displacement of preventive measures adopted to eliminate a risk may cause other (new) losses (Baker, 2002, p. 6).[10] The problem is known in the literature as 'iatrogenic injury', which in medical terminology is an illness caused by the medical system supposed to cure the patient (Spain, 1963).[11] The iatrogenic injury phenomenon introduces a trade-off between the risk generated by not acting (and embracing too much risk) and the risk generated by (over-) acting.

Can the flight ban adopted by European regulators as a response to the 2010 volcanic ash crisis be considered an over-reaction? Under an ignorance condition, it is hard to determine when precaution is excessive. In fact policymakers typically have to choose between the risk of iatrogenic injury, by adopting an over-precautionary measure (such as a flight ban), and the hazard of embracing too much risk (in this case to the harm of passengers' safety). Even if, in a state of emergency, a regulatory action designed in line with the precautionary principle may naturally lead (at least under a high level of ignorance) to a zero-risk approach, a broader governance perspective reveals that the attempt to completely eliminate risk generates new costs and harms (Wiener, 1998, pp. 78–82). It appears that for some hazards, policymakers adopt heavy and anticipative regulatory arrangements – such as those adopted in past centuries to control infections (M. Foucault, 1977, pp. 195–200).[12] In this respect, an emergency regulation opting for a flight ban has to be compared not to a riskier approach that would not close the European sky, but to an *ex ante* governance approach designed to reduce ignorance and understand aircrafts' tolerance levels to ash. From this angle an *ex post* assessment over the regulatory responses adopted by European regulators to cope (immediately) with the 2010 volcanic ash crisis shows that new costs have been generated.

In our view, a thorough policy action should not struggle to determine the amount of regulation needed, under a condition of ignorance; it should directly target, instead, such ignorance condition. In the case of the Eyjafjallajökull's eruption, the lack of sufficient information played a crucial role in pushing policymakers towards an over-reaction that ultimately emphasized the severity of the losses. A more holistic governance approach would be designed to diminish the level of ignorance, providing a larger spectrum of regulatory tools to manage the emergency. To this end a more careful allocation of risk, among different subjects (i.e. passengers and airlines), would help to acquire further information and reduce the impact of such an occurrence.

16.3.2 Avoiding Over-reaction through Risk-embracement

A look at the Icelandic eruption of 2010 shows that airlines and travellers bore the higher share of the total costs caused by this event. Unlike passengers, however, airlines (at least from a governance perspective) cannot be considered completely powerless. It appears that the lack of information is also due to the reluctant approach of airlines in furthering scientific studies to determine the effective level of ashes tolerated by aircrafts' engines (Brannigan, 2010, p. 110). Airline companies, therefore, can embrace a certain share of risk, since they are in the position to enact precautionary measures. In this sense, airlines can invest more in research and technology to better determine and/or augment the level of ashes tolerated by engines. This also would have meant a reduction of the level of ignorance characterizing these events and consequently would have allowed EU regulators to fine-tune their regulatory response. The allocation of risk should be decided through an *ex ante* governance approach (see below section 16.3) that aims at incentivizing the enactment of preventive measures. In other words, the role of policymakers, before the event occurred, should have been directed in facilitating the acquisition of information, by pushing airlines to embrace a portion of the risk. This could have also avoided regulatory overreaction, causing iatrogenic injuries.

In other words, encouraging airlines to embrace a portion of risk is meant to avoid an excessive (and *ex post*) centralized ruling from public authorities. In this sense a comprehensive governance action should, in fact, consider that not in all circumstances are individuals are powerless against large losses. A certain level of prevention can indeed be enacted by individuals. Acquiring more information is a preventive measure, because it would have minimized the impact of a large-scale loss. From this perspective, the vital matter is: 'What kind of incentives can help to acquire more information?' As illustrated below, the solution can be achieved through a governance action that calls for public and private cooperation. To clarify this point it is now necessary to introduce the main governance techniques available to cope with emerging systemic risks.

16.3.3   Governance Techniques

In sociological terms, it is important to distinguish between disciplinary and risk-based governance (O'Malley, 2004, pp. 293–5). The former is characterized by normalizing institutions and it is organized around five steps: (1) establishing an ideal norm; (2) observation of individual cases; (3) comparison between the ideal norm and the individual to isolate the problem; (4) ensure individual compliance; (5) analyze the evidence from all the individual cases in order to acquire knowledge and ameliorate governing processes. Risk-based governance, on the other hand, focuses on individuals as members of a given category of risk, determined by statistical distributions. Individual behaviours are thereby governed in accordance with their association with a predetermined group. Thus, governing risk implies taking action to prevent future hazards that are identified through rational analysis. A typical example is offered by insurance companies that classify – through actuarial analysis (based on previous records) – individuals according to different categories of risks.

Both of these governance approaches pose some difficulties when it comes to large-scale disasters and, unless they are properly adjusted, they are not suitable for emerging systemic risks. Disciplinary governance is more concerned with individual cases and it would not help to decrease the frequency of a risk, if the risk itself is not foreseeable or purely determined by nature. In this sense, tort law – the main aim of which is to create a set of incentives to minimize the costs related with the occurrence of wrongful losses (see in general Calabresi, 1970; Cooter and Ullen, 2000) – will not work. In such circumstances, in fact, the causality relation between wrongdoer(s) and losses is unclear – or there is no wrongdoer. Moreover, even if the relation between human activity and losses can be proven,[13] it might be hard to assess individual responsibilities and (as just illustrated) optimal cost distribution and eventually prevention will not be achieved. Hence, a disciplinary approach would not have the positive consequence of correcting deviant behaviours. Thus, tort law does not appear to be the most effective policy tool to cope with emerging systemic risks.

On the other hand, the lack of past record makes it difficult to create an amoral stochastic rule, as generally adopted by risk-based governance approaches. Due to the low frequency and the high impact of systemic failures, actuarial analysis can hardly be conducted. As it is generally acknowledged, in fact, the so-called 'law of large numbers' governs the insurance mechanism and drives the definition of price rates of insurance policies. To adopt a 'risk-based model of governance', however, an insurable category of risk is needed. More precisely, a risk has to be: (1) accidental, which means that losses cannot be intentionally provoked by the insured; (2) determinable, which implies that insurers are able to calculate the premium rate as a function of its frequency and the severity of the damages; and (3) independent, in the sense that the losses should not be cumulative by affecting all of the insured at the same time (Jaffee and Russell, 1997, pp. 205–10).

From the above it appears that the main concern is not only related to low-probability/high-loss ratio. Again, the excessive unpredictability of certain events poses specific challenges to the application of a risk-based model of governance. As earlier illustrated, other than other risks, emerging systemic risks do not have sufficient record, which can be used to estimate likely probabilities and expected losses. The only certainty is that the growing interconnection between people, markets and infrastructure will amplify every occurrence by turning it into a potential disaster (Kunreuther and Michel-Kerjan, 2009, pp. 3–23). The volcanic ash crisis, however, shows that the lack of information can be filled, with more scientific tests and with a higher investment in technology. Moreover, studies of the measures adopted in different countries to cope with catastrophic risks have proven that insurers and reinsurers, if acting within a regulatory framework, have a wide range of tools to expand their capacity to absorb losses and adjust a risk-based governance approach (without excessive increase of insurance premium). Yet before analysing these tools one should stress that a shift in the policy goals needs to occur.

16.4 *EX ANTE* APPROACHES AND THE ROLE OF THE INSURANCE INDUSTRY

In the light of the above, the lack of information appears to be the main issue. Due to ignorance, policymakers overreacted and due to ignorance a risk-based governance model could not be directly applied. As a consequence, preventive measures were not incentivized and losses were larger and mainly borne by travellers, becoming 'volcano refugees' and facing an increase in travel expenses.[14] In this sense the key to both prevent and compensate unavoidable losses, appears to be the reduction of the level of ignorance. This can be achieved by stimulating the appetite of the insurance and reinsurance industries, and of the financial markets.[15] This simple consideration actually implies a paradigm shift for policymakers, with relevant consequences in terms of regulatory action and risk prevention.

It is indeed necessary to move from an *ex post* approach, in which the central regulator plays a crucial role in the management of crisis and/or in absorbing losses, to an *ex ante* one, in which part of the risk related to systemic failures will be embraced by those that have the possibility to enact preventive measures. To make the *ex ante* approach effective the intervention of the insurance and reinsurance industry appears to be pivotal. Insurance companies providing coverage to airlines for this kind of losses are, indeed, interested in a careful assessment of the different levels of risk. Moreover the cooperation with regulatory bodies to verify the correctness of the *ex ante* risk assessments would discourage moral hazard and would ensure an adequate level of passengers' safety and stimulate the insurance markets. Since, for the reasons above mentioned, a risk-based governance can hardly be adopted to cope with emerging risks, some adjustments have to be implemented and a public intervention is required.

The aim is to partially shift the risk to the insurance market. Insurers will push airlines to conduct further scientific analysis, investing more in the development of new technological instruments to detect ashes, as new technologies would help to decrease the insurance premium. Travellers will benefit not only because they will have a lower probability of being volcano refugees, but also because an increase in the level of security is therefore to be expected. More information will be acquired over these geophysical events. Airline infrastructure would be less prone to a systemic failure due to this kind of occurrence. And regulatory authorities can target their action better in case of emergency.

16.4.1 *Ex Ante* Governance Approaches

In practical terms *ex ante* solutions can be implemented in different ways. A legislative or regulatory intervention is generally required to foster the private sector's role in covering a sufficiently large share of the population exposed to risk and distributing it amongst them. Thus, even if individual prevention might not necessarily be a primary goal in such a circumstance, it is true that airline companies may adopt precautionary behaviours and contribute to acquire more information. An insurance mechanism would contribute in minimizing the impact of future losses, generating positive incentives for prevention. For this reason the subscription of an insurance policy can be considered a preventive measure *per se*.

Following this approach, EU policymakers might take a different path leading to the adoption of *ex ante* regulatory measures adopted to increase the level of information and distributing the potential unavoidable losses among different industries. In this sense, by looking at the experiences of different EU member states to govern natural hazards, EU regulators can impose a mandatory insurance coverage for this kind of risk (M. Faure, 2007, p. 339).[16] The mandatory coverage for systemic risks in airlines' insurance policies, in fact, would allow insurers to gather a large sample of different risk-exposed individuals (i.e. airlines), regrouping a heterogeneous group of risks. An alternative to mandatory coverage is represented by fiscal benefits, granted to airlines when insurance policies covering systemic risks are subscribed. A price mechanism, in which precautionary behaviours adopted by airline companies are taken into account in order to calculate the final premium, might also help to create an insurance market, discouraging airlines from bearing excessive risk to the harm of passengers. This would lead to the minimization of the impact of natural disasters on infrastructures and would allow the acquisition of more information about this line of risks.

In this sense the primary goal should be the reduction of ignorance, by fostering private action to acquire more information and thus apply a more accurate risk-governance approach. This will allow to develop a variety of instruments that the insurance sector may enact, once supported by a more comprehensive approach from the public sector, to: (1) strengthen the reinsurance net; (2) spread the risk into the financial markets, through the securitization mechanism; (3) create a risk-pooling system. These tools adopted by insurers and reinsurers to cope with emerging systemic risks will now be briefly explored in order to acquire a different perspective over the governance and financial management of the unexpected losses generated by emerging systemic risks.

16.4.2 The Private Sector

Given the characteristics of extreme events, private insurance companies might not be able to provide a proper coverage over large-scale risks with unexpected damages (G. Wagner, 2007, p. 88). As a result, all these practices aim at expanding the capacity of the industry to absorb losses (see in general Monti, 2009, pp. 158–70). In addition, such solutions – combined in various ways – become particularly useful in tackling emerging systemic risks, characterized by a high level of unpredictability. In fact they help to reinforce the insurance net, while furthering the acquisition of information concerning unexpected losses.

One of the most commonly used tools to expand the capacity of an insurer is the *reinsurance* mechanism, which allows a reinsurer to pool the risks passed on by different primary insurers. As a consequence an insurer can offer higher protection to policyholders. In this sense, reinsurance companies will help to absorb large losses that otherwise could not be borne by insurers. Such techniques, however, transfer large losses to the reinsurers, which might lead – in the aftermath of a catastrophe – to a substantial rise in the insurance premiums (Scott, 2008, pp. 1054–5). To avoid an excessive rise in premiums – which will lead eventually to an increase in the ticket price paid by end-consumers – regulators can adopt a price mechanism with fiscal benefits and/or stimulate the adoption of other devices such as the retrocession (a reinsurers' insurance) or securitization.

After a series of natural disasters in the early 1990s (particularly after Hurricane Andrew), the reinsurance industry developed alternative financing methods to control prices. In particular, new financial instruments to spread the risk and to permit the reinsurance industry to acquire new forms of financing were developed. Catastrophe-bonds (CAT-bonds) emerged to cover new risks by transferring part of the risks to the capital markets.[17] With such instruments, investors assume the risk of one (or more) low frequency/high severity event(s), typically a major earthquake.[18] The mechanism triggering such financial instruments may vary and it could be more or less directly related to actual losses born by the insurer or directly related to a specific geophysical event. The assumption is that capital markets can easily absorb the losses related to such occurrences. Moreover, the fact that they are not related to the economy or to other financial instruments allows portfolio diversification, by enhancing an 'alternative risk transfer mechanism', as remarked by the World Economic Forum Report (WEF, 2009). CAT-bonds are one of the most common forms of risk transfer, although their use is still limited (Grossi and Kunreuther, 2005, p. 10). In recent times, another form known as 'sidecar reinsurance', has been developed. With sidecars, a limited liability company takes a share (if not all) of the risk together with the reinsurer, in exchange for a share in the profit or loss the business generates. This has the effect of expanding the capacity of the reinsurer (diminishing prices) and it offers a significant opportunity of profits to the investors.

Another noteworthy tool, adopted to expand the industry's capacity, is 'risk-pooling'; according to which risks held by insurers are pooled into a fund run by a consortium of insurers. More specifically, co-insurance or co-reinsurance groups offer the possibility to insurers and reinsurers to cover in joint fashion larger risks that individually companies would not be able to cover. Risk-pooling also helps insurance and reinsurance undertakings to acquire more information on new risks. Such arrangements might raise antitrust issues, as they might impose restrictions on the competition (Castellano, 2010, pp. 404–12). However, large pools of similar (low frequency) risks ensure a more stable and measurable mechanism that – also through information sharing – enables a more accurate estimation of future costs. Such pools are commonly used for different risk lines,[19] as they aim to collect individuals with different risk-exposures. Thus, individuals less exposed to risk compensate those more exposed, ensuring lower prices. Moreover, it has been proved that pools are particularly efficient and effective to cover unforeseen risks when they gather both high risks and low risks individuals since a portfolio diversification effect can be observed (Skogh and Wu, 2010, p. 35ff.). In this sense policymakers' action should aim at fostering the adoption of this instrument as they represent the optimal device to diminishing the level of ignorance characterizing new risks without increasing prices (Castellano, 2010, pp. 412–3).

16.5 CONCLUSION

This chapter shows how a new set of instruments is available to both prevent emerging systemic risks and minimize their impact. By identifying the lack of previous records as the primary issue to cope with, it is indeed possible to develop a risk-governance approach. Once airlines, the infrastructure's operators, are no longer considered powerless in enacting preventive measures, a set of incentives can be established through an *ex ante* policy action. In particular, insurance and reinsurance industries allow the risk to be distributed by reducing the level of ignorance without compromising travellers' safety. In other words, the system portrayed is an alternative to the zero-risk approach that, as illustrated by the volcanic ash crisis, can generate a costly over-reaction.

NOTES

1. From Lloyd's website: http://www.lloyds.com/The-Market/Tools-and-Resources/Research/Exposure-Management/Emerging-risks/Emerging-Risk-Reports (accessed 14 March 2011).

2. Japanese authorities, on 11 April 2011, rated the Fukushima nuclear accident a level 7 of the International Nuclear Event (INES) Scale, the same level attributed to the Chernobyl disaster.

3. Similarly the Fukushima Dai-ichi (Japan) nuclear plant, being close to a seismic zone, has been designed to resist earthquakes and to shut down automatically in such occurrences. However, a less frequent earthquake of 9.0 magnitude (MMS) – as the one occurred in March 2011 – generated a tsunami that overtopped seawalls and damaged the cooling system of active reactors, ultimately causing explosions and a leakage of radiation. On this ground the International Atomic Energy Agency (IAEA) noted that the tsunami hazard was underestimated (IAEA, 2011, p. 3).

4. For a comprehensive look at the different approaches to compensate victims of natural disasters see M. Faure and T. Hartlief (2006).

5. In this sense it is sufficient to consider that over the last 500 years, a third of the total global lava output have been erupted by Icelandic volcanoes.

6. Eurostar reported 50,000 extra passengers on 15 April 2009, and an increase of 33 per cent of users few days later.

7. The International Air Transport Association (IATA) estimates 4.3 million barrels of fuel are used per day. During the flight ban, the demand fell by approximately 1.2 million barrels per day. This has impacted the oil industry, but on the other hand generated savings for airlines (IATA, 2010).

8. ICAO, 'Manual on Volcanic Ash, Radioactive Material 14/12/07'.

9. It has to be also acknowledged that not having any victim might be seen as an indicator of the success of a policy choice made under uncertainty.

10. Professor Tom Baker also refers to a report by Franz Kafka when he was working as a clerk in the Accident Insurance Institute in Prague. The report illustrates how technical efforts to design a machine to cut wood able to protect the hands of the worker finally limited the movements of the worker, who is then exposed to other, higher, form of risk (Baker, 2002, p. 5).

11. *Nosocomial* infections are typically considered as iatrogenic injury, since they result from a treatment in a healthcare unit.

12. Similar approaches have been noted as well in modern society, for instance, when in the US in 1976, the government attempted, without succeeding, to immunize every citizen against swine flu; or when in Hong Kong in 1997, over a million chicken were compulsorily slaughtered trying to contain the 'bird flu' pandemic.

13. In the case of damages due to earthquakes (like the one affecting L'Aquila, Italy, in 2009) it is hard to consider them as 'nature-made' hazards, since building houses and infrastructures within risky area, without precautions, is a human action, which finally determines the losses.

14. Yet, as illustrated in Chapter 2 by Macrae, the same travellers were the main focus of protection of the regulatory action.

15. Swiss Re has announced at the 27 January 2011 JLT Aviation Insurance Conference in Dubai that loss of business caused by natural phenomena (e.g. volcanic ash clouds) will be insurable for the first time with a new product. This proves the interest of the insurance sector in providing this kind of coverage. Nevertheless, from a governance perspective, as will be illustrated in this work, a more comprehensive approach should be adopted not only to minimize airlines' losses, but to prevent the infrastructure failure. In this sense there is urgency for a coordinated collaboration between the private and the public sectors.

16. See, e.g., art. L125–1 of the French Insurance Code, *Code des Assurances*, which establishes that every insurance contract covering fire damages is automatically extended to those damages caused by natural catastrophes. Moreover art. L128–1 of the *Code des Assurances*, provides for the same mandatory coverage when damages are caused by technological catastrophes. In Belgium, Law of 17 December 2005 (published in the *Moniteur Belge*, 11 October 2005, 2nd edn) extended the first party

property insurance covering fire damages to natural disaster damages. For a view of the German approach to compulsory insurance scheme, see Schwarze & Wagner (2007).

17. The first experimental transactions were completed in the mid-1990s by AIG, Hannover Re, St Paul Re, and USAA.

18. For a complete account of such instruments see International Association of Insurance Supervisors Report on the developments in (re)Insurance securitization, IAIS (2009).

19. A noteworthy example is provided by the French GARET group for insurance and reinsurance of risks related to terrorist strikes.

BIBLIOGRAPHY

Alemanno, A. (2010), 'The European Regulatory Response to the Volcanic Ash Crisis: Between Fragmentation and Integration', *European Journal of Risk Regulation*, **1** (2), 101–6.

Baker, T. (2002), 'Liability and Insurance After September 11: Embracing Risk Meets the Precautionary Principle', University of Connecticut School of Law Working Paper No. 4, available at SSRN, http://ssrn.com/abstract=812926 (accessed 20 February 2011)

Becker, G. S. and Y. Rubinstein (2004), 'Fear and the Response to Terrorism: An Economic Analysis', Revised Version of February 2011, *mimeo*, Brown University.

Brannigan, V. (2010), 'Alice's Adventures in Volcano Land: The Use and Abuse of Expert Knowledge in Safety Regulation', *European Journal of Risk Regulation*, **1** (2), 107–14.

Calabresi, G. (1970), *The Cost of Accidents: A Legal and Economic Analysis*, New Haven, CT: Yale University Press.

Castellano, G. G. (2010), 'Governing Ignorance: Emerging Catastrophic Risks – Industry Responses and Policy Frictions' *Geneva Papers on Risk and Insurance – Issues and Practice*, **35**, 391–415.

Cooter, R. and T. Ulen (2000), *Law and Economics*, Boston MA: Addison-Wesley Reading.

Faure M. and T. Hartlief (eds) (2006), *Financial Compensation for Victims of Catastrophes: A Comparative Legal Approach*, Tort and Insurance Law, Vol. 14, Morlenbach, Germany: Springer-Verlag.

Faure, M. (2007), 'Financial Compensation for Victims of Catastrophes: A Law and Economics Perspective' *Law & Policy*, **29**, 339–67.

Foucault, M. (1977), *Discipline and Punish*, Harmondsworth: Penguin.

Grossi, P. and H. Kunreuther (2005), *Catastrophe Modelling: A New Approach to Managing Risk*, New York: Springer-Verlag.

IAEA (2011), 'International Fact Finding Expert Mission of the Nuclear Accident Following the Great East Japan Earthquake and Tsunami. Preliminary Summary', 24 May – 1 June 2011, Tokyo and Vienna: IAEA.

IAIS (2009), 'Developments in (Re)Insurance Securitisation, Global Reinsurance Market Report', Basel: Midyear Edition.

IATA (2010), *IATA Economics Briefing: The Impact of Eyjafjallajokull's Volcanic Ash Plume,* Geneva: IATA.

Jaffee, D. and T. Russell (1997), 'Catastrophe Insurance, Capital Markets, and Uninsurable Risks', *Journal of Risk and Insurance*, **64** (2), 205–30.

Kunreuther, H. and E. Michel-Kerjan (2009), *At War with the Weather: Managing Large-Scale Risks in a New Era of Catastrophes*, Cambridge, MA: The MIT Press.

Mazzocchi, M., F. Hansstein and M. Ragona (2010), 'The 2010 Volcanic Ash Cloud and Its Financial Impact on the European Airline Industry', *CESifo Forum*.

Monti, A. (2009), 'Climate Change and Weather-related Disasters: What Role for Insurance, Reinsurance and Financial Sectors?', *Hastings Int'l & Comp. L. Rev. and West Northwest J. of Env. Law & Policy*, Combined Issue, **15** (1), 151–72.

O'Malley, P. (2004), 'The Government of Risks', in S. Austin (ed.), *The Blackwell Companion to Law and Society*, Oxford: Blackwell Publishing.

Schwarze, R. and G. G. Wagner (2007), 'The Political Economy of Natural Disaster Insurance: Lessons from the Failure of a Proposed Compulsory Insurance Scheme in Germany', *European Environment*, **17** (6), 403–15.

Scott, S. H. (2008), *International Finance. Transaction Policy and Regulation*, New York: Foundation Press.

Skipper, H. D. and W. J. Kwon (2007), *Risk Management and Insurance: Perspectives in a Global Economy*, Oxford: Blackwell Publishing.

Skogh, G. and H. Wu (2005), 'The Diversification Theorem Restated: Risk-pooling Without Assignment of Probabilities', *Journal of Risk and Uncertainty*, **31** (1), 35–51.

Spain, D. M. (1963), *The Complications of Modern Medical Practices: A Treatise on Iatrogenic Diseases*, New York: Grune & Stratton.

Wagner, G. (2007), '(Un)insurability and the Choice between Market Insurance and Public Compensation Systems', in W. H. Van Boom and M. Faure (eds), *Shift in Compensation between Private and Public Systems, Tort and Insurance Law*, Vol. 22, Morlenbach, Vienna: Springer-Verlag.

Waugh, D. (2002), *Geography: An Integrated Approach*, Cheltenham: Nelson Thornes.

WEF (2009), *Convergence of Insurance and Capital Markets*, Geneva: World Economic Forum Report.

Wiener, J. B. (1998), 'Managing the Iatrogenic Risks of Risk Management', *Risk: Health, Safety & Environment*, **9**, 39–82.

Epilogue

Alberto Alemanno

One of the less heralded consequences of globalization is the emergence of crises of escalating magnitude that, due to their systemic impact, test our ability to organize and swiftly execute a coordinated response. Yet truly global institutions, such as the World Health Organization, the Food and Agricultural Organization, and the International Atomic Energy Agency, to mention a few, govern only specific domains and do not cover all areas of human activity. Against this backdrop, this book explored the challenges of emergency risk regulation, by initially taking the response to the volcanic ash crisis to explore the general problem of emergency response in an environment where – as recently showed by the 2011 Japan tsunami – the lines between manufactured and natural risks are increasingly blurred. A tsunami, generated in turn by an earthquake, damaged the Fukushima Dai-ichi nuclear power plant, transforming a geophysical disaster into a nuclear threat.

This book, due to its interdisciplinary approach, represents an original attempt to capture the key insights that have emerged in the different scholarly contributions to the field of risk regulation, by focusing on the notion of emergency risk regulation. Building on a diverse range of contributions, it draws lessons from the emergency regulatory response provided to the volcanic ash crisis and other contingencies and attempts at generalizing some of them to future emergency situations. In so doing, it conceptualizes the notion of 'emergency risk regulation'. Each chapter, by relying on a different disciplinary perspective, identifies a number of themes about the nature of emergency risk regulation.

If risks are a 'type of virtual reality' according to a famous definition given by Ulrich Beck, emergency risk forces the regulators to think of risk in terms of reality. This is crucial because 'risks cannot be understood outside their materialisation in particular mediations, be they scientific, political, economic or popular' (Beck, 1999).

Although we are aware that every emergency has its unique characteristics, both because of the nature of the triggering hazard and the context in which it presents itself, this book initially chose the volcanic ash crisis as a case in point for identifying the challenges of emergency risk regulation. Far from automatically generalizing the lessons learned from this recent crisis, it made an attempt at identifying the main features of emergency risk regulations by also delving in other recent contingencies. Although convinced that a more concerted study is required, the contributors to this book all seem to believe that a better knowledge of those features may contribute to a better understanding of emergency phenomena and assist policy-makers with the difficult task of addressing them.

Emergency risk regulations are generally (1) triggered by (the threat of) an unpredictable event; (2) occur under time pressure and in a situation characterized by epistemic and normative uncertainty; (3) reflect, being shaped by prevalent interests and public attitudes, the prevalent narrative; (4) require, and are conditioned by, emergency risk communication; (5) increasingly characterized by a transboundary environment; (6) question the applicability and overall adequacy of existing regulatory schemes, even those that expressly codify an emergency response to risk.

At least *prima facie*, these features are the same as those characterizing risk regulations in general. Yet the emergency context in which regulations are called to develop makes each of these characters distinctive. In particular, emergencies tend to intensify the nature, magnitude and probability of these features. Thus, for instance, if in ordinary circumstances, rent-seeking represents one of the main regulatory pathologies of risk regulation, in emergency situations, this phenomenon may deepen considerably. Under an emergency, rent-seeking becomes a 'life or death' issue for an industry, which will be particularly prone to exploit the situation to defend and promote its interests. If uncertainty is a 'business-as-usual' context for risk regulation, which tends to rely on 'regulatory science' (Weinberg, 1985), in emergency situations, uncertainty, be it epistemic or normative, relies on 'forensic science' as opposed to 'normal science'. If risk communication to be effective has to consider peoples' judgment and decision-making processes, emergency risk communication must understand how lay publics cognitively perceive risks in the immediacy of the crisis.

FUTURE PERSPECTIVES

We live in a world of bounded rationality, where full knowledge is seldom available and decisions must typically be made under uncertainty. As illustrated in this volume, in emergency risks, this rationality is even more 'bounded' by the special nature, magnitude and scale of the surrounding circumstances. Yet public leaders and risk managers are expected to act and adopt different forms of action, all urgent and comprehending the possibility of unintended consequences (Boin et al., 2005). They must invariably act without sufficient and adequate information and often face ethical dilemmas. Indeed, from a regulatory perspective, emergency risks require a prompt and immediate regulatory action, to minimize their expected socioeconomic impact. In these circumstances, even the most well-intentioned risk decision-makers are likely to make mistakes in such an unchartered territory. This volume presents ample support illustrating that, although it is remarkably difficult to prevent and predict emergency situations, we can reduce the number of those mistakes by better understanding the challenges facing emergency risk regulation. Knowing the main features of emergency risk regulation means becoming aware of the possibility that something may go wrong any time and that our response cannot always be planned. Since fear of failing to manage a risk or an imminent threat is itself a risk (Hutter, 2010), acquiring awareness of the limits of anticipatory approaches to risk may be the key in designing better risk regulations in the immediacy of an emergency. In particular, by lowering expectations and dismissing zero-risk approaches, such awareness may comfort policymakers when called upon to act in response to unknown risks.

In sum, the toolbox of risk regulation, drawing from disciplines as diverse as engineering, economics and law, should be used not to provide ready-made solutions but, by being reminiscent of previous regulatory failures, to inspire regulatory humility. The diverse and rich perspectives depicted by the chapters in this volume all remind us that regulatory humility should enlighten emergency response under the threat of a catastrophe. To paraphrase Majone's famous dictum (Majone, 1984), emergency risk regulation is a microcosm in which conflicting epistemologies, regulatory philosophies, national traditions, social values and professional attitudes are faithfully reflected. Should public leaders and risk managers all become aware of that, their task to react, manage and respond to the risk emergencies looming on the horizon might be facilitated.

BIBLIOGRAPHY

Beck, U. (1999), *World Risk Society*, Cambridge: Polity Press.
Boin, R.A. and P. 't Hart, E. Stern, B. Sundelius (2005), *The Politics of Crisis Management: Public Leadership Under Pressure*, Cambridge: Cambridge University Press.
Hutter, B. (2010), *Anticipating Risks and Organising Risk Regulation*, Cambridge: Cambridge University Press.
Majone, G. (1984), 'Science and Transcience in Standard Setting', *Science, Technology and Human Values*, **9**, (1), 15–22.

Index